"A language is not just a medium for sharing our thoughts, it's also a signal of who we are. Here, Sherry Sufi deeply explores a use of language that every historian appreciates: nationalist movements use a common language, invented if necessary, to forge diverse people into a single nation-state."

Steven Pinker, Johnstone Professor of Psychology, Harvard University, and the author of 'Enlightenment Now'.

"A perceptive analysis of nationalisms past and present. Sherry Sufi presents an engaging comparison of the use of language by different nationalist movements."

Tony Abbott, 28th Prime Minister of Australia.

"At a time when several positive new studies about nationalism and politics have emerged to contest the dominant but arcane academic terrain of postmodernist theory, Sherry Sufi has written a refreshing and invigorating book that sheds much-needed illumination on the relationship of language to national identity and how the two complement one another. His evidence comes from a range of empirical case studies that he deploys with care. His scholarship is impeccable and his writing is thankfully clear. Highly recommended."

Keith Windschuttle, Editor-in-Chief, 'Quadrant'.

"Sherry Sufi has skilfully traced the importance of language over the centuries as a determining factor, beyond ethnicity and religion, as to whether different communities come together as nations; or whether they stay apart or separate, often in conflict. His observations are as relevant to the global and regional politics of today as they were to the historical events he describes."

Colin Barnett, 29th Premier of Western Australia.

"A useful and detailed historical review of the fascinating interaction between the Hebrew language and Jewish nationalism from biblical times and up to the emergence of Modern Zionism."

Dr Colin Rubenstein, Executive Director, Australia/Israel & Jewish Affairs Council (AIJAC).

"This book delivers a comprehensive and very well researched comparative analysis of common history-and-language as the building blocks of the successful modern nation state. Through the examination of three very different case studies, Israel, Pakistan and the Soviet Union, Sherry Sufi shows convincingly how both ingredients, common history and language, are essential for the formation of a cohesive and successful nation state. Sufi provides a theoretical framework for the observation, analysis and measurement of the relative cohesion and stability of other nation states, a most important contribution to available scholarship."

Dr Asher Susser, Professor Emeritus of Middle Eastern History, Tel Aviv University, Israel.

"This is the first thorough and comprehensive attempt to critically review the complex ethno-religious and multi-linguistic landscape of the Soviet Union in many years. Sherry Sufi has managed to highlight both the successes and major challenges for Soviet leadership in developing multinational and multicultural strategies aimed at consolidating Soviet society along with the reasons why it ultimately failed to prevail."

Dr Alexey D Muraviev, Associate Professor of National Security and Strategic Studies, Curtin University, and Australia's leading expert on Russian strategic affairs.

"Based on meticulous research, Sherry Sufi offers a unique and original contribution to the study of the rise of Israel and Zionist ideology. He aptly claims that language, specifically the revival of the Hebrew language, played a crucial role in the creation of the Jewish state. This book will surely be a valuable source for scholars and students alike."

Dr Meron Medzini, Professor Emeritus of Israeli Studies, Rothberg International School, Hebrew University of Jerusalem, and former spokesman to Israeli Prime Minister Golda Meir.

"A succinct analysis of the linguistic factors that put West and East Pakistan on a collision course, ultimately leading to the establishment of Bangladesh. A must-read for those curious about the history and politics of the Subcontinent."

Dr Samir Ranjan Chatterjee, Professor Emeritus of Asian Studies, Asia Business Centre, Curtin University.

"Hebrew is a Northwest Semitic language native to Israel, which first emerged in the late Bronze Age period more than 3000 years ago, even before the rise to prominence of the ancient Israelite kingdoms. The revival of Hebrew as the vernacular of the Jewish people in modern Israel is a fascinating story, intimately related to the rebirth of Jewish national sovereignty and political independence in the Jewish homeland. Sherry Sufi explores the connection between the two, demonstrating how the adoption of modern Hebrew as the official language of the State of Israel has contributed to the vitality of the Jewish polity and the Jewish people world-wide. For the Jewish people, Hebrew is no longer simply the language of prayer, or of classical medieval literature, or of ancient religious texts, but is once again the language of daily life in Israel."

Julie Nathan, Research Director, Executive Council of Australian Jewry (ECAJ).

"Dr Sufi's treatise on the primacy of language in the historical concept of nation and the contemporary construct of the nation-state offers a unique, incisive and timely contribution to the current discourse on nationalism. Whereas that discussion is often predicated on emotive tropes emanating from both sides of the political spectrum, Sufi's extensive research presents a more rational approach that transcends the partisan cacophony frequently accompanying this topic. The accounts of how language featured in the establishment of Israel, the liberation of Bangladesh and the fall of the Soviet Union make for a captivating, engaging and stimulating read."

Dr Moshe Yehuda Bernstein, Adjunct Research Fellow, Faculty of Humanities, Curtin University, and former Director of Jewish Studies, Carmel School.

Published by Connor Court Publishing Pty Ltd.

Copyright © Sherry Sufi (2020). ALL RIGHTS RESERVED.

This book contains material protected under International and Federal Copyright Laws and Treaties. Any unauthorised reprint or use of this material is prohibited. No part of this book may be reproduced or transmitted in any form or by any means, electronic or mechanical, including photocopying, recording, or by any information storage and retrieval system without express written permission from the publisher.

CONNOR COURT PUBLISHING PTY LTD
PO Box 7257
Redland Bay QLD 4165
sales@connorcourt.com
www.connorcourtpublishing.com.au

ISBN: 978-1-925826-86-9 (pbk.)

Cover design by Ian James.

Front cover picture: Flemish School, 17th Century, The Tower of Babel, Wikimedia Commons.

Printed in Australia.

FROM CAVEMEN TO COUNTRYMEN

THE LINGUISTIC ROOTS OF NATIONALISM

HOW LANGUAGE MAKES & BREAKS NATION-STATES

SHERRY SUFI PhD

FOREWORD BY PROFESSOR GREG BARTON

ABOUT THIS BOOK

This book is an adaptation of my PhD thesis. It is a modest contribution to the combined study of language and nationalism. Language is a uniquely human phenomenon. It enables sociability, cooperation and preservation of cultural content. It assisted the transition of nomadic cavemen from the hunter-gatherer age to fixed political territories with written laws. From ancient city-states to medieval empires, rulers have long sought to integrate masses into common *political* forms in order to rule them. Since dynasties ruled by divine right in a 'might makes right' world order, the politically facilitated mobilisation of the masses into common *cultural* forms was not strictly necessary. Yet the last two centuries of industrialisation have seen a gradual transition out of this landscape. Large multiethnic, multireligious empires began to fracture into compact nation-states. Nationalism, as a political concept, assumes that the rulers in fixed political territories should be of the same cultural community as those they seek to rule. As a result, the masses now need to be mobilised into a common cultural form (nation) in order to be integrated into a common political form (state). Still, human populations who share the same geographical territory are too often divided along ethnic, linguistic, religious, or sectarian lines. How then can this integrated *cultural-political* form (nation-state) be best achieved? As laid out in this book, my argument is that a shared *history-and-language* remains the most efficient formula for nationalists, not the alternative route of *exclusive* appeals to ethnicity, religion, sect, or ideology. This book surveys and compares three very different cases of the use of language by three different nationalist movements, each of which resulted in a different outcome.

As shown in Case Study 1, when *both* ingredients are present, the nation-state thrives. Israel is an example. Zionism provided the historical narrative of Jewish suffering and yearning to return to

Jerusalem. Lexicographer Eliezer Ben Yehuda provided the revived ancestral language, Hebrew. Together the formula helped integrate Israel's ethnically diverse Ashkenazi, Sephardic, Mizrahi, and Ethiopian varieties of Jews as modern *Israelis*. As shown in Case Study 2, when only *one* ingredient is present, the nation-state splits. The Muslim nationalist movement in the Subcontinent adopted the Urdu language. But its historical narrative was based on *differentiating* its members from anything that remotely resembled Hinduism. The modified right-to-left Arabic-script was a marker of the Muslim identity. This worked well for the ethnic Punjabi-speakers, Urdu-speakers, Pashto-speakers, Balochi-speakers, Sindhi-speakers and other ethnic minorities in West Pakistan. The Bengali language was written in the left-to-right Brahmi script associated with Hindu culture. The Bengalis sought autonomy and eventually seceded to form Bangladesh. As shown in Case Study 3, when *neither* ingredient is present, the nation-state disintegrates. The Soviet Union was an *ideological* experiment. Its subjects neither had a shared history nor language. Soviet pioneers did not promote linguistic assimilation right from the beginning. By the time they reversed this policy, it was too little, too late. The conclusions of these case studies help us make sense of the rise and fall of many other nation-states around the world.

ACKNOWLEDGEMENTS

No one committed to the pursuit of wisdom and understanding could possibly downplay the importance of constructive criticism.

So before others, I thank those who disagreed with my ideas over the years. Nothing has done more to deepen my understanding than being challenged.

I thank the Australian Association for Jewish Studies (AAJS) for the invitation and opportunity to present my research on Hebrew and Israeli national identity at its 30th annual conference in 2018.

Likewise, I thank the NSW Jewish Board of Deputies for the generous opportunity to travel to Israel on a study tour in October-November 2018 as part of its Joshua Berger Family Fellowship. Observations from the program certainly helped refine my thoughts on language and nationalism in modern Israeli society.

Sherry Sufi PhD
Perth, Western Australia

ABOUT THE AUTHOR

Dr Sherry Sufi is a Western Australian author, columnist and political commentator. He holds a Bachelor of Arts in Philosophy, a Diploma of Information Systems, a Master of Arts in Politics and International Studies, a Master of History, and a Doctor of Philosophy for which he received an award for outstanding research. He fluently speaks, reads and writes multiple languages.

He has made appearances on Sky News Australia and 2GB radio. His articles have been published in *The Australian, The West Australian,* Fairfax media, *PerthNow, The Spectator* and The *Jerusalem Post*.

He was the recipient of the Berger Fellowship award to visit Israel on a study tour through the New South Wales Jewish Board of Deputies in 2018.

He is an outspoken advocate for democratic values, civil liberties and free speech. He is the Editor-in-Chief of the Liberal Party of WA's policy journal *The Contributor* which he co-founded in 2014.

He has organised and hosted many panel discussions and public seminars on topical issues, including an unprecedented debate on the Israel-Palestine conflict that featured prominent leaders from Australia's Jewish and Palestinian communities.

Since 2015, Dr Sufi has served as Chairman of the Policy Committee for the Liberal Party of WA at the state level.

In 2019, he was awarded a Meritorious Service Award by the Liberal Party of Australia at its annual WA State Conference in recognition of his unwavering commitment to the party.

The views expressed in this book are his own.

www.sherrysufi.com

FOREWORD

This book does that thing that all good books need to do. And that is, to make us *think* by engaging us in a compelling narrative. That a common language enables sociability, cooperation and cultural creation and preservation appears so natural as to be beyond contention. Yet in being self-evident, it is also often overlooked. As a result, the central role of language in nation-building is too seldom examined. Sherry Sufi's book makes a valuable contribution towards addressing this gap.

Beguilingly approachable and engaging, this book does not set out to be a definitive work. What it does do, however, is to force us to engage seriously with central issues in nation building. Throughout the book, Sufi reminds the reader that it is important to set aside emotions, tribal loyalties and personal biases in order to attempt to look at the nations of the world as neutral observers.

In a 2017 Pew survey of 14 nations, he points out, respondents said that the most important marker or element of national identity was language. Common speech communities consistently benefit from greater sociability. And this is intuitively recognised by those who share the bonds of a common language. Religion and language have long been linked. Language is not just about communication, it is also about culture and identity. Throughout human history this has been bound up in religion and with perceptions of shared history. For this reason, having access to a lingua franca, pidgin or creole, language of trade is not the same as truly sharing a common language.

Sufi persuasively makes the case that shared history and language is the most efficient formula for nationalists to build a sense of nationhood. This does not stop many from making exclusive appeals to ethnicity, religion or ideology but these simple demands, he cogently asserts, lack the compelling power that comes from wrapping them up in a sense of shared history built around a common language. With both ingredients present, he argues, the nation state thrives. When one element is absent the task of nation building in the collective imagination becomes that much harder. And when both elements are absent the project ultimately becomes unsustainable. To illustrate this theory, Sufi explores three case studies.

The first case study is entitled *How Hebrew re-created the Jewish State*. It examines the seminal contribution of lexicographer Eliezer Ben Yehuda that led to the 'one nation and one language policy' of 1913. Without the resurrection of Hebrew, the modern Jewish state would have struggled to develop and maintain a coherent national identity and culture. Israel represents a powerful case of language bringing together a disparate collection of people with widely varying views of religion, ethnicity and historical trajectory. The remarkable story of the successful creation and implementation of modern Hebrew is a story about language and nationhood without parallel. In hindsight, it is difficult to conceive of how modern Israel could have become such a powerfully self-aware nation without this element of a common language. And yet, as Sufi unpacks in his engaging narrative, the case for a modern nation of Israel in which citizens all speak modern Hebrew was by no means self-evident to most of those leading the movement to establish the new state.

Sufi's study drives home the importance of the people of this complex nation of diverse origins speaking a common language. Not only does it provide a common medium for Israeli citizens of diverse religious, ethnic and cultural identities via a resurrected language, until very recently, it was but an artefact of history, literature and religion. Modern Hebrew has now completely transcended those origins and in doing so served as a way of uniting people divided on other fronts.

The second case study is entitled *How Urdu turned East Pakistan into Bangladesh*. The combination of a common language and a common history can be immensely powerful. This can clearly be seen in the inverse. The case of Pakistan represents an attempt to build a modern nation and construct a modern sense of history that ignores or rejects the role of a common language. Once again, the author considers the linguistic and other forces driving the friction that led to East Pakistan splitting from West Pakistan.

To tell the story, Sufi examines the political circumstances of Muslim-Hindu relations in the Subcontinent under British rule. For centuries, Muslims across the region have lived diverse lives that have involved strong elements of common religious and linguistic identity but without having a common, shared, history. Urdu was by no means spoken by the majority of Muslims in South Asia at the beginning of the 20th century but the vast majority did share in common the Arabic script written right-to-left. The significant exception, however, was in Bengal on the eastern edge of the Subcontinent. There, Hindus and Muslims alike shared a common Bengali linguistic heritage that was both rich and ancient.

The Arabic script helped give a common identity in West Pakistan and paved the way for an increasing number of educated Muslims to unite around the common use of Urdu. Ironically, it did much the same in India itself where roughly as many Muslims remained as those who lived in West Pakistan. Few in West Pakistan were native speakers of Urdu (less than 4% at the time of partition) but their mother-tongues of Pashto, Balochi, Sindhi and Punjabi were written in right-to-left Arabic script. The scripts of Hindu Indians (Hatvanki, Khojki, Gurmukhi and Devanagari) were all variants of a left-to-right Brahmi script.

In East Pakistan, Bengali speakers shared neither a script nor a common history with their compatriots in West Pakistan. Sufi does not make a simplistic argument for the case that East Pakistan was destined to split simply because it did not share a common sense of history wrapped around a common script and unifying language. Rather, he eloquently unpacks the various deep-seated reasons why these factors made a decisive contribution to the drift to Bengali independence.

Pakistan's founder M.A. Jinnah famously, and presciently, stated: "Let me make it very clear to you that the state language of Pakistan is going to be Urdu and no other language. Anyone who tries to mislead you is really the enemy of Pakistan. Without one state language, no nation can be tied up solidly together and function." Bengali literature has a rich tradition stretching back until the 11th century. More recently, the Bengali Renaissance of the mid-1800s saw the emergence of evocatively powerful writers such Ram Mohan Roy and Rabindranath Tagore.

Ironically, the Partition of India, and of Bengal, removed any reason for Muslim Bengali speakers in East Pakistan to resent Hindu Bengali speakers in West Bengal. At the same time, the government of Pakistan went out of its way to prevent Bengali from being used for official purposes. This all contributed, Sufi observes, to perfect storm conditions in which: "Secession was the result of a complex chain of events that began with Pakistani refusal to give Bengali official status, and which, eventually granted in 1956, came as too little, too late. Mutual mistrusts were deeply entrenched by this stage."

The third case study is entitled *How Russian ended the Soviet Experiment*. This final case study makes a compelling argument in the negative, for the importance of a shared history and language. The USSR shared neither a common past nor language from the beginning. Communist ideology and authoritarianism, Sufi observes, both contributed to the collapse of the USSR: "Gorbachev's reforms were well-intentioned, but the Soviet Union had by this stage become a megastructure sitting on top of conflicting national identities. These reforms removed the lid."

The genius of this book is that it plants a seed that quickly sprouts and puts down roots in our thoughts. It provokes us into reflecting on generally overlooked aspects of nation formation. What roles do languages like English, Spanish, French and German play? Should Hindi be seen as an incomplete success whose unfulfilled potential mirrors the unfulfilled potential of Indian democracy? Why has modern Mandarin Chinese been so much more successful than Hindi? Why does Malay remain very much a community language and lingua franca in Malaysia, while in Indonesia, it has bloomed into a successful common language of a new archipelago nation? And in what ways has the Indonesian language contributed to the success of Indonesian democracy?

In this digital age of accelerated globalisation, and rapid economic and social transformation dominated by the rise of the global south, led by Asia, it is more important than ever that we reflect on the role of language in shaping identity and connecting people.

Professor Greg Barton
Faculty of Arts and Education
Alfred Deakin Institute for Globalisation and Citizenship
Deakin University

PREFACE

It all started more than two decades ago. One afternoon, our school was out on an excursion at the Perth Zoo in 1998. I was walking around with our class group, with a discman in my pocket, and headphones plugged into my ears like many cool kids in the nineties, listening to Savage Garden's first album. As we came to a stop, I'd hit pause to listen to what our geography teacher had to tell us, then resume play as we continued the tour by foot. We reached a cage with orangutans. I turned off the music and began listening to our teacher attentively. I recall him saying, "Now *that* right there is our primate cousin. She shares a 96% genetic similarity to us. That's evolution for ya!" The usual drop kicks were like "Hmm meh, whatever". The nerds were like "Wow, how fascinating, Sir!" I was somewhere in between. As we kept walking, I resumed play on my discman. The next track that came on was the hit *'To the Moon and Back'*.

One random thought led to another, as it ever does. In a weird and wonderful way, the lyrics of *that* song kind of got me thinking. If the teacher was right, and we and the orangutans did share common ancestry, how was it that those poor creatures were trapped inside a cage, while we had quite *literally* flown to the moon and back? (Thanks, Neil Armstrong!). It seemed logical enough to deduce that, *if* evolution was true, then it followed that the offspring of our common ancestors would have to have veered off on completely separate trajectories at some point in the distant past. Not that I could locate that point of divergence on some chronological timeline of history at the time. Yet that didn't stop me from speculating. I kept pondering if there was a secret ingredient that only *we* developed along the way, which our primate cousins did not. I wondered, could such an ingredient explain our complexity, as opposed to their relative simplicity? Yes, there is. It's called language. That was the *one* exclusive property of human existence that sets us apart from *every* other living being.

It gave us the ability to go beyond mere signalling. Meaning, we now had the capacity to formulate and comprehend a near infinite number of sentences by simply rearranging a finite vocabulary. So we think, we talk, we read, we write. No doubt, the emergence of language was the single greatest turning point in human history. It was the point at which our own set of early ancestors departed from other primates. Our distant cousins came out the other end as chimps and orangutans, still hopping from one tree branch to the next. We came out the other end as humans who built ships, explored the seas, conquered the earth, made unthinkable leaps forward, including perhaps the *most* unthinkable of all, our trip to the moon and back.

I grew up with a fondness for cricket. My earliest memories of the game would be the 1987 world cup, although I don't recall much. I have closely followed every world cup since then. 1992, 1996, 1999, 2003, 2007, 2011 and at last, 2015 where I have fond memories of watching the Aussies beat the Kiwis live at the MCG in the final. A rather recurrent and relevant observation worth sharing is that, through these many world cups, I distinctly recall hearing countless Pakistani friends repeating the mantra "Doesn't matter if we don't win the world cup, as long as we don't lose to India!". Equally fascinating was the fact that I would see an identical attitude among countless Indian friends who would repeat the same mantra inversely, "Doesn't matter if we don't win the world cup, as long as we don't lose to Pakistan!" At a pub with a mixed crowd of Pakistani and Indian friends during the 2003 cricket world cup, I recall seeing how what started out as light hearted banter eventually morphed into a punch up over this rivalry.

I really began wondering, why? To be fair, there are no two countries on earth that have greater cultural affinity with each other *despite* belonging to two completely separate religious traditions and civilisational identities than India and Pakistan. The art, the culture, the language, the cuisine, the music, the literature, the architecture and even the sense of humour are more alike than English and Australian cultures believe it or not, and any unbiased Pakistani or North Indian person would tell you as much. Pakistani kids not only grow up watching Indian Bollywood films, they idolise Indian actresses and actors as their role models. Indians grow up singing along to Pakistani rock music as if it was their own. Yet, despite all that common cultural synergy, it is *so* important to beat each other on the sporting field and even end up in a pub brawl over it? I wondered, was there a secret ingredient that explained this rivalry? Yes. Nationalism is the *one* exclusive force which can, at its best, inspire great struggles for freedom and justice and, at its worst, cause unthinkable violence and bloodshed. The sporting field and the olympics have become by far the most vivid representation of nationalist sentiments.

Think about it: Another person may share the same ancestry as us, follow the same religion as us, speak the same language as us, yet if she or he is trapped on the other side of an arbitrary fence, that person is a *foreigner* to us. Consider the example of the Portuguese and the Spanish. By religion, both are Catholic. By language, both speak a descendant of Middle Latin. By geography, both share the Iberian Peninsula. By ancestry, both belong to the same gene pool. So why is a Portuguese person different from a Spanish person? The only major difference I could think of was a linguistic one. Even though Portuguese and Spanish are closely related languages and knowing one often helps understand the other, at some point, Middle Latin would have to have evolved into separate branches. One dialect became Portuguese, and the other evolved into Spanish. With change in speech came a difference of ethnic identity, which then became the basis for different national identities.

It is *this* shared interest in language and nationalism that eventually led to my interest in pursuing this theme as the subject of what started out as my PhD thesis, which now forms the basis of this book. Could it be that the two were correlated? As you may glean, reading through the chapters of this book tells you about *how* the author thinks, reasons, and draws his conclusions. Reading this preface on the other hand, tells you about the author himself. We are, after all, the sum of our experiences and observations in life. It is often these casual moments that we look back at, many years if not decades later, and end up realising, what a turning point that was. With the benefit of hindsight, this is how I look back at both the 1998 language story from the zoo and the 2003 nationalism story from the pub during the cricket world cup. In producing any book of a serious nature, the challenge for the author is not what to include. Rather, it is determining what to exclude. Every piece of scholarly work is the result of a judgement made by the author in consultation with other experts involved in the editorial and publishing process about its contents, structure and methodology. The author has to be judicious about the range of literature drawn on for the purposes of writing a book. The argument presented here is no exception. The literature reviewed in the first chapter on nationalism, and in the second chapter on language, was carefully selected from the range of key ideas in the marketplace of academic debate in these two fields. It draws on a range of earlier classical works by prominent scholars in the areas of nationalism and language. The same goes for the three case studies. Yet these chapters are to neither be taken as an *anything-and-everything* you need to know about the two fields, nor as a supposed database of *anything-and-everything* that has ever been said within the two fields. Such an expectation would be as unrealistic as it would be unreasonable. The intention was to acknowledge and draw on some of the earlier works in relevant fields as a means to explain to you, the reader, some of the key concepts and assumptions that help us make sense of language, identity and their relationship with nationalism. If by the time you're done reading, you walk away with a clearer understanding, then this book has done its job.

The chapters with the three case studies were selectively chosen because each of those tells the story of a distinct attitude towards the use of language in the nation-building and state-formation processes. Those chapters show us examples of complete success (Israel), partial success (Pakistan) and complete failure (Soviet Union) of nationalist efforts to mobilise the masses into common cultural and political forms using a common language (Hebrew, Urdu and Russian, in that order). The conclusions from my arguments presented in these chapters could be used for making sense of many similar language-based nationalist experiments around the world. There are plenty around.

Since this is a book that concerns language, it is only appropriate to take this opportunity to point out how important I believe is the role of writing in plain language. There is a perception among non-academics, that academics use "big words" and "ramble on" among many other interesting charges. Simplistic as these may sound, having read countless research papers and attended many seminars, I could vouch that this perception isn't entirely wrong. Many academics could be doing more to talk and write in an accessible way. Using big words doesn't prove how smart we are. In fact, when we have a choice between two words, such as "so" and "therefore" and we even *know* they both mean *exactly* the same thing, why do we continue to opt for the *less common* of the two terms? I'm all for academic writing that displays a high level of sophisticated thinking. But let's not forget, that's *not* mutually exclusive with the use of plain language. In writing this book, I have avoided these pitfalls and kept my writing style as plain as possible. While my argument would inevitably be of interest to academics and students of history, international relations, political science, sociology, and cultural anthropology, my *main* target audience here is, in fact, the general public. For too long, academics have written in a style and manner that only appeals to other academics. What's the point of creating a secluded community of intellectuals that is disconnected from the masses at large? What use is an idea if it's only heard by a tiny minority? It is hoped here with utmost sincerity that more members of the general public will have greater appreciation for understanding the role that language plays in making and breaking nations.

Since this is a book that concerns nationalism, it is only appropriate to take this opportunity to point out how important I believe is the role of setting aside our emotions, our tribal loyalties, and our personal biases, and in fact looking at the nations of the world as neutral observers. Another challenge for the researcher are the limitations of one's vantage point. As fallible observers, we see the world through the prism of our own life experiences and preconceptions. That makes it all the more important to study the ideas that are diametrically opposed to ours. Responsible care was taken to ensure as much neutrality in producing this work, as was humanly possible. Neither is this the first book written on the combined study of language and nationalism, nor will it be the last. Neither are its chapters comparing Israel, Pakistan and the Soviet Union the only ones ever produced within the field, nor will they be the last. This book is a modest contribution to this converging area of research. It is hoped that the arguments presented here will lead to new frontiers of discovery within the fields of language and nationalism. Enjoy the read.

TABLE OF CONTENTS

1. Nationalism:
   Cavemen to Countrymen   25

2. Language:
   Armoury of the Mind   61

3. Case Study 1:
   How Hebrew re-created the Jewish State   91

4. Case Study 2:
   How Urdu turned East Pakistan into Bangladesh   131

5. Case Study 3:
   How Russian ended the Soviet Experiment   161

6. Conclusion:
   Linguistic Roots of Nationalism   205

Notes   217

Bibliography   233

1

NATIONALISM: CAVEMEN TO COUNTRYMEN

"Men love their country, not because it is great, but because it is their own"
Seneca

The last century saw mighty empires that once stretched across multiple continents left fractured into pieces. This was not accidental. Given the colossal size of territories they ruled, empires were generally multilingual, multiethnic and multireligious. The cultural settings of the ruling class did not always match that of those they ruled. What tore empires apart in the end was the idea that the ruling class should be from the same cultural in-group as the people it seeks to rule. This idea was nationalism. As a political concept, it has been both a blessing and a curse for humanity at the same time. At its best, it has inspired the greatest of struggles for freedom and justice. At its worst, it has motivated the most gruesome forms of violence and ethnic cleansing. The world's first large scale global conflict featuring modern industrialised weapons, World War I, was triggered by the assassination of the Austro-Hungarian Empire's heir presumptive, the Archduke Franz Ferdinand, by Serbian nationalist Gavrilo Princip in Sarajevo on 28th June 1914.

Nationalism has motivated many to kill and die for its cause. Yet whether it is a modern construct or an outgrowth of a primordial instinct rooted deep within human nature remains the subject of widespread debate. Either way, it remains one of the most pervasive ideological currents of our time. Its visual reminders are all around us: flags, coats of arms, national anthems, passports, military parades and heroic tales of founding figures. When seeking statehood, nations of the world define their quest for liberation with *different* cultural settings. Nations could be defined by an ethnicity, multiple ethnicities, a religion, multiple religions, a political ideology, or a combination of all. Yet the need for a common cultural bond remains a crucial factor in constructing a national identity, and in keeping the nation-state together. To that effect, this chapter explores the idea of nations and nationalism. Let's get started by defining nationalism. There are two possible meanings. In the first sense, it refers to the political efforts pursued by organised movements on behalf of cultural in-groups to achieve self-determination. British sociologist Ernest Gellner described this sense as: "...primarily a political principle, which holds that the political and the national unit should be congruent."[1] This implies that the *ruling class* in a sovereign state must be of the same *cultural settings* as those it seeks to govern. In the second sense, it refers to the patriotic sentiments expressed by members of *cultural in-groups* to celebrate and ensure their cultural self-preservation. Gellner describes the second sense as an outgrowth of the first. For him, "Nationalist *sentiment* is the feeling of anger aroused by the violation of the principle, or the feeling of satisfaction aroused by its fulfilment."[2] These two definitions are interwoven and treated as such throughout this book. In a nutshell, nationalism is a political concept that seeks to connect a distinct *nation* with a sovereign *state*.[3] The renowned British philosopher Isaiah Berlin explained the concept as follows:

> By nationalism I mean something more definite, ideologically important and dangerous: namely the conviction, in the first place, that men belong to a particular human group, and that the way of life of the group differs from that of others; that the characters of the individuals who compose the group are shaped by, and cannot be understood apart from that of the group, defined in terms of common territory, customs, laws, memories, beliefs, language, artistic and religious expression, social institutions, ways of life, to which some add heredity, kinship, racial characteristics; and that it is these factors which shape human beings, their purposes and their values.[4]

One observation that is clear from Berlin's definition is that nationalism can be configured around a range of different core ingredients. This chapter deals with some of these. Hans Kohn defined nationalism as the: "...process of integration of the masses into a common political form. Nationalism is unthinkable before the emergence of the modern state."[5] What Kohn means by *modern* is the kind of political rule that emerged in the late 1700s, with the emergence of public education systems and print capitalism, processes furthered and complemented by both the American and the French revolutions. This period saw European and American societies take a radical shift from agrarian economies to rapid industrialisation, factory work and increased literacy. The implication was that large scale collective identities were required that went beyond one's mere township or village. So goes the argument that nationalism came about to fill this need to facilitate much larger identity groupings.

Hugh Seton-Watson defines nationalism as: "...a doctrine about political organisation that puts the perceived interests of the nation above [...] everything else, and a movement (usually a political party or several parties) whose professed aim is to promote the interests of the nation."[6] This is a relevant point, because not all cultural in-groups in the world necessarily produce nationalist movements, only some do. Seton-Watson's definition acknowledges the political activism that can often come with nationalism when people are mobilised to act politically. This is a central theme throughout this book. As nationalism seeks to connect *nations* with *states*, it is equally crucial to define both these terms. The concept of the *nation* as it is understood today first appears in the writings of German philosopher Johann Gottfried Herder in the late 18th century. He speaks of his idea of the *volk* (or the *people*) as:

> ...not simply the people of a country, but a metaphysical entity defined relationally as that which produces a particular, art, culture, set of great men, religion and collection of customs. All of these things are taken, not as products of individual men but as *manifestations* of the spirit of the people, or *volksgeist*.[7]

Kenneth Minogue explains that, for Herder, the: "...people are always found in divided groups which have evolved a language and culture in response to their environment and which express their own national character. In the succession of generations, a people elaborates and develops that culture, and each individual man is what he is because one or another culture has stamped itself upon him."[8] As Minogue acknowledges, a people's concept of *what* they are often is a response to their environment. French historian Ernest Renan in his essay *What is a Nation?* argued that a nation was: "...not the simple sum of the individuals who comprise it; it is a soul, a consciousness, a person, a living result. This soul may reside in a very small number of men; it would be best if all could participate in it; but what is indispensable is that, through governmental selection, a head is created that stands vigil and thinks while the rest of the country does not think and is hardly conscious." Renan continues that the nation: "...presupposes a past, it is summarised, however, in the present by a tangible fact, namely, consent, the clearly expressed desire to continue a common life."[9] Renan's emphasis on the *past* is crucial for understanding nationalism in the modern sense. Some nations define themselves on ethnic grounds, others on religious grounds and yet others on ideological grounds. It is naïve to expect that these core ingredients should be identically manifest across different national identities in the world. Yet the one commonality that is necessary in each case is that they *all* have a past. Even ideological forms of nations, such as the Soviet Union (dealt with in chapter five: Case Study 3) imagined a history when its people didn't share one. What Berlin's emphasis on *memories*, Herder's emphasis on *volksgeist* or the *spirit* of the people, and

Renan's emphasis on people having a *soul* or a *consciousness* suggest, is that a national identity must pre-exist in the consciousness of *multiple* people for it to constitute a nation. There is a deep and important point of connection here with the possibility of language itself.

As we will see in the next chapter, if a language only existed in the mind of one person, it would not constitute language in the second and third senses that we define. It would be a language in the first sense, and an impossibly private one at that, as Wittgenstein discussed in his *Philosophical Investigations* §§244–271. The essential idea is that language mastery is mastery of a normative practice, and that one person alone cannot ground or sustain such normativity. They would be unable to distinguish what *is* right from what merely *seems* to them to be so. The principle of multiplicity applies to nations and national identities. By their definition, they are *shared* by other people. If a single individual invented an identity label to refer to her or himself based on her or his relationship with a particular region, and a particular history, with its own mythological content that was not shared by anyone else, would this self-made label constitute that individual's *national* identity? No, because the entire point of nationalism is to connect *multiple* people(s) together with each other who, on some level, are bound together by a shared mythology or concept of a common past. There is no criteria on how many members are needed at a bare minimum in order to constitute a nation. The Jewish people are considered a single nation when there are arguably only 15 million of them in the world, as are the Chinese and Indian people whose numbers go beyond 1 billion each. This most emphatic expression of the need for a shared past comes from British historian Eric Hobsbawm who famously remarked that:

> Historians are to nationalism what poppy-growers in Pakistan are to the heroin-addicts: we supply the essential raw material for the market. Nations without a past are contradictions in terms. What makes a nation is the past, what justifies one nation against others is the past, and historians are the people who produce it. So my profession, which has always been mixed up in politics, becomes an essential component of nationalism.[10]

From Moses parting the Red Sea to rescue the ancient Israelites out of Egyptian bondage to the Australian diggers fighting the Ottoman Turks at Gallipoli, national mythologies are constructed based on a mixture of perceived and actual historical events. It would be too simplistic to expect that national mythologies must be based on facts. Obviously, the further back a particular story goes in time, the harder it is to ascertain its veracity. It does not matter either way as far as a sense of nationhood is concerned. In their 1983 publication *The Invention of Tradition*, Eric Hobsbawm and Terence Ranger argued that many traditions that: "...appear or claim to be old are often quite recent in origin and sometimes invented."[11] This is a contentious proposition and has been treated as such within academia. Some traditions are ancient, like the epic of Mahabharata, the Upanishads and the four Vedas of Hinduism (Rig, Atharva, Samma and Yajur), or the stories of the Jewish tanakh. While the stories about highland clans, bagpipes and kilts in the Scottish identity may well be more recent 'inventions' to use Hobsbawm's own term. Either way, it neither mattered to the Hindu nationalists in the Subcontinent nor to the Zionists whether the Vedas or the Jewish Torah stories were fairy tales or not. Nationalists tend to view their national mythology as an *actual* history on a single, linear trajectory. Ernest Gellner sums it up elegantly when he observes that:

> 1. Two men are of the same nation if and only if they share the same culture, where culture in turn means a system of ideas and signs and associations and ways of behaving and communicating.
> 2. Two men are of the same nation if and only if they recognise each other as belonging to the same nation. In other words, nations maketh man; nations are the artifacts of men's convictions, loyalties and solidarities.[12]

Gellner's point about *shared* recognition is thought provoking. If people do not see each other as belonging to the same nation, then it follows that they are not. In a similar vein, Anthony D. Smith describes a nation as: "...a named human population sharing an historic territory, common myths and historical memories, a mass, public culture, a common economy and common legal rights and duties for all members, the nation is a multidimensional concept."[13] Like Herder, Kohn, Berlin, Gellner, Hobsbawm and Seton-Watson, Smith's emphasis on common history and culture is not unique. As far as nationalism is concerned, that shared *history* does not necessarily have to be based on actual events. It could be based on implausible fairytales. Factual history is not a prerequisite condition of national identities. The past as imagined by nationalists can be, and often is, based on a combination of facts and myths. Elie Kedourie notes that: "...nationalists make use of the past in order to subvert the present."[14] The subversion part here refers to nationalist struggles from foreign rule. For most of human history, people's sense of identity was primarily based on the village or town they lived in or the religion they followed. The state in which people lived was, for the most part, an empire and it was rare for the rulers to be of the same religious or cultural settings as their conquered subjects. Sociable communities could be formed at the local level, when people had conversations with their local butcher, or barber, or cobbler. These were *actual* communities, who too often spoke a different dialect of the same language that was spoken several kilometres up the road. In this sense, language was a marker of *regional* identities. Before the Industrial Revolution in the late 1700s, there were no trains, cars, or airplanes. Walking, riding a horse or being dragged in a carriage, or chariot if one was wealthy enough to afford one, were the primary means of transportation. Unless one was an explorer or a soldier, leaving one's village or township was rare. Someone living in Paris had no need to think of someone in Sauvignon as part of their community or group identity. When the ruling elites did need to mobilise the masses, for instance, during times of war, the natural ingredient to do so with was religion.

After the Industrial Revolution started, societies across Europe and America not only began to shift from an agrarian to an industrial economy, but as a parallel consequence, more people began moving out of villages, often forced by enclosure, into major cities in search of factory work. The steam engine made it possible for ordinary people, not just explorers and soldiers, to move around at will. With rapid advances in technology, the quest for work in other cities and railway tracks connecting towns, suddenly people in Paris had more of a reason to think of people in Sauvignon as being the same as them, even if the accent or dialect of French spoken was different. This is the sort of post-industrial backdrop that resulted in the emergence of the modern nation-state. Benedict Anderson's central argument in his 1983 publication *Imagined Communities* is that national identity was the perfect replacement for the religiously dominated worldview that defined people's group identities through most of the Middle Ages. The invention of the Printing Press in 1453 had resulted in the rise of literacy. Equipped with the ability to read and write, over time people became interested in politics and gradually started mobilising into organised political groups. As newspapers became popular, people read the same stories, identified the same characters, entering and exiting the narrative at different stages, and this created the sense that the nation was a continuous story, the political organisation of groups of people as both ancient and modern placed together on a linear trajectory.

For national identities to work, people did not need to belong to actual communities where all the members knew each other. They simply needed to naturally feel, or be made to feel by the ruling elites, that they belonged to the same nation. Anderson makes this point more emphatically than most other scholars: "I propose the following definition of the nation: it is an imagined political community - and imagined as both inherently limited and sovereign."[15] He goes on to argue that a nation:

> ...is *imagined* because the members of even the smallest nation will never know most of their fellow-members, meet them, or even hear of them, yet in the minds of each lives the image of their communion.[16]

Anderson's observation that nations are *imagined communities* is exceptional. This is because it is both factual and simple at the same time. Whether a nation is based on one or more ethnicities, or one or more religion, it *imagines* itself as a community based on a shared past as argued by Herder, Kohn, Berlin, Gellner, Hobsbawm, Seton-

Watson and Smith. Scholar of the Middle East, Bernard Lewis too defines the nation as: "...a group of people held together by a common language, belief in a common descent and in a shared history and destiny. They usually but do not necessarily inhabit a contiguous territory; they often enjoy, and if they do not enjoy they commonly seek, sovereign independence in their own name."[17] Lewis spent much of his academic life writing about Islam and the Arabs. It is not surprising that his definition acknowledges that a nation does not necessarily have to inhabit the same contiguous territory. There are 22 independent sovereign states with an Arabic-speaking majority population. Regardless of what outside observers might think, there certainly have been countless Arab scholars that have argued that the Arabs are a single nation.[18] The same can be true of the Anglosphere that is, the English-speaking nations, or the Hispanosphere that is, the Spanish-speaking nations. By this stage, the basic concepts of nations and nationalism are clear. Since nationalism seeks to combine the political and cultural boundaries of a sovereign territory, it is equally crucial to define the *state* itself. The most celebrated definition was presented by German sociologist Max Weber, who defined the state as:

> ...that agency within society which possesses the monopoly of legitimate violence. Violence can only be applied by the central political authority, and those to whom it delegates this right.[19]

The best definitions are often those that are not convoluted in their meaning. Too often, definitions of political concepts can include miscellaneous qualifying properties as prerequisites. For instance, a definition that argues that a nation has to have a common religion means that all one has to do is to point to some examples of nations with multiple religions and the definition fails. Often the best definitions are those that make the fewest complex assumptions. Weber's concept of a *state* is as exceptional as Anderson's concept of a *nation*. Weber is essentially saying that a state is a territory where one particular ruling authority, as opposed to a rival authority, gets to administer and police the state. The territory upon which such an apparatus exists *is* the state. Where that territorial jurisdiction ends, is where the state ends. Weber's definition of the state is not time-sensitive. It could be applied across all timeframes. Ancient empires like Greece, Rome, Assyria were all *states* by this definition. At their own points of geographical origin, each of these ancient empires also constituted *nations* as defined by Anthony D. Smith who argues that nations are primordial.[20] Yet because they were expansionist empires, which did not always seek to assimilate their conquered people, not all of the subjects they ruled were necessarily part of the same *nation*. Gellner explains Weber's definition by pointing out that: "Violence may be applied only by the central political authority, and those to whom it delegates this right. Among the various sanctions of the maintenance of order, the ultimate one - force - may be applied only by one special, clearly identified, and well centralised, disciplined agency within society. That agency or group of agencies *is* the state."[21] So, a state requires institutions in order to function, for instance: bureaucracies, a judicial system, a military or religious organisation.[22] International law relies on the definition of statehood as enshrined in the Montevideo Convention on Rights and Duties of States (1933). Its Article 1 states:

> The state as a person of international law should possess the following qualifications: a) a permanent population; b) a defined territory; c) government; and d) capacity to enter into relations with the other states.[23]

The last of these points is crucial. It is the criterion that prevents rogue separatist groups and terrorists from declaring true or real, rather than merely nominal, statehood. Even the so-called Islamic State in Syria and Iraq (ISIS) that declared a *caliphate* in 2014 had a permanent population, a defined territory and a government. What it did not have was the capacity to enter into relations with the other states. The international community's shared rejection of ISIS played a role in cornering self-proclaimed caliph Abu Bakr Al-Baghdadi's regime. This was a clear case of a government that *wanted* to see itself as a state, but could not, because no one would recognise it as such. There are also examples of governments with only partial recognition as states. The Palestinian Authority which controls Area A and partly controls Area B in the West Bank is recognised by 138 out of the 195 sovereign nation-states with United Nations membership. Although most Western countries do have diplomatic ties with the Palestinian Authority, they do not officially recognise it as a sovereign state. These examples show how recognition by other states has become a crucial part of the criteria for sovereign statehood in the present world. As Peter B. Evans and Dietrich Rueschemeyer argue: "We consider the state to be a set of organisations invested with the authority to make binding decisions for people and organisations juridically located in a particular territory and to implement these decisions using, if necessary, force."[24] The two go on to observe that the state: "...cannot escape being an instrument of domination. The interrelations between the various parts of the state apparatus, on the one hand, and the most powerful classes or class fractions, on the other, will determine the character of the overall 'pact of domination.'"[25] Indeed, as Article 8 of the same Convention states: "No state has the right to intervene in the internal or external affairs of another."[26] This is a core feature of sovereignty.

Here, Michel Foucault makes a somewhat cynical observation: "Maybe, after all, the state is no more than a composite reality and a mythologised abstraction, whose importance is a lot more limited than many of us think."[27] This assertion may be interpreted as suggesting that sovereignty is an illusion because weaker states are susceptible to being controlled by stronger states. It remains true that states can be and often are subordinate to foreign hegemons.[28] Critics have often accused the United States of meddling in the affairs of other sovereign states and seeking to install puppet regimes friendly to American interests. This occurred through a combination of covert operations such as the 1953 overthrow of Iran's Prime Minister Mohammed Mossadegh, who was democratically elected, through a coup d'état jointly orchestrated by the United States and the United Kingdom, as well as through overt operations such as the overthrow of Iraqi dictator Saddam Hussein in 2003. Some may argue that today the same is in play with Venezuela. Indeed, these violations of sovereignty are part and parcel of the United States-led world order that has existed since the conclusion of World War II. Of course, the United States did not, at any rate, turn Iran after 1953 or Iraq after 2003 into the 51st state of America. It instead preferred comprador-style regime change to further its interests. It neither annexed the territories it invaded, nor sought direct rule over the populations of the invaded states. Despite Foucault's cynicism, these acts of meddling do not altogether erode state sovereignty as a fundamental political concept in today's world.

Now that the concepts of a *nation* and *state* have been explored, we turn our focus back to nationalism. In essence, when nationalism is taken to its logical conclusion, the independent territorial unit that emerges on the world map is a *nation-state*. This term is preferred by scholars for a technical reason. It serves a purpose its colloquial equivalent term *country* does not. The *nation* part refers to the default *cultural* settings. The *state* part refers to the default *territorial* settings. The terms nation and state are frequently expressed interchangeably.[29] Politicians in particularly tend to refer to their countries or states as *nations*. This practice is acceptable in vernacular speech. Yet in technical terms a state is, as earlier defined, a sovereign territory and a nation is, as earlier defined, a collection of people or an *imagined community* with a shared history. Robert Lane Greene observes that: "Americans tend to use 'nation' as a synonym for 'country', but political scientists and historians, as well as many Europeans, tend to use the term for a much more specific phenomenon: a group of people who feel they belong together, whether they have a country of their own or not. Nations tend to share several things: a sense of common history, a religion, cultural customs, some geographic continuity and of course a language. And though all of these can be powerful the *two most powerful of all tend to be religion and language*. Where people share the same faith and the same language, they tend to consider themselves a nation."[30] Ethnicities are generally impenetrable. One cannot simply opt-in or opt-out of an ethnic background. Group membership is determined by perceived ancestry. Ethnicity works well as the base level identity for individuals.

Yet if a nationalist movement seeks to represent ethnically diverse populations, it ends up requiring a higher level grouping that *is* penetrable. This is where Greene's emphasis on the importance of religion and language becomes relevant. One can opt-in to a religion through conversion, or for that matter, opt-out through apostasy. One can learn a new language. That said, there is no universal formula for determining what core elements should form a *particular* nation in the first place, or who gets to be a part of the cultural in-group, let alone *how* statehood is to be achieved and managed. These configurations can and ultimately do vary from one national identity to another, as does the method by which sovereign statehood is sought. George Washington led the American revolutionaries to victory against the British Empire and achieved statehood for the thirteen original colonies in 1776 through an armed struggle. Mahatma Gandhi achieved statehood for the Indians from the British Empire in 1947 through his civil disobedience as enshrined in his pacifistic philosophies of *ahimsa* and *satyagraha*.[31] The Zionist movement achieved statehood for the Jewish people in 1948 through sustained land purchases, diplomacy, revival of their ancestral language (discussed in chapter three: Case Study 1), resettling the land and armed struggle. Scottish nationalists attempted to secede from Great Britain through a referendum in 2014 that was unsuccessful.[32] Catalan nationalists tried to secede from Spain through a referendum in 2017 that was successful, but not sanctioned by the Spanish government.[33] There are multitudes of other examples. The point is that the method by which statehood is sought varies.

Nationalist movements determine the rules and boundaries of their national kinship and set their own political agenda. Israel is a state with its national settings rooted in a religious Jewish past that has evolved to function as an ethnicity over time. Pakistan is a state with its national settings rooted in a form of religious Muslim past *specific* to the Subcontinent region comprising of multiple ethnicities.[34] India is a state with many ethnicities and religions with its national settings rooted in a cultural Vedic past. There are multitudes of other examples. The point is that the method by which a national identity is configured also varies. Some nationalists seek co-existence alongside other *cultural out-groups* on the same territory. Israel for instance calls itself both Jewish and democratic, a fifth of its population is made up of Arabs who have democratic rights and the Arabic language has special recognition. Canada is another example of a binational state with parallel English and French identities. Other nationalists seek the removal of *cultural out-groups* from the territory. The only common denominator across all nationalist movements is the basic desire for statehood. A national identity could be constructed based on *any* random cultural configurations ranging from ethnic to religious, or even ideological. Chaim Gans observes that:

> ...common descent (or a myth of common descent) is an essential characteristic of ethnic groups but not of national groups which only share a common language, religion, customs, history or ties with a particular territory (none of which is necessary). Many movements of cultural nationalism did indeed grant the myth of common descent an important practical role in their agendas. This perhaps justifies calling the present nationalism 'ethnic' for purposes of historical classification.[35]

The distinction between ethnicity and nationality can often be confusing for the specialist and the non-specialist alike. There are three reasons for this: 1) The presumption that identity groupings are, or should be, biologically determined. This is true for ethnicity, but not necessarily for nationality. 2) The tendency to mistakenly think of the two *terms* as being synonymous with each other, even though they have distinct meanings. 3) Language groups with or without states are often thought of as potential *nations* of themselves when in actual fact, ethnicity is likely the more appropriate label. Ernest Gellner confounds the difference between the two. While he correctly argues that most nations are not likely to demand a state, in trying to estimate the numbers of *potential* new states that may *hypothetically* result from these *potential* nations, he ends up using language as the primary criterion. Having a distinct language alone does not warrant sufficient grounds to think of a cultural in-group as a nation. Ethnicity and nationality are both cultural constructs. Out of the two, ethnicity has come to be perceived as biologically determined through ancestry, more so than nationality. Ethnicity and nationality may both be premised on actual or imagined ancestral origins. The fact is that human group identity or kinship is a *multitiered* phenomenon. An individual's sense of *imagined community* can be based on ethnicity, religion or civilisation, sect, culture, language, a particular region or a philosophical ideology. As a result, there is no single recipe for manufacturing a national identity. Nationalist movements can and usually do seek to build nations based on any one or more of these tiers of kinship. Each of these can be considered as both sociable and imagined communities of their own. Sociable, because their members can interact with each other using a common language. Imagined, because many will never know each other personally as Benedict Anderson elegantly puts it.

To assert that group identity matters to individuals on a deeply personal level is to state the obvious. Still, it is crucial to note that it is often up to the individual to determine which tier of her or his multitiered identity should serve as their default setting. Someone in Cairo may choose to identify as an *Egyptian* (nationality), or an *Arab* (ethnicity), or a *Muslim* (religion), or a *Sunni* (sect), or a North African (region), or an African (continent). Someone in Calcutta may choose to identify as an *Indian* (nationality), or a *Bengali* (ethnicity), or a *Hindu* (religion), or a *Brahmin* (caste). Someone in Sydney may identify as an *Australian* (nationality), or an *Anglo-Celt* (ethnicity), or a *Christian* (religion), or an *Anglican* (denomination). Note that Arab, Bengali and Anglo-Celt are all ethnic markers of an individual's identity. There is an implied expectation that one is born into these cultural in-groups, rather than gaining membership through naturalisation, assimilation or conversion. Arab happens to be an ethnicity that transcends political borders across 22 independent states. Bengali is an ethnicity that has its own minority state within India in the province of West Bengal as well as another independent nation-state of Bangladesh, which seceded from Pakistan in 1971 (as explored in chapter four: Case Study 2). Likewise, an Anglo-Celt is an ethnicity that can be found anywhere within the British

Isles or its colonial extensions: the United States, Canada, South Africa, Zimbabwe, New Zealand and Australia. While most Anglosphere states welcome new migrants[36] and let them acquire citizenship through a naturalisation process, these migrants do not become Anglo-Celts by ethnicity, they become Americans, Canadians, Australians and New Zealanders by nationality. This again reinforces the point that ethnicity is an *impenetrable* tier of group identity.

For the purpose of classification, migrants to the Anglosphere often end up prefixing their identity with their chosen tier of ethnicity, nationality, religion or sect. For instance, a Beirut-born migrant in Sydney might identify as a *Lebanese* Australian, or an *Arab* Australian, or depending on her or his faith, either a *Maronite Christian* Australian or a *Shiite Muslim* Australian. In migrant diasporas, ethnic differences can often be overridden by the nationality at birth which then starts acting as an ethnicity of itself. Pakistanis living in Pakistan differentiate each other on ethnic grounds as Urdu-speakers, Pashtuns, Punjabis, Balochis, Sindhis among many other minor ethnic groups. Pakistani linguist Tariq Rahman makes the observation that:

> Identity is an elusive category. A person might define himself or herself in terms of sex (male or female); family role (son, daughter, wife); occupation (weaver, or julaha); tribe or clan (Mughal, Pathan, Arain, Sheikh); economic class; or some other self-defining label. Such labelling is part of self-perception and also perception by others. Sometimes, one's own perception might be different from that of others. They may see one as a Pakistani, whereas one thinks of oneself as an Indian, Bangladeshi, or Asian.[37]

Rahman's assertions are sound. Similar attitudes exist among many other national groups, Afghans and Indians included. Yet Pakistani migrants living in the Anglosphere rarely identify themselves by their ethnicity. The Pakistani nationality takes over as a quasi-ethnic identity. So a Pashtun Pakistani migrant in Manchester would generally refer to her or himself as a Pakistani Brit, or an Asian Brit, or a Muslim Brit, but rarely ever as a Pashtun Brit. The few that do tend to identify with the original ethnicity are the ethnocentrists who may well consider ethnic Pashtuns from Afghanistan and ethnic Pashtuns from Pakistan to be a single nation separated by an arbitrary border drawn by British coloniser Sir Mortimer Durand in 1893. After arriving in the UK, the ethnocentric Pashtun might well identify as a *Pashtun* Brit, but that would be a rare occurrence. Generally people go up from their base level identity to a higher tier and the label *Pakistani* then becomes a prefix and starts acting like one's ethnicity in the West. As to which identity grouping matters more to the individual depends on the individual. It works the same way for nationalist movements.

If they so aspired, nationalists could literally manufacture a nationalist cause based on one's ethnicity, religion, sect or any other tier of human identity. Any territory can potentially be attached to *any* group identity, indigenous or otherwise. It is often assumed that continuous inhabitation of land is a prerequisite to nationalist activity. This is not correct. The entire colonised world is a prime example of national identities based on settler narratives. North and South America today predominantly speak English, Spanish, Portuguese and French and indigenous native American languages have been pushed into the background. This supersession of local identities results from centuries of European conquest and colonisation of the Americas. The same is true of other settler colonies created by the British Empire such as parts of South Africa, Zimbabwe, New Zealand and Australia. The State of Israel is a *re-indigenised* state where, as the story goes,[38] the indigenous Jewish people have been able to return home after 2,000 years of exile and become a demographic majority.

American political scientist Samuel P. Huntington identifies civilisation as the highest level of human group identity.[39] It is more often than not defined by a common religion or cultural values. Those Muslims living in the West who choose to identify as *Muslim* American, *Muslim* Brit or *Muslim* Australian instead of Turkish American, Pakistani Brit or Lebanese Australian are essentially those who choose to put their religious or civilisational identity above both their ethnicity and nationality at birth. Often migrating to a Western country leaves many in an environment where their political allegiances or cultural affinities may switch boundaries from ethnicity to nationality acting as ethnicity to religion or civilisation acting as ethnicity. Whatever an individual chooses to prefix before her or his adopted demonym *becomes* their sub-identity. As explored in the next chapter, common language creates sociability. A Bengali-speaking Indian migrant in the United Kingdom could easily mingle in the local Bangladeshi community as if they were from the same place, even though they arrived in the UK on two separate national passports. In a similar vein, a Farsi-speaking Iranian migrant in Australia could easily mingle in the the local Afghan community. A Spanish-speaking Venezuelan migrant in America could comfortably mingle in the local Puerto Rican community. In fact, migrant communities in the West either do assume a *pan-ethnic* character enabled by shared vernacular language, or a religiously based *civilisational* character enabled by common reference to shared liturgy.

When a Venezuelan person is living in Caracas, the group identity would not typically stretch out far enough to consider a Puerto Rican, a Mexican or an Argentinian as her or his *own* people, or *volk* as Johann Gottfried Herder put it. Unless, if one happened to be an ideological pan-nationalist, which would be the exception rather than the rule. This is not out of dislike for Puerto Ricans, Mexicans or Argentinians, but because a Venezuelan living in Venezuela does not typically hear much about, let alone comes into close contact with Puerto Ricans, Mexicans and Argentinians. This makes for a weak case to lump them all as part of the Venezuelan imagined community as Anderson puts it. These nationalities do not generally register on each other's radar. A Muslim Egyptian living in Cairo would typically not come into contact with, let alone hear a great deal about, Indonesians. Yet migration to a Western country changes all that. When migrants meet others from different nation-states who speak their language, it is generally a fascinating experience for them. This formation of sociable communities can, and usually does, transcend national borders. It redefines how people identify each other. In the

United States, migrant Venezuelans, Puerto Ricans, Mexicans or Argentinians simply become *Hispanic* Americans. A Pew Research Center survey in 2013 found that Spanish was: "...the most spoken non-English language in the United States.[40]

In a similar vein, the Egyptian and the Indonesian in Sydney become *Muslim* Australians. Islam as a religion discourages racism and racial disunity. Muslims often boast of this fact with great pride. Except, when Pakistanis living within Pakistan attend the mosque on Fridays, they only see other ethnic varieties of Pakistanis. For that matter, when Arabs anywhere in the 22 Arabic-speaking states, or Indonesians, or Somalis, or Bosnians or Turks go to the mosque to pray, they *predominantly* only come into contact with other Arabs, other Indonesians, other Somalis, other Bosnians or other Turks. Yet migration to the Western world offers the opportunity to meet Muslims from other nationalities, races and ethnic backgrounds they had never met before. Attending a mosque on Friday in London, New York, Toronto, Auckland or Sydney enables the faithful Muslim to *truly* come to terms with the *cosmopolitan* nature of Islam. So the idea that Islam is colour-blind and the *ummah* or global community of Muslims are one *volk* as Herder would put it, starts to perpetuate a sense of a *civilisational* imagined community.

Both ethnic and national boundaries get disregarded in that mode of thinking. Islam goes from being a religious identity to a quasi-national identity with a shared civilisational past. Many begin to envision the idea of a pan-Islamic state stretching from Morocco to Indonesia. Pakistanis, Moroccans, Bosnians, Turks, Indonesians and Somalis all come from different ancestral roots, speak different languages at home, have different physical characteristics and come from different national identities. Yet when they walk into a Mosque on a Friday, they recite their *Jummah* prayers in classical *Fusha* Arabic and identify Arabic calligraphy on the walls of the Mosque. They connect with each other through the same liturgical language and sharing the same ideographs in Arabic that evoke the same nostalgias. As a result, migrant Muslim diasporas in the West often become laboratories for quasi-nationalist experiments.

No discussion on religion or civilisation as potential markers of a group identity can afford to leave sectarian identity out. Both the Christian and the Islamic worlds have experienced some of the longest lasting and most gruesome forms of wars over sectarian divisions. Christianity began as a Messianic first century sect of Judaism, but evolved separately into a religion of its own over time. The relations between Jews and Christians had for centuries been fragile ever since. What began as a sectarian difference became a religious and civilisational one. Within Christendom, there were two main branches of Christianity to begin with, which officially split up in the Great Schism of 1054 leaving Western Catholics on one side and Eastern Orthodox on the other. The Latin-speaking Holy Roman Empire became the administrative centre of Catholic Christianity while the Greek-speaking Byzantine Empire became the administrative centre of Orthodox Christianity, until its conquest by the Muslim Ottomans in 1453. The administrative centre of Orthodox Christianity eventually shifted from the now-lost city of Constantinople to Moscow which proclaimed itself as the 'Third Rome'.[41] The year 1517 led to yet another split within Western Christendom marking the start of the Protestant Reformation led by Martin Luther. This resulted in a series of violent wars until the Treaty of Westphalia was signed in 1648. This period remains one of the most tumultuous in early modern history marking rampant bloodshed between Catholics and Protestants across Europe.

If the Irish Republican Army's political activism and terrorism is any indication, sectarian divisions have been real within Europe until more recent times. Islam too split up into Shi'ite and Sunni branches almost immediately after its founding Prophet Muhammad's death. The initial point of divergence was political, but over time, jurisprudential and doctrinal differences also widened. Sunni Islam came to establish itself through the Umayyad dynasty in Damascus, while Shi'ite Islam established itself through the Abbasid dynasty in Baghdad in the early Middle Ages. After the US invasion of Iraq in 2003, the shi'ite-sunni patchwork in Iraqi society became more militant and volatile. The Islamic State in Iraq and Syria (ISIS) was in fact a hardline sunni nationalist group that took advantage of the power vacuum from the collapse of Iraq's existing government and joined forces with breakaway rebels fighting Syrian dictator Bashar Al-Assad across the border. The on-going rivalry between Sunni-ruled Saudi Arabia and Shi'ite-ruled Iran is another manifestation of a sectarian struggle that has found its way into a competition for regional hegemony. In short, sectarian identities are real and can turn politically explosive. This is why sectarianism remains one of the core ingredients behind which nationalist movements could potentially mobilise the masses in an effort to seek statehood.

Racial identity is not directly relevant to the subject of this book. Yet it cannot be left out of the discussion on identity because, in recent times, it too has become attractive for some nationalist causes. Whether one believes race is a biological or social construct, physical differences in human appearance are real and can be observed by the naked eye. These differences can sometimes compliment ethnicity, nationality or civilisation, not only as markers of identity, but of *typicality*. France is home to many French citizens of African descent. More than half of France's soccer team at the 2018 FIFA World Cup in Russia was made of African Frenchmen. Those players are as French as anybody both in the legal sense, as well as the linguistic sense. Yet they attracted many comments from critics about the changing face of French society.[42] This is partly because they did not constitute what a typical Frenchman is supposed to look like. By contrast, former French soccer player Zinedine Zidane was a Muslim of Algerian descent who had a Caucasian Mediterranean appearance. Zidane blended in and was often mistaken as an authentic representation of a typical Frenchman. The idea of *typicality* in any concept of ethnicity, nationality or religion remains a highly contentious and arbitrary matter. To claim to have found the *median* appearance in any diverse spectrum of appearances and to insist that this particular stereotype defines a certain identity group is to necessarily discriminate against the *mean* and the *mode* appearances. Group identities are and should be taken as social, political and cultural constructs.

Defining an identity grouping based on racial lines is a form of historical revisionism. Before the start of the European age of discovery with the founding of the New World by Christopher Columbus in 1492, Europeans began coming into close contacts with other humans with starkly different physical appearances to their own. These were types of humans which Europeans had never previously interacted with. As many of the natives of the newly explored lands across the Atlantic and the Pacific Oceans were technologically less advanced than Europeans and their societies were far less politically organised than European and other old world societies, many Europeans proceeded to assume that the natives were biologically inferior to themselves. This phenomenon is described as scientific racism. It came to manifest itself in great pieces of literature from the 18th and 19th centuries. Alfred Wallace and Charles Darwin discussed it in their theories of natural selection. Gregor Mendel's ideas on genetics, Johann Blumenbach's taxonomy of human races and Arthur de Gobineau's treatise on the inequality of races are examples of these. These theories went hand in hand with Darwin's theory of evolution and Herbert Spencer's notion of the survival of the fittest. These notions only helped reinforce the old world order within which might was right. Under these new 'scientific' realisations that the races of the world were not equally designed by evolution and that the Europeans were at the top of the food chain, various European empires used these conclusions to rationalise their exploration and settlement of new colonies around the world. There is little evidence to suggest that physical appearance or race was the primary marker of *national* identity *before* the emergence of the theory of scientific racism.

If world history on almost any continent is any indication, people with the same physical appearance have caused more violence and bloodshed to each other, than to those with different physical features. Europe and Sub-Saharan Africa are prime examples of this. The English and the French, for instance, both tend to be of a Caucasian appearance, both of Christian origins, both from Western Europe, both use the Latin script to write their languages, both share a similar diet and cultural lifestyle and yet it never occurred to them to think of each other as one race, one *volk* or one imagined community. From the Battle of Hastings (1066) to the Battle of Waterloo (1815), the English and the French have a long history of *not* thinking of each other as an imagined community. The most violent and bloodiest example of their rivalry was the Hundred Years' War from 1337 to 1453. It was only during World War I (1914-1918) that the English and the French at last forged an alliance of convenience to mobilise the Arab nationalists against the Ottoman Empire and to carve up the map of the modern Middle East to further their economic interests. The English and the French despised and fought each other for over eight centuries despite sharing more than enough cultural commonalities to literally satisfy the criteria of a single nation put forward by almost every scholar discussed so far including Anderson, Herder, Kohn, Berlin, Hobsbawm, Seton-Watson, Greene, Smith and Lewis.

Bear in mind that Berlin's criteria for a nation were: "common territory, customs, laws, memories, beliefs, language, artistic and religious expression, social institutions, ways of life, to which some add heredity, kinship, *racial characteristics*; and that it is these factors which shape human beings, their purposes and their values."[43] If we went through each of those, the French and the English could be considered one nation. When we take into account the Norman period when a French dialect was the language in England, it even, to a degree, satisfied the criterion of linguistic commonality. Yet these are and always have been two separate nations because, for whatever reason, they choose not to think of each other as the same nation. As Gellner points out: "Two men are of the same nation *if and only if they recognise each other as belonging to the same nation.*"[44] This Anglo-French rivalry is a strong argument against any suggestion that somehow commonality of physical appearance, or what Berlin described as racial characteristics can bind people together as one volk. At least, it has not done so historically.

These are the kind of arguments present-day white nationalists are either unaware of or wilfully disregard. Europeans who might share the same physical appearance have never thought of each other as one volk or an imagined community and do not exactly have a shared past. There is no common European myth that everyone can relate to. If one were to be constructed, like most nationalist movements a significant amount of cultural differences and internal rivalries between different European dynasties would have to be wilfully discarded in order to project a common national mythology. Charlemagne was a hero for the French. He slaughtered thousands of Saxons. Can the contemporary descendants of Saxons in today's Germany consider Charlemagne to be their hero? Pope Urban II commissioned the First Crusade from 1095 to 1099 through his Papal Bull *inter gracias* to reclaim Jerusalem. He was not only Catholic, but the epitome of the kind of parochialism that the Protestant Reformation sought to fight against from 1517 onwards. Can Protestant Europeans then consider Urban II to be a celebrated figure of *their* national memory? One of the greatest moments in English history was its triumph over the Spanish Armada in 1588. It was the moment that put English naval supremacy on the world map. Can the Spaniards, humiliated by the English, consider the English triumph over the Spanish Armada as a moment of *their* own triumph? They were, after all, the defeated party. Adolf Hitler's regime murdered six million Jews and many Poles, Slavs and Gypsies. Can *anyone* in Europe consider him to be their hero? In short, European history is so fraught with internal divisions that even the most optimistic pan-European nationalist could not manufacture a shared past and consciousness without running into manifest contradictions. This is one of the underlying reasons why the European Union, much like the Soviet Union before it, does not appeal to ethno-nationalists. Many have predicted that Brexit could be the beginning of the end of the European Union.[45] Time will tell.

What is evident is that people who might share the same racial characteristics and ancestries *too often* continue to identify each other as *foreigners*. The entire map of Europe and Sub-Saharan Africa are two prime examples of that. The Rwandan Genocide in 1994 claimed the lives of up to one million ethnic Tutsis by the ethnic Hutu government. Yet again, this gruesome act of mass murder was committed by one Sub-Saharan African cultural in-group against another Sub-Saharan African cultural in-group which shared a: "...common territory, customs, laws, memories, beliefs, language, artistic and religious expression, social institutions, ways of life, to which some add heredity, kinship, racial characteristics"[46] with its murderers. The Hutu and Tutsi of Rwanda are collectively known as Banyarwanda, a subdivision of the Bantu peoples of central Africa and even share the same language. What both white and black nationalists are attempting to do is to manufacture a modern kind of a national consciousness that has *never* existed throughout history. Neither have white Europeans ever been a single nation nor have black Sub-Saharan Africans been a single nation. By comparison, India which is ethnically, racially, linguistically and religiously far more diverse than both Europe and Sub-Saharan Africa not only has a stronger claim to a shared sense of nationhood, it is seven decades ahead of the European Union in holding its 1.2 billion citizens together as Herder's one *volk* and as Anderson's imagined community.

It is clear by this stage that human identity is a multitiered phenomenon. These tiers could be based on ethnicity, religion, civilisation, sect or culture. It is entirely up to the individual subject, depending on their circumstances at hand, to determine *which* of these tiers of her or his identity matters more to them in *what* given situation. Some feel a greater affinity to their religious or civilisational group identity than to ethnicity, others may be the exact opposite. If one conclusion is logical to draw from these observations, it is that nations and national identities can potentially be whatever it is that the particular nationalists in charge *want* them to be. A single ethnicity could start its own nationalist movement, as could a particular religious sect, or a group of ethnicities and religious beliefs. There is no hard and fast rule on how cultural in-groups should determine their parametres. This is why there are different forms of nationalisms, with wide-ranging attitudes both before and after statehood has been achieved. If nationalists seek to represent an impenetrable cultural in-grouping that outsiders cannot opt-in to nor opt-out of, that is generally described as *ethnonationalism*. Due to the prefix 'ethno' it is often mistakenly assumed that ethnonationalism is about preferential treatment of a single ethnicity above others. This is not necessarily how ethnonationalism works. Consider Britain's example where the ethnonationalist attitude is fairly uniform in its opposition to multiculturalism and mass immigration, but it is, in general, perfectly comfortable in accepting what it considers to be Britain's indigenous ethnicities of English, Welsh, Scottish and Irish. These are different ethnic groups within British society, but the ethnonationalist does not put one above the other, nor tries to imagine a Britain without a particular ethnicity. Rather, ethnonationalist thought is happy to accept English, Welsh, Scottish and Irish as valid representatives of the British national identity.

This goes back to the earlier point that, sometimes, a national identity *can* function as an ethnic identity of itself. Other examples of ethnonationalism may involve a single ethnic group wanting its own state. The Kurdish example in Iraq or Catalan example in Spain are cases in point. These are pre-statehood forms of ethnonationalism, based around a common ethnolinguistic identity. The form of nationalism practiced in most Anglosphere nations is civic nationalism. Its core philosophy is that national identity should not be confined to biological inheritance, rather it can be achieved through naturalisation and anyone of any ethnicity, race or religion can be a part of the nation through migration. Great Britain, United States, Canada, New Zealand and Australia all practise this form of civic nationalism. Yet each continues to have many dominant ethnonationalist voices right-of-centre in their political landscape. While *ethno* and *civic* are the two main forms of nationalism that still continue to feature in political debates, especially in the Western world, other forms of nationalism have been defined. Some use the term supranationalism to refer to multiethnic or what some may perceive as multinational states like the Soviet Union used to be from 1917 to 1991 or what India has been from 1947 till present day. Civic nationalism is generally a post-statehood nationalism. Even the Anglosphere countries that practice it were ethno or supranationalist at the time of their making and had restrictive immigration policies. Civic nationalism entered the picture much later through the rise of multiculturalism. The only example of pre-statehood civic nationalism is pan-Islamic nationalism. Although statehood in the form of a Sunni Islamic Caliphate has not been achieved, this form of national identity based on the Islamic notion of the *ummah* is open to all. Outsiders can opt-in regardless of ethnicity or race, provided they support the cause. In general, pre-statehood nationalisms tend not to be of a civic nature. Most ethnonationalists or supranationalists tend to view their cause as struggling against an imperial power or a foreign occupier to achieve independence such as Catalans and Kurds, or they exist in a diaspora wanting to return to a distant homeland such as Jews.

Today the world map comprises of 195 nation-states based on their membership of the United Nations. Yet modern *nation-states* are rarely configured as precisely as the term might suggest, if taken literally. Neither does every nation in the world have its own sovereign state, nor does every sovereign state necessarily only comprise of a single nation. Ernest Gellner points out that the number of potential nations: "...is probably much, much larger than that of possible viable states. If this argument or calculation is correct, not all nationalisms can be satisfied, at any rate at the same time. The satisfaction of some spells the frustration of others."[47] As a result, the territorial settings of world states do not always match the cultural settings. There are states with a single nation, eg: Japan and Israel.[48] There are nations without a single state, eg: Catalonians and Kurds. There are nations with multiple states, eg: Arabs and Anglo-Celts. There are states with multiple nations, eg: Canada and

South Africa. Suffice it to say, the modern world is a mosaic of ambiguous territorial configurations. As Gellner points out, this is because: "...very many of the potential nations of this world live, or until recently have lived, not in compact territorial units but intermixed with each other in complex patterns. It follows that a territorial political unit can only become ethnically homogeneous, in such cases, if it either kills, or expels, or assimilates all non-nationals."[49]

It is often assumed that nationalism is about empowering majority rule. This is a simplistic view. In some cases, nationalist endeavours represent the majority demographic while in others, they represent a minority demographic. The numbers vary from one situation to the next. If members of the cultural in-group that a particular nationalist movement seeks to represent *do* happen to be the demographic majority by default, then they may use that fact to advantage to legitimise their demands. Nelson Mandela's case in South Africa is a prime example. Since blacks were the demographic majority, his African National Congress argued that white minority rule had to end and it did. If members of the cultural in-group of a particular nationalist movement seeks to represent *do not* happen to be the demographic majority by default, then they may seek to become the majority. How they go about achieving this varies from one case to the next. The Jewish case in Ottoman Palestine is a prime example. From the 1880s, Zionist thinkers began encouraging Jews from Europe and Russia, where Jews were being persecuted at the time, to start purchasing land in Ottoman Palestine and set up farming communities known as *kibbutzim,* and they did.

No universal formula was applied in drawing the borders of the world's 195 sovereign states. These borders were imposed on the world through human agency. Each nation-state is the product of very different and unique political circumstances. Some have emerged organically (eg: Japan), but most were artificially drawn from the spoils of decolonising empires. The cultural configurations within territorial units were always destined to be ambiguous due to the multiethnic and multireligious nature of population demographics within empires. In the minds of contemporary observers, thinking about the age of empires can often conjure up the image of an ancient way of governing societies placed in the distant past. It may remind us of ancient regimes like Alexander the Great's Hellenic Empire in the third century BCE, or Augustus Caesar's Roman Empire in the first century BCE. What is often forgotten is that the age of territorial empires did not disappear too long ago. Empires were around literally less than a century ago. At the outbreak of World War I (1914-1918), most of the world's territories were still under the control of one European imperial power or another. The major players were the: British Empire, Spanish Empire, French Empire, Portuguese Empire, Austro-Hungarian Empire, Russian Empire and Ottoman Empire. Ruling dynasties with ports along the Atlantic coast became great naval powers in the centuries that followed America's discovery by Christopher Columbus in 1492. The English, French, Spaniards and Portuguese fought each other militarily as well as the natives of the new world. The colossal sizes of these empires were the result of centuries of territorial expansion through warfare. This also meant the absorption of many different ethnic and religious minorities. Andreas Wimmer and Yuval Feinstein note that:

> Kings, theocrats, and imperial elites attempted to extend their states' boundaries irrespective of the ethnic backgrounds of those who came under their rule.[50]

Ruling elites without port cities along the Atlantic coast struggled to keep up with maritime colonisation. They compensated by expanding their dominions in-land. The Austro-Hungarians expanded across central and southern Europe. The Russians went eastward across the Ural Mountains through Siberia to the Sea of Japan. The Ottoman Turks ruled most of the eastern Mediterranean coast, the Levant and most of the Arabian Peninsula. Richard Pomfret points out that: "The great nineteenth-century empires were multicultural, and their collapse would lead to subdivision, just as with the Hapsburg Empire in Europe. Dividing the spoils looked set to be a messy business in all cases."[51] By the end of World War I, the Austro-Hungarians, Russian and Ottoman empires had all disintegrated. British, French, Spanish and Portuguese empires had also begun to dissolve into smaller units due to nationalism. Wimmer and Feinstein note:

> ...the global ascent of the nation-state over the past 200 years was a discontinuous process, unfolding in various waves linked to the break-up of large empires.[52]

Territorial conquests were the lawful norm during the age of empires, or the old world order as it has been called. It was a fundamentally different world to ours. In their 2017 publication *The Internationalists: How a Radical Plan to Outlaw War Remade the World*, international law experts Oona A. Hathaway and Scott J. Shapiro point out that acquiring territory by the use of force was first attempted to be prohibited through the Kellogg-Briand Pact (1928). The idea was to put an end to war. Yet the pact did not take effect immediately as World War II (1937-1945) still broke out less than a decade since its signing. The aftermath of World War II saw the intention of the pact brought into force through the United Nations Charter. This was to be a turning point in world history. For the first time, war was outlawed. Once a measure of first resort, war was to now become a measure of last resort. Disputes between nations were to be resolved through diplomacy and negotiations, rather than violence. It was determined that this prohibition on conquests would not apply retroactively. Future acquisition of territory by force were to be deemed illegal, but territories gained through conquest *before* the Kellogg-Briand Pact would not be reversed. 1928 became the cut-off for lawful conquests. By the turn of the 20th century, much of the colonies under the possession of European colonial powers had in fact been conquered and settled prior to this date. Yet nationalism had come into full force across the literate world by this stage. People were more educated and conscious that their imperial rulers did not represent their cultural settings. The only way to rectify this, it was argued, was to gain independence. This resulted in the long and slow process of gradual decolonisation.

NATIONALISM: CAVEMEN TO COUNTRYMEN

In recent centuries, many of the intellectual elites across Europe had begun to doubt the very idea of empire. As a result, decolonisation and nationalism ended up working in tandem, as complementary forces. On the one hand, were the European imperial powers, challenged from within. On the other hand, the rise of literacy, modernity, print media and the influence of European nationalist thought came to influence the nationalist elites among native populations across the colonies under the imperial rule of European powers. People began to be mobilised and started demanding statehood. Mahatma Gandhi and his struggles to liberate India from the British Empire is perhaps the most fetishised example of an anti-colonial nationalist movement. Most decolonised nation-states neither gained their independence from the same imperial power, nor did they gain it at the same time. There was never a *common* recipe to create nation-states with identical cultural or political configurations. These states were often created as part of a territorial carve up by the departing European imperialists. Power was transferred into the hands of select local elites who happened to have had the good will of the key decision makers in the departing imperial government. It must be noted that different nationalist elites used entirely different arguments to define the *nation* for which they had sought a sovereign *state*. Across much of the Arabian Peninsula, multiple states were created as gifts to the families of tribal warlords that had allied themselves with the British and the French Empires in their joint quest to dismantle the Ottoman Empire. The Hashemite family of Jordan and the Al-Saud family in what became Saudi Arabia are prime examples. The same was true of the other Gulf states and appointed dynasties.

The nation-states of Arabic-speaking North Africa resulted from local struggles against the colonial French, Italian and British Empires. In the case of decolonised states, often the case was, whoever happened to be the first to start a nationalist movement got to decide how the nation was to be configured. In the Subcontinent, there were many different religions and ethnic groups. There could have potentially been dozens of different ethnic or half a dozen religious nation-states when the British Empire left. Instead, two distinct forms of nationalisms emerged that were based on a religious identity. Pakistan for Muslims and India for the Hindus.[53] Of course, because the Hindu and Muslim populations were not territorially separate from each other, but in fact, too often interwoven into the same town, village and district, it was not always possible to create *exclusively* contiguous territories to accommodate the demands of both Muslim and Hindu nationalist elites at the same time. It was this interplay between the often competing national demands within the same territory on the one hand, weighed up against the logistical impossibility to simultaneously satisfy both on the other hand that is, in part, responsible for the ambiguously configured national borders. In short, there were two types of *specific* ethnic and religious communities that ended up being absorbed into a more *general* form of nationalism. One, those who did not have nationalist movements of their own. Two, those who had nationalist movements but held no clout among the political elite in the dying days of the imperial colony. Wimmer and Feinstein argue that:

> ...nationalist movements emerge through an imitation process driven by the extraordinary success and global dominance of the first nation-states. Nation-states are subsequently created around the world wherever a power shift allows nationalists to overthrow or absorb the established regime, quite independent of whether domestic modernisation processes have readied a society for nation-building.[54]
>
> ...a power shift is more likely when nationalists have had ample time to mobilise the population and delegitimise the old regime or when the established regime is weakened by wars.[55]
>
> Diffusion of nation-states among neighbours or within the same empire also empowers nationalists by providing a model to follow and new alliance partners on which to rely.[56]

Some nations did not have a choice over their state borders. They were determined by outside forces without much consultation with local leaders. The British Empire for instance, created Belgium, which is not a distinct nation, just to leave behind a buffer zone separating France, Germany and the Netherlands. This resulted in different ethnic groups who spoke different native languages coming together under these artificially enforced borders by a foreign power, forced to live together by sheer happenstance, and ruled over by an arbitrarily appointed monarchy. Other nation-states are essentially *shrunken* former empires: Britain, Turkey, Russia, France, Spain and Portugal. These were all mighty empires in their day but went through decolonisation. Most of their ethnic and religious diversity was in the remote parts of the colonised territory. As the empires disintegrated, the territorial possessions shrunk and defaulted back to the original territory of the founding state. As things stand at present, with the exception of Britain - where there are English, Welsh, Scottish and Irish ethnic varieties - most of the other shrunken empires remain relatively homogeneous in their population composition.

There are nation-states where natural borders were determined by physical geography more so than other factors. Iceland, Australia, New Zealand, Madagascar, Japan and Sri Lanka are examples of this. The nation states that were either never conquered by a foreign power or only conquered for a short period of time tend to receive their borders from the political developments *around* them, as opposed to those within. This would include Japan, Ethiopia, Iran, Afghanistan, Thailand and China. These are nations without the prolonged history of foreign occupation other nations have had to endure. Japan may strike some as the odd one out since it was temporarily occupied by American forces from the end of World War II in 1945 until 1952. Still, it was never colonised by a European imperial power despite coming into close contact with Jesuits from the Portuguese Empire as early as 1543. With the exception of Japan which is a collection of islands devoid of artificial borders, the rest of these nations emerged as a result of events around them, as opposed to events within. The best example is the Durand Line established in 1893 that separates Afghanistan from what was then the North-West Frontier Province of British India, what is now Pakistan. The British Empire wanted to leave a buffer zone between itself and the Tsarist Russian Empire, as a security barrier.

The border separating Afghanistan and the North-West Frontier Province of British India was negotiated between British diplomat Sir Mortimer Durand and Afghan Emir Abdur Rahman Khan.[57] Although Afghanistan was to be an autonomous region, its foreign affairs were handled by the British Empire. This arrangement meant that members of the same ethnic group, Pashtuns, were left stranded across two different sides of an international border.

Under the old world order or *ancien régime* as British historian Eric Hobsbawm called it, the borders of empires were constantly expanding and shrinking based on perpetual warfare. When wars were won, new territory was seized from the losing team. When wars were lost, old territory was ceded to the winning team. As the United Nations Charter in 1945 went about adopting the spirit of the Kellogg-Briand Pact (1928) to prohibit war and future territorial conquests, international borders at the time were to be deemed frozen. Yet the process of decolonisation did not occur overnight. Many nations across North Africa continued to gain independence from their European colonisers right through the 1950s and 1960s. There were still territorial gains. India annexed Goa in 1961. Israel captured the West Bank, Gaza, Golan Heights and the Sinai Peninsula in 1967. Bangladesh was created through war in 1971. East and West Germany reunified in 1990. The collapse of the Soviet Union saw 15 new nation-states emerge on the world map from 1991 onwards. Hong Kong was ceded back to China in 1997. Wimmer and Feinstein make the observation that:

> ...secessions from established nation-states will continue to occur, as the recent creations of Kosovo, East Timor, and Montenegro illustrate. And the few existing non-national states in the Middle East and elsewhere might experience a constitutional revolution in the future. Overall, however, we do not expect new waves of nation-state creations to sweep over the world.[58]

Indeed, there is no shortage of separatist movements around the world. Many nations have attempted to secede from their current states to form their own distinct nation-states. The Scottish independence referendum in 2014[59] and the Catalan independence referendum in 2017 are prime cases.⁶⁰ There are many more who demand states, the Kurds and the Palestinian Arabs fall in that category. The evolution of human societies has seen our species transition from hunter-gatherers to city-states to empires to nation-states. Although we have travelled through different stages of development, the tendency to form sociable communities has been the common denominator. Once upon a time, we shared a roof with our fellow *cavemen*. We hunted and gathered. Sat around a bonfire and told stories. Today, we share a roof with our fellow *countrymen*. Gellner identifies three stages of development, essentially lumping together the city state and the empire into a single stage as he remarks that: "Mankind has passed through three fundamental stages in its history: pre-agrarian, the agrarian, and the industrial. Hunting and gathering bands were and are too small to allow the kind of political division of labour which constitutes the state; and so, for them, the question of the state, of a stable specialised order-enforcing institution, does not really arise."⁶¹

He is correct in pointing to the lack of statehood during the hunter-gatherer stage. This is because settling in one place and building attachment to a fixed territory is what statehood is about. If sociable communities of people were to constantly be wandering from one territory to another, or occupy territories on regular seasonal bases, it would be impossible to create an enduring monopoly over the use of force. Gellner goes on to stress this point further and asserts that: "By contrast, most, but by no means all, agrarian societies have been state-endowed. Some of these states have been strong and some weak, some have been despotic and others law-abiding. They differ a very great deal in their form. The agrarian phase of human history is the period during which, so to speak, the very existence of the state is an option. Moreover, the form of the state is highly variable. During the hunting-gathering stage, the option was not available."⁶²

To sum up, nationalism has, no doubt, been a powerful force in the modern world. From the non-violent ethnonationalism of the Scottish and Catalan referendums to the supranationalism of Brexit, to the violent religious-civilisational nationalism of ISIS and Boko Haram, the recent surge in nationalist activity suggests that nationalism will likely continue to be a powerful force in decades if not centuries to come. In defining and analysing nationalism, nations, states and the multiple tiers of group identity, this chapter sets the conceptual framework within which the central argument of this thesis – that a shared language forms the backbone of the nation building process – is to be understood.

2

LANGUAGE: ARMOURY OF THE MIND

"To know another language is to possess a second soul"
Charlemagne

In the current world order, it is no longer feasible for nationalist movements to seek to create a common cultural form by exclusively appealing to ethnicity, which is impenetrable for outsiders, or to religion, which could be converted to, but not forced on outsiders in this day and age. So it follows that language becomes the most obvious and attractive tool to mobilise the masses and integrate them as members of a shared cultural-political form. There is substantial support for this view in the results of a 2017 Pew Research Centre cross-national survey of 14 nations which found in every case that, what was taken by citizens to be the most important marker or element of national identity was language.[63] No doubt, language has been and continues to be a desirable operating system for strategies of nation-building. This is achieved by facilitating appeals to common cultural myths, legends, ancient stories, literature or poetry. The same applies to state-building. That is achieved by enforcing a national language, an education system, written laws and bureaucratic documents. As discussed in the last chapter, nationalism requires the: "...integration of the masses into a common political form."[64] This chapter defines language and discusses its centrality to the human experience. It also examines its ability to create and shape sociable communities through its capacity to record and preserve knowledge and to act as a marker of one's group identity on various levels. In an age where ethnicity and religion can no longer promise to deliver robust national solidarity, it is language that has become the most feasible tool for nationalist movements in manufacturing and maintaining national identities.

The story of humanity, as of any extant biological species, is a story of successful adaptation. In the face of challenges we either go under, as most species have done throughout history, or we adapt, improve and survive. This need for adaptive change is manifest across all aspects of our collective experience. Politics and governance, society and community, law and ethics, customs and values, art and literature, medicine and technology: each is a part of the human tale of self-preservation and information sharing, as we build and live through our sociable communities. Early hominids stuck together and learnt to understand the laws of nature through trial and error. We inherit the sum of their observations. In other words, we do not need to repeat the same mistakes committed by our distant ancestors. We have over time accumulated great wisdom as it has been transmitted through oral tradition, cave paintings, written alphabet, printing press, and now, the world wide web. Other living beings, including those who share 96% genetic similarity with us, have not been able to achieve all this. Our distant cousins, chimpanzees and orangutans, today live more or less the same lives they did 10,000 years ago. We, on the other hand, have flown to the moon and back. There is a force without which none of this would have been possible. That force is our ability to speak amongst ourselves. As such, language is more than simply a tool for communication. It shapes the cognitive algorithms that let us think, analyse, ascribe meaning to objects and concepts, appreciate humour, exercise creativity, convey feelings and make deliberative choices. It is the medium that enables us to interpret our observations, to be able to judge and draw conclusions. Those who share a language have greater sociability than those beings that do not. This is because we can form *speech communities*. It is in this sense that what we speak and how we speak it becomes the distinct marker of our identities. Alyssa Ayres argues that:

> Language plays a central role in creating boundaries of belonging that shape, or rather are shaped by, choices of national identity. Despite the fact that language is a very pliant facet of one's social self, widespread and indeed formalised linkage of language with ethnicity has created our current world of nation-states.[65]

Exploring this nexus between language, community and identity is the main focus of this chapter. Without this understanding, we would not be able to appreciate why language remains so attractive to nationalist movements. Language is the evolutionary response to the human need to exchange thoughts and information in order to maximise our prospects and quality of survival through adaptive change. For philosopher Daniel C. Dennett: "There is no step more uplifting, more momentous in the history of mind design, than the invention of language. When Homo sapiens became the beneficiary of this invention, the species stepped into a slingshot that has launched it far beyond all other earthly species."[66] No doubt, the spread of language has had profound impact on human societies. Culture could not be preserved across time without language, nor could language evolve independently of culture. This relationship is symbiotic. Language not only constructs cultural narratives through folklore, it also preserves and conveys them to future generations. It embodies vital ingredients that form the basis for an individual's ethnic, religious or national identities.

Through access to common knowledge and shared communication, speakers of a shared language are able to evoke actual and perceived ancestral narratives and lay down the framework for determining social norms and values. Language helps us develop sociability and unique interactive relationships with different members of the family and community. It embodies distinct cultural characteristics and psyches of social groups creating a sense of exclusive belonging. It is not an understatement to say where there is no common language, there is a lacking sense of community. Co-founder of the Wired Magazine

Kevin Kelly once remarked that: "The creation of language was the first singularity for humans. It changed everything. Life after language was unimaginable to those on the far side before it."[67] More than two thousand years before us, it was Aristotle who in his seminal work *Politics* first identified language as the medium of moral perception, enabling differentiation between right and wrong. (*Politics* 1. 2. 1253al 14). As Richard McKeon observes:

> Language, as a function of man, is a frequent subject of inquiry in the course of Aristotle's scientific investigations; for language not only has a natural basis in man's bodily organs and psychological powers, but it is, in turn, one of the natural bases of the virtues and of social and political relations, and it constitutes the natural means of imitation in the art of literature and the matter of which literary works are formed. In addition to such inquiries into the foundations of language in human organism, moral agent, and aesthetic object, Aristotle turns his attention to questions concerning the operations of language, for it can be put to various uses, and it can in any of them contravene as well as accomplish the purpose for which it is directed.[68]

This explains why religion has an indispensable relationship with language. It is commonplace that for the vast majority of peoples through almost all of human history, religion has been the system of ideas and practices that speech communities articulate and deploy to provide deeper meaning to an otherwise mysterious existence. Religion is the first known phenomenon that enabled humanity to build morality and to learn to differentiate between right and wrong. As a result, religion has been essential in the creation and maintenance of social structure and hierarchy. It seems equally clear that the preservation and transmission of religious beliefs, teachings and customs would be inconceivable without sacred scripture being scribed using language. The continuation of rituals and worship would be equally unthinkable without the use of prayer and liturgy using language. It is through language that adherents maintain their connection with the rest of the religious community and to the shrines central to their belief systems. The Jewish concept of *Am Yisrael* (nation of Israel) in liturgical Hebrew and the Islamic concept of *Ummah* (nation) of believers in classical (fushaa) Arabic are prime examples. Sabbath services in Hebrew enable Jews in the diaspora thousands of kilometres apart from Jerusalem to commune with that land. Sunday mass in Latin enables Catholic minorities in India to preserve their unique traditions and commune with the Holy See at the Vatican. Friday *khutbah* in Arabic at mosques in Xinjiang enables the Uighur Muslim minorities in China to commune with the Holy Ka'aba in Mecca. William Safran argues that:

> Language is a marker of ethnic identity; a vehicle for expressing a distinct culture; a source of national cohesion; and an instrument for building political community. Yet the relationship between language and ethnonational identity is a contested matter. There is no question that language is one of the elements defining collective consciousness, the others being religion, history, common descent, and territory.[69]

Of course, the long early history of religion in the self-constitution and social articulation of speech communities did not, of itself, depend on written language. Yet it remains clear how the stability and relative permanence of such writing systems acts to strengthen the power of religion in human communities at the same time as it opened up other forms of semantic or social articulation. The beginnings of the Bronze Age in the late Neolithic period saw the birth of humanity's first systems of writing, hieroglyphs of Ancient Egypt and the Cuneiform of Sumer. Although their concurrence is indisputable, whether or not one influenced the development of the other remains the subject of widespread debate. The emergence of written language and the rise of early river valley civilisations in the Ancient Near East is far from coincidental. That accumulated body of information and skills transmitted by earlier hunter-gatherer speech communities in the region inevitably paved the way for the birth of permanent settlements in designated territories. This was a massive leap away from the nomadic lifestyle of the past. Situated on the Nile, the Euphrates and Tigris, and the Indus, these early river valley civilisations featured small agrarian communities with domesticated animals, pottery, central government, basic laws, common currency and trade. This marked the first time in history where common language, now a mixture of the spoken and the written, would become the marker of one's social membership of an organised community. With some caution, Joshua A. Fishman makes the observation that:

> Language serves as an important instrument for protecting collective identity and communal cohesion. It is important because it marks the "at-homeness" of a people threatened by cultural homogenisation. It has helped to preserve the identity of the Tamils in Sri Lanka; the Turks in Cyprus; the Quebecois in Canada; the Ibos and Fulanis in Nigeria; and the Bamileke in Cameroon. However, language may not be sufficient, because linguistic differences do not always demarcate ethnic groups.[70]

That language should have this profound ability to unite or divide sociable communities is not new knowledge. One of the earliest narratives that embodies the power of language is the Old Testament story of the Tower of Babel in Genesis Chapter 11 verses 1 to 9. In a world with only one language, a group of settlers from the East come to settle in the land of Shinar. With the use of bricks, the settlers decide to build a city comprising what could literally be thought of as an ancient skyscraper. First century Jewish Roman historian, Flavius Josephus, explains in his *The Antiquities of the Jews* that the building was viewed by God as an affront, a manifestation of the contempt Nimrod, the King of Shinar, felt towards God.[71] The fact that God decides to teach people a lesson is hardly surprising in light of his consistently punitive character manifest throughout the Old Testament. What is both intriguing and relevant is *how* God chooses to inflict his punishment:

> "6 The LORD said, *'If as one people speaking the same language they have begun to do this, then nothing they plan to do will be impossible for them.* 7 Come, *let us go down and confuse their language so they will not understand each other."* 8 So the LORD scattered them from there over all the earth, and they stopped building the city. 9 That is why it was called Babel - because there *the LORD confused the language of the whole world.* From there the LORD scattered them over the face of the whole earth."
> – Genesis 11:6-9[72] [italics are mine]

Make no mistake, this is an omnipotent, omniscient and all-powerful God, quite capable of wiping out entire cities, sending down plagues and curses, and casting terror into the hearts of people. Yet of all the options available, that he should choose to confound the languages of people as the punishment for an act of architectural audacity tells us something about the mindset of those who forged this narrative in the first place. It is reasonable to assume that the authors of this passage knew that common language was the backbone of a community. The Tower of Babel narrative rests on the assumption that if humans spoke *different* languages, they would no longer be able to form sociable communities and cooperate with one another on a project like the construction of this tower that dares to reach out to the heavens above. As it happens, the same remains true in the real world today. Where there is no communication, there is no cooperation, and *optimum* communication occurs where there is *common* language.

Given its multipurpose characteristics, modern humans are fortunate to be endowed with the faculty of language. Humans, orangutans, chimps and gorillas all belong to different genera of the same biological family: *hominidae*. The intrigue does not lie in the fact that we speak while our evolutionary cousins do not, in fact they too make certain sounds. The intrigue is that we speak with *grammar* while they do not. At some point in the distant past, through mutation and natural selection, we, but not our fellow hominidae, came to express and transmit information through the semantic and communicative possibilities opened up by the advent of grammatical speech. For millennia, language has been the centrepiece of the human experience, and not merely because of its essential nature as a medium for communication. It has equally been the source of intrigue and perplexity for philosophers, linguists, grammarians, historians, sociologists and anthropologists alike. Efforts to understand language from wide-ranging vantage points and its ability to bind us together into communities, nations and tribes, have resulted in many competing theories.

Fascinated by its complexity, some 19th century Indo-European linguists concluded that language was an organic lifeform itself. Friedrich von Schlegel described it as 'ein lebendiges Gewebe' which means 'a living tissue' and Wilhelm von Humboldt as 'Organismus der Sprache' which means 'an organism of language'. When Charles Darwin's 1859 publication the *Origin of Species* became available in Germany, August Schleicher offered a view regarding the organic nature of language in an unequivocally literal sense.[73] As George Van Driem points out, while this vitalist concept began to die down as more scientific methods of examining language emerged over time,[74] these 'organic' origin theories, much like the Tower of Babel story, still remain fascinating insights into the minds of those that have attempted to grapple with the mysterious nature of language as a uniquely human phenomenon.

On the level of personal competency in daily use, we know *what* language is and *how* it functions. Yet devising an unambiguous definition can still be challenging. There is an abundance of different views, though most are not mutually exclusive. This chapter aims to provide a workable and generally acceptable definition of language. Linguist Graeme Trousdale says: "A dictionary definition of the terms 'language and 'dialect' is a useful place to start, because dictionaries typically provide definitions on which at least some people in the community agree. One function of a dictionary is to represent what most speakers of a given variety will accept as an accurate meaning of any given concept."[75] Trousdale goes on to cite the *Oxford English Dictionary* which defines language as:

> The system of spoken or written communication used by a particular country, people, community, etc., typically consisting of words used within a regular grammatical and syntactic structure.[76]

Linguist Martin Montgomery, defines language as: "...a set of interlocking relationships in which a linguistic form takes on the meaning it does by virtue of place within the total system of signs".[77] In their book *An Introduction to Language*, Victoria Fromkin, Robert Rodman and Nina Hyams define language as: "...a system that relates sounds or gestures to meanings."[78] They go on to point out that "Talking birds such as parrots and mynahs are capable of faithfully reproducing words and phrases of human language that they have heard, but their utterances carry no meaning."[79] As far as its functionality is concerned, using language expresses a speaker-intention: that the listener is to do or think X. And one way (not the only one, but a common one) to understand this, is through a process in which the speaker's mind or brain directs her or his speech organs to encode, by vocal movements, that which originates in the speaker's brain, expecting that the listener will receive this encoded information through their senses (hearing, sight, or even touch) and that their brain will then decode it, and end up doing or thinking X *as intended* by the speaker. This speaker-intention, as expressed in language (the medium of information transmission) results in a stream of sound with its own rhythms, tones, pauses and other building blocks.

Information transmission such as speaker-intention clearly involves sociability in two connected ways. In the first place, information is transmitted, and in the second, that information is only transmissible *as long as* the speaker and the listener share, and know they share, the same code - a condition that itself involves the capacity to correct or incorrect uses of the coding medium (concepts). For instance, to understand the english sentence, "Please pass me the red pen", one must know what the speaker's words 'red' and 'pen' refer to, and to know further that 'please' is the marker of a polite request, and that 'pass' designates a certain action or performance. While most human languages, on a deep level, deploy in their own structured ways the same grammatical components (subject/verb/predicate), the meanings of words and concepts can sometimes vary considerably. This is why religious exegetists often respond to textual criticism by pointing out that the scripture makes sense in its original language and that its authentic meaning gets lost in translation.[80] Sometimes, this is actually the case. Other times, it is an excuse to substitute for one's inability to respond to legitimate criticism with reason and logic. Either way, it follows that such ambiguity over scriptural interpretation is less likely to occur where religious adherents share the same language.

In his dialogue *Cratylus*, Plato addresses whether names are conventional or natural. He reflects on whether words are simply arbitrary signs or if they have an intrinsic relationship with the subject which they refer to.[81] In the end it is not clear what exactly he concluded, as the dialogue seems for the most part to be defending naturalism, only for Socrates to admit at its end that a naturalist account cut free from conventionalism is manifestly inadequate when it comes to understanding the semantics of names. It is not surprising, given the power and the ultimately inconclusive nature of the *Cratylus*, that from Plato onwards, countless thinkers have attempted to theorise over the nature of sense, words and meaning. That, for many of them and for modern thinkers on language, it was the conventionalist account that has proved most popular. So, describing language, Charles Hockett suggests that its: "...meaningful units are made of meaningless parts", where this "meaninglessness" is not a matter of lacking semantic value, but rather the fact that that value is not an intrinsic value of the relevant "meaningful units" considered in themselves and alone, but is "arbitrary" in that it consists in our shared agreement about the correct and incorrect uses of these sounds or signs in language use.

So, the sounds, as it were, the mere vocable blasts, or inscribed squiggles 'red' and 'pen' mean nothing of their own. The use of the label 'red' to describe the colour of human blood and the label 'pen' to describe the object we use for writing rest on implied agreement that those words should correspond to the objects that they do in the minds of the speaker and the listener. Most words are not invented with deliberate intent. They originate and evolve over time through an organic process of inter-communication. Of course, none of us was there to witness the birth of most English words we use daily, but this is not always true. Consider the case of internet slang such as 'lol' (acronym for 'laughing out loud') or the verb 'to google' something, which means looking something up on the search engine called Google, or 'brb' (acronym for 'be right back'). That words derive their meaning from an implied, but normative, agreement between different agents remains as true of abstract concepts as it is of concrete concepts. There is neither intrinsic nor universal value, for instance, in words such as "courage" or "bravery" or "chivalry" or "magnanimity" except what has been ascribed to them in the folklore of the culture in consideration. Most native speakers using such terms inherit their meaning as imparted by the practices that produced them. Recognising the arbitrary nature of words, Ferdinand de Saussure asserts that:

> Theories suggesting that the simple fact of using these sounds in language means *ipso facto* we should inquire into their production are completely arbitrary, imprudent even, until we have established the importance and nature of the role they play within the very particular entity that we call language.[82]

When one says "duck", we only think of a duck because we have an enculturated tradition or practice of picking out ducks with the term "duck". A typical high school graduate has, through enculturation, roughly 60,000 words in their mental lexicon. These come with cultural baggage and connotations. The great hallmark of our species is the long term memory and capacity to store sounds and words. De Saussure's idea was that language could be examined in the present, as opposed to being studied from a historical vantage point. William Hamilton described language as: "…little else than a registry of the factitious unities of thought".[83] His use of the term 'factitious' is indicative of the inherently artificial and subjective nature of meaning. This constitution of shared meaning through the "arbitrariness" of convention as we encounter it through the enculturation practices of various cultural situations means we cannot assume that all languages may be neatly - and without loss or distortion of meaning - mapped onto each other. The Belgian philosopher Antoon Vandevelde goes on to write:

> Doubtlessly, there are languages with totally different structures, with totally different roots than our Indo-European languages. This makes the acquisition of these languages much more difficult, but one can hardly say that Finnish, or Basque, or Hungarian, or Tamil native speakers are for instance by nature unable to understand Western philosophy or that they are for essential reasons handicapped to contribute to it. Even Derrida, Heidegger, James Joyce and Verlaine have been translated in various languages […] Most literary and

philosophical work can be rendered more or less faithfully in most languages and the expressive part in language is largely unconscious.[84]

Meanings are essentially *concepts*. They can vary across different cultures. It follows that Vandevelde's view is overly simplistic. Consider that Muslim scholars have often struggled to accurately translate the word *taqwa* into English because no english equivalent exists. Instead they are forced to explain the meaning of the term by amalgamating what, to a native English speaker, seem like two distinct and even contrary Western concepts of 'love' and 'fear'. Islamic scripture urges believers to demonstrate *taqwa* that is simultaneous feelings of love and fear towards God. Of course, rather than to try and translate the term, we might simply import it into English unchanged, but this should not occlude the obvious fact that while the same word will now be in use in both languages, the emotional response and conceptual connotations evoked in the minds of the speaker and the listener will vary according to their native linguistic tradition and competency. As can be seen, Vandevelde tended to see things differently, but even he conceded that:

> Each word is a condensation of a whole history, an etymological history, that in some way, that is not always fully elucidated, is connected to the history of ideas and practices of a language community.[85]

Let us illustrate this point further by looking at the concept of "romantic love". In English, this is a reasonably straightforward concept, drawing on courtly tradition and novelistic narratives from Helen of Troy to Romeo and Juliet. It picks out a kind of erotically infused and deep commitment of the narrative line of one life to that of another. Yet when we turn to the Subcontinent, we find that Hindi has many words for what we, as English speakers, would understand as romantic love in: *pyar, prem, ishq, ashiqi, muhabbat, chahat, dillagi* to name a few. Most Bollywood films tend to be centered around romantic themes. An individual who grows up with Hindi (or Urdu, essentially the same spoken language)[86] is far more *likely* to have a more emotionally sensitive and dramatised concept of romantic love compared to Western Europe's much more cynical and measured concept of the same. The conventional arbitrariness of meanings enables native language speakers to identify those like themselves as belonging to the same sociable community. This also explains why sense of humour varies across different cultures. In order for people to laugh, they have to *get* the joke with the accompanying cultural connotations. Western slapstick humour from Charlie Chaplin to Jim Carrey has far greater appreciation in cultures where English is not the first language in comparison to dry witty British humour. One does not need to know any particular language to appreciate slapstick, because it evokes the basic human ability laugh at exaggerated physical activity as it creatively impinges on our expectations of normality. Someone takes a tumble after stepping on a banana peel, and we laugh. Someone's pants fall down before the King or the Mayor, and we laugh. This is more or less universal. Yet comprehending the sort of dry British wit one sees portrayed in shows like *Monty Python, Yes Minister, Keeping Up Appearances, Some Mothers Do 'Ave 'Em, Fawlty Towers, The Young Ones* or *Blackadder* is a different ballgame. There is a punchline, which requires a degree of familiarity with aspects of native Anglophonic culture in order to *get* the joke. This is more likely to happen between native speakers of the same language.

Obviously the risk of ambiguity is higher in cross-cultural communication than in native level communication. Native level communication standardises abstract concepts, enabling speakers to imagine roughly the same idea simultaneously. In this sense, native speakers of the same language end up constituting a *distinctive* cultural grouping. The English-speaking world, or Anglosphere, is a prime example. People from the British Isles, America, Canada, the Caribbean, Australia, New Zealand, the Falkland Islands, and English-speakers in South Africa and Zimbabwe appreciate each other's films, television, art, literature, music, and humour. This creates a sense of *cultural commonality* that transcends geographical barriers and facilitates, for instance, their governments in establishing military alliances, allowing easy travel access for citizens, and economic cooperation. The same is true of Spanish across Central and South America, or Arabic across North Africa and the Middle East.

At this point, let us cast these ideas about language, its conventional use and essential sociability, in more precise terms by distinguishing more clearly the three senses of the term "language" central to my argument: 1) any natural language, 2) a specific natural language and 3) language as a form of specialised content and expression, such as the language of politics, law, art or science. Each of these clearly plays a role in defining an individual's sense of sociable community, of group identity and as a result, of her or his own identity.

In the first sense, language refers to any natural language. It is the use of mutually intelligible signs or symbols as the means for communication. Now, some non-human animals too possess means of conveying information. Some, like the dance bees perform to indicate the location and amount of food supplies, can be quite elaborate. But as noted by Victoria Fromkin, Robert Rodman and Nina Hyams, animal communication is not complex and rich with conceptual meanings like human language.[87] For centuries, scholars have agreed that language is a *distinctly* human faculty that distinguishes us from other living beings. This view remains widely accepted today despite research to the contrary by some dissenting linguists. Still, those who no longer argue that humans are the only animals capable of possessing language, agree there are complex features inherent within human language that do set it apart from other means of communication, animal or artificial. It is here then with natural language that we find the core of that sense of a human community and identity that sets us apart from the rest of nature. Joshua A. Fishman points out that:

> In essence, it is the *use* of language which sets humans apart from other members of the animal kingdom.[88]

In the second sense, language refers to a *specific* language, a determinate and determinable grammatical symbolism that enables individuals to convey thoughts through verbal utterances using a pre-existing database of identifiable symbols commonly referred to as *vocabulary* eg: English, Mandarin, French, Arabic or Hindi. Here, we find language functioning not merely to separate the human from the non-human or animal, but from other human beings in terms of their historical, cultural and often ethnic and national identities. The distinction between language and dialect can sometimes appear elusive. Linguists often speculate when it is that a dialect deviates so far from the standard pronunciation of a language that it becomes a language of its own. Urdu and Hindi, Spanish and Portuguese, Farsi and Dari, or Dutch and Afrikaans are considered distinct languages even though their speakers can, to varying degrees, not only comprehend, but often be able to have mutually intelligible conversations with each other. Some Australians may struggle to comprehend thicker varieties of Irish accents despite both being native speakers of English. Yet this does not make Irish a separate language since it is only the pronunciation and tone that vary, the grammar and vocabulary remains the same. Contemporary languages such as Italian, Spanish and French trace their origins back to Latin, once the language of the Roman Empire. Contemporary Hebrew, Aramaic and Arabic trace their origins back to Proto-Semitic. Languages in both categories deviated from their parent languages, Latin and Proto-Semitic at some point in the distant past, beginning with variations in pronunciation and later evolving (or devolving, depending on the observer's vantage point) to the extent that speakers could no longer comprehend each other by default.

Yet there is a further point. While languages may differ and shade into various dialects, it is also the case that one language can have multiple names, and multiple languages can have one name. For instance, until the partition of India and Pakistan in 1947, the word *Hindustani* was generally used to describe the languages now recognised as *Hindi* in India and *Urdu* in Pakistan. Though Urdu uses the *Nastaleeq* variant of the right-to-left Arabic script and Hindi uses the *Devanagari* variant of the left-to-right Brahmi script for writing, their spoken vernaculars remain essentially identical. Pakistanis watch Bollywood films in Hindi as if they were listening to Urdu. Indians watch Pakistani soap operas and rock music as if they were listening to Hindi. Yet these are classified as two different languages for arbitrarily defined political purposes – a theme that is explored in chapter four: Case Study 2. An inverse example is found in China. Various dialects of Chinese

Mandarin are so different from each other that speakers often cannot understand each other. Outside observers are often typically struck by the fact that everything on Chinese television is subtitled, *in* Chinese, yet these dialects are all classified as Mandarin.

In the third sense, language is a content-based system specific to certain subjects, disciplines or faculties of knowledge. This includes legal language, scientific language, economic language, religious language, medical language or political language. For instance, the sentences "in legal *language* 'force majeure' means an act of god" and "in political *language* 'porkbarelling' means the use of taxpayer funds to pander to voter interests in pursuit of garnering support".[89] Such specific languages are subsets of language in the broader senses yet clearly impact on our ideas of community, fellowship and identity. In particular, such restricted language domains allow for ever more rigid and defined identities. In part, this is simply a function of the specialisation of language involved, but such specialisation also means a system replete with inherent ideological content amenable to use by concentrated cliques for conveying selective meaning, and for generating distinct modes of thought, within social cliques. Nowhere is this practice more prevalent than in religious and political communities where language is used for the establishment, maintenance and dissemination of orthodox beliefs.

In an instance of such a specifically defined ideologically loaded sub-language that seeks to displace all other levels of language in community and identity formation, we have Newspeak, the fictional language featured in the novel *Nineteen Eighty-Four* by George Orwell: a controlled language created by the totalitarian state as an instrument to limit the citizen's thoughts, individuality, and inner expression intended to render literally unthinkable and unsayable any potential threats to the regime.[90] Naturally, as a limiting ideological device of conformist identity, newspeak might aim at such an impossibility of thought and expression, but until such time its major device is to label all thought and expression outside of the newspeak limits as "thought-crime." This condemnatory labelling is rather familiar, of course, in everyday life. Various academic, media and political elites devise and deploy labels in order to express hostility to their critics.

Once a neologism is introduced in political vernacular, its use can be stretched to serve ulterior purposes. Often, legitimate criticism aimed at Islamists is mistaken as criticism aimed at mainstream Islam or Muslims and labelled 'Islamophobic'. There are many similar examples. Critics of same sex marriage may attract the label 'homophobic', just as critics of third wave feminism can attract the label 'sexist', and defenders of human dignity and free expression be condemned as 'Cultural Marxists.' Language in this third sense is an incredibly powerful tool in politics. This in turn makes it an attractive vehicle for both the nation-building and state-building processes. All a particular regime or interest group has to do, is to have sufficient cultural power that it can invent a label, ascribe set connotations to it and by repeating it enough number of times, have its intended meanings penetrate popular culture. This tactic may be intellectually disconcerting, but it remains common in the political arena.

These three senses of language are interwoven. To recap, the first sense deals with language as a tool for communication. Language in this sense enables individuals to form and maintain sociable *human* communities. The second sense deals with specific natural languages. Language in this sense forms the basis for ethnic, religious (in the liturgical sense) or national identities. The third sense deals with language as a specialised conceptual framework, and as such, with a narrower sense of identity. Each of these definitions is crucial to the central argument of this book. Let us then bring these senses of language together. In the first, and most general, sense of language as that which marks us out as a human community, language is simply an arrangement of symbols we call words. When arranged correctly, the sentences that make up communication convey meaning, as intended by the speaker. The rules that assign sense and meaning to sentences are grammar (assembly), phonology (sounds), semantics (meaning), and pragmatics (use). Like other facets of human development, these rules have been refined through thousands of years of natural and cultural selection. That these two senses – natural and cultural – come into play here is no accident.

As Charles Darwin said of language in this sense:

> It certainly is not a true instinct, as every language has to be learned. It differs, however, widely from all ordinary arts, for man has an instinctive tendency to speak as we see in the babble of our young children; while no child has an instinctive tendency to bake, brew or write. Moreover, no philologist now supposes that any language has been deliberately invented; each has been slowly and unconsciously developed by many steps.[91]

For the most part, it is true, language in this sense operates at the instinctive level. There is little conscious effort involved. Morphology is the study of the methods that enable us to construct complex words using prefixes, affixes and suffixes from simpler base words. Phonology on the other hand deals with combining consonants and vowels into the smallest of words. Accent is the inheritance of a foreign phonology. It is what makes us talk differently. This is why foreign accents can sometimes be undesirable. Noam Chomsky notes that the main puzzle on the level of natural language as such that requires an explanation is the creativity, productivity, the ability to understand new sentences language speakers exhibit. Apart from clichés, every new sentence is one constructed from scratch. Yet when we hear one for the first time, we can comprehend it. This is not because we have simply memorised a bunch of words. What it suggests is that we internalise words *with* the rules of grammar.

It is because different natural languages have distinct ways of facilitating their grammatical internalisation of words that it is tempting to think, in an overly radical rejection of Vandevelde's view on the essential oneness of meaning(s) across languages, that different languages mean, in some kind of a literal way, different worlds. This was the intimation of Edward Sapir who first proposed what would eventuate into the most contentious of theories in linguistics. It was the idea that languages in some way reflected the social realities and thought patterns of their speakers. Benjamin Whorf built on the ideas of Sapir, leading to the concept that would be referred to as the Sapir-Whorf Hypothesis. Its central argument was that people's languages shaped the way they perceived the world.. In so doing, they supposedly *created* that world being perceived by its observer. One potential problem with this idea may be that breaking up the world into linguistic entities in this way, so that each is external to the other, seems to imply that languages themselves are external to each other. But clearly, they are not, or else they would be blank to each other. Yet the possibility of translation proves that they are not. More fundamentally, as does the fact that an infant picks up whatever language she or he is exposed to in any regular environment. We have a common, shared, human facility for natural language, and for whatever of those languages we are enculturated into.

Indeed, the younger the human, the easier it is to learn a language. The older we get, the harder it gets. From an evolutionary standpoint, Charles Darwin noted that the *larynx* had to descend in order to allow food to pass through with ease, leading to the danger of choking. As to why our species evolved devices such as a throat and a mouth, that make us vulnerable may be seen as an evolutionary compromise to enable us to communicate and to better survive through information sharing. Like its speakers and because of those speakers, language has itself undergone major evolutionary stages over time. It facilitates the flow of information in the world and enables us as rational agents to participate in the interactive process. It enhances our ability to *compute* information. It enables us to comprehend the use of pragmatics. That is, context and other information in order to make sense of our surroundings. We essentially interpret the sentence: "If you could pass me the tomato sauce that would be wonderful" as an *instruction* saying "give me the tomato sauce". As many experts have observed, the miraculous thing about language is that it lets us express an unlimited range of ideas by simply re-arranging a limited vocabulary. Is is through language that we build a sense of interdependency with others. British philosopher Paul Grice's *Cooperative Principle* argues that people cooperate in order to bring meaning across properly. In essence, we transmit our 'communicative intention' using the following four maxims: 1) Honesty - people want to hear the truth, 2)

Information – people tune out if you are not telling them something of value, 3) Relevance – people wonder what is in it for them, and 4) Clarity – people want to hear what is clear and understandable.[92] It is on these maxims that our sociability rests, and from these arises the conditions of our various (self-)identities. As Linguist and Cognitive Scientist Steven Pinker notes, language has been thought of, in figurative terms, as the original 'wiki' that combines the inputs of multitudes of people and has an indispensable impact on human consciousness, identity, and community. It systematically influences how one perceives and conceptualises the world.

There are, of course, major disagreements between linguists as to how natural language (or particular natural languages and their relative domains) arose in the first place. In one camp are linguists who argue the primacy of biology in explaining what language is and how it emerged in humans. These linguists view human language as the product of a minor genetic mutation with major significance for human development. They argue that as a result, humans possess all the basic understanding we require from birth to create and reproduce language within our brains. The linguists who disagree instead point to the gradual evolution of language from prior communication tools. These linguists place greater emphasis on the role of culture in creating and reshaping languages. They point to the fact that over 6,000 of them are spoken today worldwide to dismiss arguments that all human language can be traced to a single point of origin. These competing perspectives are essential to understand, if only to distinguish clearly between approaches to language that imply or rest on a ground of an undifferentiated human linguistic capacity and as a result community, and those who, looking at cultural factors, encourage a more differentiating conception of linguistic community.

Among the key elements of human language is the ability to form thousands of vocalisations and combine them into utterances that contain complex information. Without this ability, language would not have emerged as the stimulus producing sociability and holding communities together with a common identity. Yet in order to develop this ability, profound physiological changes had to occur. The most important of these occurred in the early stages of evolution approximately 3.5 million years ago. Around that time *Homo Australopithecus* developed the ability to walk erect on two feet. This phenomenon is known as bipedalism. Some scholars speculate that the changes that allowed this to happen also led to changes in skull size, allowing for the lowering of the larynx. This, they argue, was a necessary prerequisite to facilitate the vocalisation of vowels. The lowering of the larynx and the development of an L-shaped vocal tract allowed for the emergence of more sophisticated means of oral communication. Linguist Jean Aitchison makes the point this way:

> Perhaps we need to ask why humans, alone of mammals, acquired the ability to speak. The answer may be convergence. Humans, like other apes, began with the advantage of good hearing, combined with the habit of habitual vocalisation. Then humans began to walk upright, acquiring an L-shaped vocal tract which allowed them to produce stable vowels and a clear output.[93]

Besides complex use of sound, human language is also distinguished by its use for more than simple need-based purposes and its sensitivity to context and audience. Where almost all other animal species use oral communication either to issue general warnings, alarm calls, or discovery of resources, typically food, humans use speech to work cooperatively, and assist others with fulfilling wants and exchange ideas. This ability to interact with our environment in complex ways sets language apart from all forms of animal communication. It enables us to accumulate knowledge over time and preserve it for the benefit of future generations. As Michael Corballis notes in *The Recursive Mind*, the development of human language gives human beings not merely the ability to truthfully share information, equally and at the same time, it gives them the unique ability to lie. That is, to deliberately mislead another through communication. It also allows us to produce such internally contradictory statements as "This sentence is false", a statement whose truth value cannot logically be determined.[94] This capacity for lying, as well as truth-telling, is unique to human language, and it clearly impacts on the content and meaning of claims of identity and community.

As human language emerged well before the development of written communication, it is impossible to determine exactly when the first humans used structured sounds to communicate beyond the relaying of basic information. The general consensus among scholars is that human language could not have emerged more than 100,000 or so years ago. That was the turning point that allowed for the lowering of the larynx that enabled vocal sounds to form in a sequential manner. Many evolutionary biologists argue that the precursors to modern *Homo Sapiens* lacked the anatomical features, in particular the shape and placement of the larynx necessary to produce the multiplicity of sounds that complex human language comprises of today. It was not until the peak activity period of the Neanderthals from 60,000 to 25,000 years ago that the needed anatomical features began to develop.

Noam Chomsky argues that human language emerged as the result of a single, abrupt change. In his 1965 publication *Aspects of the Theory of Syntax*, Chomsky first argued that human language emerged, fully formed, as the product of a genetic shift in the human makeup that occurred at a singular point in time. He notes that while all animals have ways of communicating information, in other species the methods are a little more than codes and lack the sophistication and complexity of human communication. At the same time, Chomsky notes that although we know that humans with the capacity for producing language first emerged in Africa hundreds of thousands of years ago, there is no evidence in the fossil records of humans possessing a complex symbolic communication system any earlier than somewhere between 60,000 and 100,000 years ago. In Chomsky's view:

> You have propositional attitudes; descriptions of possible organisations and interactions between people; possible physical events, and so on. And that's available to you if you have internal language; we all know it, just by introspection. We all have that capacity. And presumably our hominid ancestors at that point had the

same capacity.

One thing we're pretty certain about is that existing humans are virtually identical in this respect. Which means that whatever it was that gave us this capacity – it couldn't have happened later than about fifty thousand years ago, which is about when the trek from Africa starts. In fact it's likely that whatever happened led to the trek from Africa. Hominids physically very much like us were there for hundreds of thousands of years – as far as the archeological record shows. And it began with a small group, one of many small breeding groups. And that one suddenly exploded all over the world. It's hard to imagine that that's not related to the same developments that led to the human capacity to innovate.[95]

Humans endowed with this ability spread fairly rapidly beyond Africa, appearing first in southern Eurasia and later in Australia and nearby Pacific islands. In terms of evolutionary time, according to Chomsky, this development occurred suddenly after a few hundred thousand years with little or no notable change in the makeup or talents of human beings. In *The Science of Language*, Chomsky explains how he reached this conclusion:

> Nothing much seems to have changed [in human development] for hundreds of thousands of years, and then, all of a sudden, there was a huge explosion. Around seventy, sixty thousand years ago, maybe as early as a hundred thousand, you start getting symbolic art, notations reflecting astronomical and meteorological events, complex social structures…just an outburst of creative energy that somehow takes place in an instant of evolutionary time – maybe ten thousand years or so, which is nothing.[96]

The most plausible explanation, though one that should be viewed with a critical eye, is that a slight genetic shift occurred in a *single* individual that gave that person the ability to form complex utterances conveying something more than simple coded statements of warning, identification, or direction. That individual then transmitted that genetic advantage to its offspring, who then passed on this apparently dominant trait to succeeding generations, which then facilitated unprecedented progress and development, as well as binding individuals together in the form of sociable communities.

There are other linguists who support this kind of emergence theory, if not the idea that language arose first as an isolated idiolect. Most of them argue that all human languages are descendants of a single *proto-language* that emerged at a specific point in time. Among these linguists is John McWhorter, whose book *The Power of Babel* is an extended exploration of how all the world's languages descended from a single tongue that emerged no sooner than 100,000 years ago. In the introduction to his book, McWhorter notes that fossil evidence of traits that could be considered distinctly modern human date back no farther than 35,000 years. But he accepts the view that it is most likely that the human capacity for language first emerged sometime around 100,000 years ago. McWhorter observes that:

> ...it would appear that human language can be traced back at least 150,000 years. Yet there remains the problem that only just 35,000 years ago do we see the kinds of cultural explosions among human beings that mark them as indisputably "us." The possibility theoretically remains, then, that language did not arise right when sapiens did, but instead only arose, say, 35,000 years ago.[97]

Chomsky and those who agree that language remains a uniquely human trait argue that the change occurred after the genus *Homo* diverged from the evolutionary path of other apes. The trait Chomsky identifies as the origin of complex communication through language is an ability to perform a mental function called *Merge*.[98] Simply put, this is the ability to combine two discrete objects into a single object, essentially a set comprised of both. Merge makes sophisticated communication possible by stripping its symbols of almost all meaning. Instead of a single utterance transmitting the information "Dangerous predator ahead! Avoid this location!" the sender can combine symbolic elements that have much more limited meaning in and by themselves to form statements with the necessary complexity. This concept meshes somewhat uneasily with the standard Darwinian theory of natural selection, by which many small changes over a long period of time create significant physical or mental features.

Linguist and Cognitive Scientist Steven Pinker agrees with Noam Chomsky about the innateness of language, but spends much of his book *The Language Instinct* arguing against Chomsky's other idea that language emerged suddenly from a single genetic mutation.[99] Other critics go further than that, suggesting that human language evolved not from sudden or gradual genetic changes, but from earlier, less sophisticated forms of human communication that reflect the social and cooperative nature of human society. Linguist and Psychologist Michael Tomasello argues that human language rests on a foundation of more primitive gestural communication.

In his *Origins of Human Communication*, Tomasello argues that pointing and pantomiming are the basic building blocks on which the entire language edifice is built. Put simply, these are methods of non-verbal communication that both humans, who otherwise could not transmit information between themselves and others, that gives the gestures added meaning use to this day. Tomasello rejects the idea that all 6,000 or so world languages somehow descended from a single proto-language that arose along with the first modern humans. Explaining pointing and pantomiming as the first uniquely human forms of communication, Tomasello argues that:

> The social-cognitive and social-motivational infrastructure that enabled these new forms of communication then acted as a kind of psychological platform upon which the various systems of conventional linguistic communication (all 6,000 of them) could be built.[100]

He bases his assertion on research conducted by himself and his colleagues on great apes, in particular chimpanzees, who display learned gestural behaviours that are designed to attract the attention of a specific recipient with a goal in mind. These learned gestural behaviours have become 'innate' considering that chimps that are not raised where such behaviours can be observed still adopt them, and chimps that are taught new gestures fail to spread them to their peers. Yet more importantly, they depend on a feedback mechanism. The chimp is attuned to the recipient's current state and anticipates a specific response to the gesture. Besides gestures intended to produce a specific response, which other animals also display, chimps also engage in gestural communications that are meant to attract the attention of the recipient but not necessarily elicit a specific response. These gestures are instead meant to call the recipient's attention to the chimp's own mental or physiological state first, then to act in response. Some chimps go one step further, engaging in gestures that are referential, not designed to elicit a predetermined response, such as offering unwanted food to another. Tomasello argues that these gestures are a bridge between primate and human gestural communication and point to the evolution of human language via similar human gestures. The next step, which humans took, was to point towards things without the expectation of a response in return from the recipient. This sort of helpful pointing, which apes do not engage in, was the first instance of cooperative communication on the part of humans.

Likewise, linguist Daniel Everett in his *Language: The Cultural Tool* dismisses Chomsky's understanding of language as a faculty generated by a sudden shift in the human genetic makeup at a singular point in human evolution.[101] Instead, Everett sees language as bound up with the evolution of human society as it arises from the shared development of a "theory of mind." As humans came to recognise that members of our fellow species had minds that worked as ours did, we began to cooperate for self-defence, sustenance and a host of other mutual needs. With the desire to cooperate came the need to communicate. Language emerged as an effective means of communication. Animal communication predominantly takes place to ensure the survival of the species. Such communication usually serves one of two purposes: To inform other members of the species where food could be obtained and to inform other members of the species of a nearby threat to their survival. As such, the 'statements' made by most animals are highly directive and of a broadcast rather than targeted nature. In addition, the younger species also often attempt to locate their mothers by communicating their presence by means of a vocal call.

On the other hand, human communication not only performs a much wider range of functions than that, it actually performs them in different ways. An ape who desires food might point to the food with the intent to tell the recipient of the pointing to bring the food to the ape. A human, on the other hand, might ask another, "May I have a glass of water?" with the expectation that the hearer will respond, "Yes, you may. Help yourself." Or a human might say to another "I'm famished" and receive a response like, "There's a restaurant on the corner. Let's go eat." Human exchanges differ in that they are not necessarily directives – they do not have to command the hearer to do something – and that they rely on a great deal of trust: the utterer issues the utterance with the expectation that the recipient will voluntarily respond with favour. These facets of human communication are outgrowths of human evolution into a species that relies on a high level of cooperation with others to thrive. This view is an indication of the extent to which sociability is innate to the human experience.

Yet human vocal communication goes beyond requests for help and cooperation. We also use language to express our current mental state, to describe objects to others, to discuss events and ideas, and to share reminiscences about past occurrences, we think about hopes and fears for the future. These aspects of communication extend well beyond all other forms of animal communication, and only human language, in the second sense, makes them possible. For one human to understand another, there must exist some pre-established ground rules for structuring and carrying out the exchange of information. At its base, language is the set of ground rules that have emerged among groups of humans that enable communication to occur. Each of these languages sets one group of humans apart from another. They are usually connected in some way to the shared experiences and memories that contribute to group cohesion, as sociable communities. To that extent, language is more than a set of rules. It is a framework for building and preserving culture and transmitting its shared values and understandings for future members of the cultural in-group.

A prime example of the role culture plays in shaping language comes from isolated indigenous peoples in places such as Australia or the Amazon rainforest. The languages spoken often lack words for numbers beyond a simple "one," "two," and "many." The language of the Pirahã tribe in Brazil lacks these numbers.[102] Indigenous Australians who spoke the Warlpiri language only acquired words for numbers through their contact with Englishmen after 1788 which necessitated their learning to count and words for numbers. They simply incorporated the English number words into their own language.[103] The cultural functions of language tend to get short shrift from those researchers who argue that language is innate, for their focus is more on the features of the world's languages that bind them together as opposed to those that set them apart. Similarly, those who focus on the cultural function of language tend to be dismissive of arguments that make any claim to a universal language faculty or any aspects of it. This basic split between two competing groups of language theorists informs the on-going debates over how and when language first appeared on the human timeline, and over the nature and use of language.

In short, sociability is the backbone of a community. People have a group identity because they talk, socialise and share information. As the central argument of this book rests on the premise that language is the principal tool that enables individuals to form sociable communities, it is important we discuss a unique feature that helps serve this function. That feature is *phatic communication*. The term *phatic* was first coined by anthropologist Bronisław Malinowski in the early 1900s from the Greek word *phanein* which means, to show oneself or to make an appearance. As understood by Sociolinguists, the phatic is a form of communication which, despite not transmitting any new propositional information or knowledge, still remains an inherent part of the nature of human communication using language. Individuals across all world cultures engage in phatic communication. For example, on hot days we all know how often we hear (and say ourselves) to an audience that already knows this fact, "Gee, it is hot today!", just as on rainy days we are prone to saying to each other "It's raining". While syntactically these utterances may appear fact-stating as the hearer already knows the information, there is nothing new to be transmitted.

So when someone asks "what is going on?" The answer is a matter, as it were, of checking or registering that "we are on the same wavelength" and as such, we are in the *same* world, together. If, for instance, on a very hot day, we express how hot it is, and the hearer gives us a strange look insisting that it was *not* hot, we have already lost our bearings when it comes to talking with and understanding our interlocutor. Or if not, we may assume they are simply hostile to us as when, on a sunny morning, one is walking and says to another person out strolling, "It's a beautiful day today!" and they respond firmly "No, it is not a beautiful day!". We can see how that very common yet often ignored phatic dimension of our communicative lives marks out and often repeatedly confirms that we are attuned with each other, that we have the same shared default "settings". This enables us to be at ease with each other securely, as co-members of the one language community. Since phatic communication reassures us that we are in the same position, as fellow occupants of the same world, it is in this sense an inherent property of language. It enables individuals to publicly and socially reaffirm their attunement with each other and the common world we inhabit. And as we have seen in the previous chapter, and will see in our three case-studies, how phatic communication plays a central role in the identity formation that is nationalism.

We have so far examined the uniqueness and centrality of language to the human experience. In so doing, this chapter placed particular emphasis on the way that language on its various levels presupposes and constructs a sense of community. It follows then that national identity is bound up with the development and articulation of the modern state and state system. We now turn our focus to three case-studies that compare and contrast three distinct uses of language in the nation-building and state-building processes. The first of these is what could aptly be described as the world's oldest continuous nationalism, encapsulated in the story of the revival of Hebrew, the creation of the modern Israeli identity and the rebirth of the Jewish state.

3

CASE STUDY 1

HOW HEBREW RE-CREATED THE JEWISH STATE

As we saw in the first chapter, nationalism as a political concept is about a nation having its own sovereign territory. By definition, there is no nationalism *without* attachment to, or yearning for, a specific piece of land. Many nations can and certainly do exist under the sovereignty of rulers from cultural out-groups, but these are *either* nations without a nationalist movement, *or* their nationalist movements are currently in the process of seeking statehood. As discussed in the second chapter, language is uniquely human, it creates sociability, it helps preserve cultural content and remains a marker of human identity. In light of our shared discussion on nationalism, as an idea that binds people with land, and on language, as a tool for nation-building, there could be no better proof of both propositions than the story of the revival of Hebrew and the rebirth of the Jewish state of Israel. With the age old Jewish attachment to Jerusalem and the hills of Zion that predate the birth of the modern Zionist movement, Judaism is, in many respects, the world's oldest form of nationalism.

When Pope Francis visited Jerusalem in 2014, Israeli Prime Minister Benjamin Netanyahu told him during their meeting that "Jesus was here, in this land. He spoke Hebrew" to stress the connection between Judaism and Christianity. Somewhat surprised by this statement, the Pope looked up and, pointing his finger, corrected the Prime Minister with one word: "Aramaic!" In turn, Netanyahu recovered, following up with "He spoke Aramaic, but he knew Hebrew!" As the *Time*

Magazine reporting the story notes: "The correction was gentle, even playful – typical Pope Francis style. Everyone smiled and laughed."[104] Hebrew is today the official language of the world's only Jewish state, Israel. It is common knowledge that Jesus was born into a Jewish household. It is not counter-intuitive to then assume that Jesus must have been a native speaker of Hebrew. Yet the Pope's little known encounter with the Israeli PM remains fascinating for two reasons: One, the Pope was correct. Jesus was a native Aramaic speaker. Two, the encounter is a reminder that Aramaic's displacement of Hebrew as the spoken vernacular by first century Judea is not common knowledge. While there is great debate among scholars over how many languages Jesus spoke, there is widespread agreement that his *native* tongue was Aramaic.[105]

How is it then that Jesus Christ, a man born in Bethlehem into a Jewish household during Roman occupation some 2,000 years ago was speaking *Aramaic* as his native tongue? There is no national story more central to the shared study of language and nationalism than this. Hebrew was the language of the ancient Israelites, the ancestors of modern Jewry. Not only the language itself, but in fact *how* one spoke it was often the marker of one's identity. As the traditional story goes,[106] in the centuries following the Babylonian exile, Hebrew eventually came to be replaced with Aramaic and became a dead vernacular language with no native speakers left. For almost 2,000 years, its use was reduced to liturgy and worship, or for use by scholars, until its eventual revival a century before our own time. The story of the birth, death and resurrection of the Hebrew language goes hand in hand with the triumph of political Zionism. Indeed, the establishment of the State of Israel on 14th May 1948 remains the best example of a modern nation-state successfully managing to absorb an ethnically diverse Ashkenazi, Sephardic, Mizrahi, and Ethiopian Jewish population[107] that had made *aliyah* to their promised land from far away places, into a common Israeli national identity through the use of their ancient ancestral tongue brought back to life in modernity.

Hebrew is a language that continues to mystify many around the world. For the Jews who speak it and those who do not, it is the language of their ancient Israelite ancestors, as well as the language of liturgy and worship. For Christians and Muslims, it is the language of the Ten Commandments and the Torah, which both faiths believe to be a divine revelation. Yet Hebrew as a spoken vernacular went extinct for two millennia and was only revived over a century before our own time by Russian-born Jewish lexicographer Eliezer Ben Yehuda. This makes Hebrew's story fascinating in its own right. To say that there are many dead languages in the world today, including several that still hold religious significance, is to state the obvious. Latin in Catholicism and Sanskrit in Hinduism continue to be used by adherents of these faiths in liturgy and worship. Yet neither of these has any *native* speakers left. Catholics around the world speak many different tongues from Italian to English and Spanish among others. Hindus in India speak India's national language Hindi alongside one or more native tongues depending on their ethnic or provincial identities. Even at the Vatican City, the seedbed of Catholic Christianity, Italian remains the spoken vernacular instead of Latin and was recognised as such in 2014 when Pope Francis decided to take official status away from Latin.[108]

Without the revival of Hebrew, the story of Israeli nationalism could well have taken a radically different turn. It has enabled Israelis of all stripes with ancestries in Europe, Russia, North Africa, Arabian Peninsula, Persia, Ethiopia, and India to come together as 'Israelis' and connect as one *volk* to put it in Herder's terms.[109] It has been an outstanding example of the successful integration of the masses into a common political form as Kohn put it.[110] Through revived Hebrew, Israelis today form sociable communities, develop distinct slang terms along with a unique sense of humour, and enjoy cinema in a shared national consciousness. In the diaspora, the Sephardic Jews generally spoke Ladino or Arabic and Ashkenazi Jews generally spoke Yiddish or Russian. For the Zionist project to work, it needed a common language yet pioneer Theodor Herzl was late in realising this. The other Zionist pioneer Leon Pinsker did stress the importance of language, but never came up with a plan on what that language would be in seeking a Jewish state. As this chapter shows, the revival of Hebrew was a bottom-up movement, rather than top-down as it often is in cases of other nationalisms. Its revival was started by lexicographer Eliezer Ben Yehuda who was not officially part of the Zionist movement.[111] The Jews, like the Bedouin Arabs, are a Semitic people who trace their ancestry to the ancient Middle East. Historically known as the Hebrews or Israelites, the Jews could best be described as a cultural in-group that has both an ethnic and a religious component. They are a self-conscious imagined community as Anderson would put it, bound together by a shared past.[112] This sense of national history is predominantly grounded in the Jewish faith. As the evolution of the Jewish identity has occurred over the centuries, the ethnic and religious components have submerged and become largely inseparable from each other. The closest present-day comparison would be the Sikh people of the Indian province of Punjab. They too may be considered both an ethnicity and a religion at the same time.

What constitutes a Jew in today's world is unique. This is because the rules for eligibility differ considerably from the conventions of other religious communities. By contrast, Christianity and Islam are religions without any ethnic or ancestral component. When one stops believing that Jesus died for their sins, they are no longer a Christian. When one stops believing that Muhammad was the last and final prophet of God, they are no longer a Muslim. So the Christian and Muslim identities are ideological in their make-up. It does not work like that in contemporary Rabbinic Judaism. If one is born of maternally Jewish ancestry then one is Jewish, even if one no longer believes in God or the Torah.[113] This means that the contemporary Jewish identity accommodates atheism and agnosticism. A Jew may abandon her or his faith in the existence of God, yet still be considered a Jew. Under normative Jewish law, this emphasis on determining one's identity as a Jew despite apostasy from Judaism applies across several generations. This is well-documented in Shulchan Aruch, Even Ha-Ezer 44:9.[114]

Technicalities aside, in actual practice keeping track of the Jewish identity can be difficult across the ages once traditions have been abandoned. This in part explains why there are no Jewish Christians, Jewish Muslims, Jewish Hindus, or Jewish anything else. If one Jewish person converted to another religion, they may yet continue to be considered Jewish for the time being, but if across future generations, that person's descendants went on to raise their children with a separate set of beliefs, it would be impossible to keep track of one's Jewish ancestry despite the ruling in Jewish law.

Many Muslims from the Middle East claim descent from the historical Jews who converted to Islam from the seventh century onwards during the spread of Islam across North Africa and the Middle East. Such claims are usually neither demonstrable, nor falsifiable and in fact remain historically plausible. It is true that large numbers of Jews did begin converting to Islam both during its founder Prophet Muhammad's own life time as well as afterwards. But these claims mean nothing as far as the present-day Jewish identity is concerned. Those cases would not be considered Jewish. Although the Jewish identity functions like an ethnicity, it is not homogeneous in its composition. In the first century when the diaspora began, the subdivisions among Jews were based on *sectarian* divisions, notably the Pharisees, the Sadducees and the Essenes. These feature quite vividly in the Christian New Testament. Yet today's Jewish people make up ethnic subvarieties from a diverse range of backgrounds with wide ranging physical characteristics. There are Russian, Ethiopian, Indian and Chinese Jews among other varieties that are all considered one people or one volk, 'Am Yisrael' or the 'nation of Israel'.

There are three major ethnic subdivisions. European Jews are referred to as the Ashkenazim (named after a character in the Old Testament by the name of Ashkenaz). Moroccan, Algerian, Greek, Spanish, and Turkish Jews are referred to as the Sephardim (named after Sefarad, the Hebrew term for Spain - many claim descent from the Jewish expulsion of 1492 under the Alhambra decree). Middle Eastern, Iranian, Central Asian, and Subcontinental Jews are referred to as the Mizrahim (which literally means 'Easterners' or Orientals). The Ethiopian and Chinese Jews are in classes of their own.[115] These subdivisions result from 2,000 years of being scattered around the world, facing different challenges under different rulers and through interaction with local cultures and people forming hybrid sub-identities. The Jewish identity, which acts as an umbrella overarching these internal varieties, rests on its own national imagination grounded in stories passed down through the generations and written in the Tanakh (or Old Testament) and the Talmud. As with the history of any people, the further back we look through the historical and archaeological record, the more the boundaries between myths and facts end up being blurred. Yet it remains crucial to understand collective national mindsets and group identities as their group members seem to understand their own past.

Indeed, scholars of anthropology, folklore, and behavioural sciences differentiate between an *etic* approach which looks at a social group, community, or culture through the eyes of the outside observer, and an *emic* approach which looks at the same through the eyes of the subject, as an insider. As discussed in the first chapter, the 'imagined communities' Benedict Anderson talks about, that form the basis of national identities are not always based on fact, evidence or verifiable realities. More often than that, the national consciousness is a combination of myths and facts. Yet the only way to develop a coherent and proper understanding of how collective national or cultural mindsets work is by arranging both the myths and the facts on a single timeline. To use a Western comparison, this is like placing the story of Medieval characters Robin Hood (a mythical legend) and Richard the Lionheart (a historical figure) on the same historical tapestry.

Too often, outside observers struggle to understand what motivates a group of people to take the steps they do to fulfil their nationalist aspirations. After all, it is easier to dismiss parts of what somebody else considers to be their legitimate history when the observer is not part of that cultural in-group. To avoid going down such a rabbit hole, this chapter takes an emic[116] approach for the understanding of the Jewish identity and its relationship with the Hebrew language in the liturgical and vernacular senses. So, from an insider's point of view, the Jewish story begins over 4,000 years ago in the ancient city of Ur in present-day Iraq. Paganism at the time was the dominant form of religious practice. Against this backdrop of idolatry emerges the Prophet Abraham. He forges a special relationship with one God, later revealed as *Yahweh*. This God promises the land of Canaan to Abraham[117] and his descendants who come to be known as the Israelites. God tells Abraham to:

> Leave your country, your family, and your father's home for a land that I will show you. I'll make you a great nation and bless you. I'll make you famous; you'll be a blessing. I'll bless those who bless you; those who curse you I'll curse. All the families of the Earth will be blessed through you.[118]

This is about the most emphatic expression of a primordial form of nationalism grounded within religious thought. In the centuries that followed, Abraham's descendants came to be held captive in neighbouring Egypt. God raises a saviour Prophet, Moses, to set the Israelites free from Egyptian bondage. Moses leads the Israelites across the Red Sea into the Sinai Peninsula where he is given a special revelation from God, the Ten Commandments.[119] This marks a defining moment in Jewish history, as Moses encounters God at Mount Sinai, God identifies himself with the statement: "ehyeh asher ehyeh" which translates as: "I am, that I am." God to the Israelites was referred to by many labels, from *Elohim* to *Adonai* or *HaShem*. The third of these commandments given to Moses was: "You shall not take the Lord your God's name in vain". The four Hebrew letters Y-H-W-H that represented "ehyeh" or the "I am" part of God's declarative statement to Moses came to be the beginning of the sanctification of Hebrew as a language. Even in English, when Jews talk about God they often spell it as 'G-d' in case the paper it is written on is put to use that desanctifies God's name, for instance stepping on it, or using it to wipe the floor. No matter where Jews have lived throughout history, as soon as one walks into a Synagogue and sees writings on the wall in Hebrew, they feel a sense of connectivity to a nation that goes beyond their local village or township.

Nationalist proclivities can be seen early on in the Jewish narrative. After the death of Moses, his successor Joshua is instructed by God to conquer the promised land. This involved having to fight other ethnic groups that are mentioned in the Torah, notably: the Hittites, Amorites, Canaanites, Perizzites, Hivites and Jebusites. Joshua is told to wipe these people off the face of the planet till no one's left alive anymore, to take their land and establish God's kingdom.[120] The fact that this passage in Deuteronomy identifies other ethnic groups by name is a strong indication of the Jewish sense of national distinctness. Not only did the Israelites in ancient times know they were different from the rest, they had a strong attachment to the territory they saw as promised to their forefather Abraham. Joshua obeys God and establishes the first Kingdom of Israel in the conquered land of Canaan, ushering in a period of prosperity with many exemplary Jewish Kings including Saul, David and Solomon. King Solomon built a holy sanctuary for the worship of Yahweh in the city of Jerusalem between 970 and 930 BCE beneath which lay the sacred stone tablets with the Ten Commandments inscribed in the Hebrew language.[121] This site is called the Temple Mount in Jerusalem. Today two Islamic mosques, the Dome of the Rock and Al-Aqsa sit atop the site. These were built in the seventh century of the common era by conquering Arabs. Without a doubt, God's promise of land to Abraham, the story of Moses leading the Israelites out of Egyptian bondage across the Red Sea, then Joshua leading them back into the promised land continue to be entrenched deeply in Jewish consciousness.

Modern nationalism, as seen in the first chapter, attempts to connect a self-conscious people with a cultural imagination to a specific territory. This is why the terms 'nation' (reference to a people) is often combined with the term 'state' (reference to a land) to form the term 'nation-state' which remains the more technical expression for referring to a sovereign country on today's world map.[122] The Jewish attachment to what it perceives as the "promised land" is the oldest continuing case of territorial nationalism. Yet the story of this attachment and the role played by the Hebrew language along its path of survival and self-preservation has been one fraught with immense upheavals. Not long after Joshua's conquest, the Israelites were plunged into a bitter civil war and the Kingdom split into two. Israel in the north and Judah in the south.[123] Judah or *Yehuda* was one of Abraham's great grandsons through his son Isaac and grandson Jacob. From his name, the Anglicised terms *Jew* (Yehu) or *Jewish* (Yehudi) are derived, which historically meant a member of the specific tribe of Judah.[124] Over time, these terms have come to refer to *any* descendant of the Hebrews or Israelites regardless of which of the twelve tribes their ancestry may otherwise stem from.

Hebrew continued to be the language of religion and of community for the ancient Israelites. In Judges 12 the pronunciation of one Hebrew consonant becomes a matter of life and death. The ancient Israelites used language, accent and pronunciation as markers of group identity. The most powerful expression of this tendency is the story of the Gileadites who went to war against the Ephraimites over mispronunciation. Unable to tell apart each other based on physical appearance and attire, they relied on language. The Ephraimites pronounced the word for an ear of grain as "Sibolet" and the Gileadites as "Shibolet". The actual story in the book of Judges is:

> The Ephraimite forces were called out, and they crossed over to Zaphon. They said to Jephthah, "Why did you go to fight the Ammonites without calling us to go with you? We're going to burn down your house over your head."
>
> Jephthah answered, "I and my people were engaged in a great struggle with the Ammonites, and although I called, you didn't save me out of their hands. When I saw that you wouldn't help, I took my life in my hands and crossed over to fight the Ammonites, and the Lord gave me the victory over them. Now why have you come up today to fight me?"

> Jephthah then called together the men of Gilead and fought against Ephraim. The Gileadites struck them down because the Ephraimites had said, "You Gileadites are renegades from Ephraim and Manasseh."
>
> The Gileadites captured the fords of the Jordan leading to Ephraim, and whenever a survivor of Ephraim said, "Let me cross over," the men of Gilead asked him, "Are you an Ephraimite?" If he replied, "No," they said, "All right, say 'Shibboleth.'" If he said, "Sibboleth," because he could not pronounce the word correctly, they seized him and killed him at the fords of the Jordan.
>
> Forty-two thousand Ephraimites were killed at that time. Jephthah led Israel six years. Then Jephthah the Gileadite died and was buried in a town in Gilead.[125]

From very early on, we see concurrent evidence of both the sanctity of the Hebrew language in the religious sense and its importance as a point of differentiation between the cultural in-group and the cultural out-group. In 721 BCE, an Assyrian invasion into Israelite territory occurred under the command of Assyrian King Sargon II. It was customary in those days for the conquered people to worship the gods and goddesses of their conquerors. The conquerors would in turn incorporate any local deities into their pantheon of multiple deities, a phenomenon known as polytheism. What set the Israelites apart from other people in those times was their strict monotheism.[126] Israelite refusal to worship any deity other than their own unique God *Yahweh* the God of Abraham, Isaac, Jacob, and Moses, and their refusal to allow their own god to be appropriated by their conquerors was seen as an act of defiance.[127] Angered conquerors would retaliate harshly inflicting severe punishments. The most common of which was forced expulsion to desolate territories outside of Jerusalem, the centre of all Jewish activity.[128]

The Assyrians expelled large numbers of Jews to Upper Mesopotamia, in the northern parts of present-day Iraq. In ancient Judaism, the predominant means by which Jews worshipped God was through animal sacrifices and burnt offerings at the Temple in Jerusalem, built centuries earlier by King Solomon. In exile, this could no longer be done. So, returning to the promised land and staying close to the

Temple Mount becomes a central feature of diaspora Jewish thought. An apt comparison would be the contemporary Islamic attachment to Mecca, in Saudi Arabia. Muslims can only perform the annual pilgrimage of *Hajj* in Mecca alone and not anywhere else. Just as there can be no Hajj in Sydney, London or New York as there is no Holy Ka'aba in those places, in ancient Judaism there could be no daily Jewish worship as prescribed in the Torah anywhere except the Temple in Jerusalem. What kept the Jews connected to their religion and sense of community was continued use of the Hebrew language for prayer and liturgy. In exile, they continued to recite the *Shema* in Hebrew, that is 'Shema Yisrael, Adonai Eloheinu, Adonai Ekhad' which says 'Hear O Israel, the Lord our God, is one God.'[129]

Bernard Spolsky notes that: "In 605 [BCE] the Babylonian king Nebuchadnezzar defeated the Egyptians, and set out to gain control of the Middle East".[130] Then, in 597 BCE, the Babylonians invaded Jerusalem.[131] Large numbers of Israelites were again sent into exile in Babylon. This time, the Jewish Temple gets destroyed in 586 BCE. This became a major turning point in Jewish history marking the end of what is understood as *First Temple* Judaism. It is during this period of Babylonian exile that Jews came to develop a belief in the idea of a Messiah, a special figurehead to be sent to earth as a helper from God. His mission would be to bring the Jews out of *Galut* which is the collective term for foreign occupation, exile or enslavement. It refers to a political circumstance where Jews are ruled by non-Jews regardless whether that occurs within Jerusalem or elsewhere in the world. It is during this period that Aramaic gradually started to replace Hebrew as a native spoken vernacular among the Jews all over the ancient near east.[132] The middle part of the Book of Daniel in the Old Testament is written in Aramaic which was considered the language of diplomacy at the time as well as the native tongue of the ruling elite in the Medo-Persian Empire.[133] R. H. Charles proposed the theory that the entire book of Daniel was likely written in Aramaic, but that later chapters were translated into Hebrew. H. C. Leopold argues against this explanation on linguistic grounds. C. Hassell Bullock points out that the Aramaic segments were written in the language of the empire for their consumption.[134] What is evident by this stage is Aramaic infiltration into Jewish religious writings, a language that held no religious significance for the Jews. This transition was the result of political pressures in exile.

In 539 BCE, the Persians invaded Jerusalem.[135] They practiced Zoroastrianism which is also a monotheistic religion. This might explain a part of the reason why they were less hostile towards the Jews compared to previous pantheistic invaders. Persian King Cyrus not only allowed the Jews of Babylon to return home to Jerusalem, he in fact went so far as to allow for the Jewish Temple to be rebuilt in 516 BCE. Meanwhile, the expectation for the arrival of a *Messiah* continued to be a common feature of Jewish thought during this period of *Second Temple* Judaism. Next came the Greek invasion led by Alexander the Great around 332 BCE as part of his campaigns against the Persian Achaemenid Empire. This ushered in a period of the cultural *Hellenisation* of Jewish thought. Bernard Spolsky notes that: "During the Hellenistic period (332-165) BCE there continued to be ostraca (pieces of pottery) written in Aramaic, and there are Aramaicisms in the Septuagint."[136] Yet the major factor that kept Jewish identity attached to its religious and cultural imagination was the continued recitation of the Torah in the Hebrew language. Following the death of Alexander the Great, the Hellenic Empire in the near east branched off into two factions: The Ptolemies whose stronghold was Egypt and the Seleucids whose stronghold was Greater Syria, or the Levant region as it is understood today. While many Jews continued to remain wedded to the eschatological belief that the Messiah would come and rescue them from Galut, some Jews did take their emancipation in their own hands and sought independence through guerrilla warfare. The Maccabean Revolt against the Seleucids and Hellenised Jews from 167 to 160 BCE remains a case in point. A small group of Jewish nationalist rebels, the Maccabeans, in fact managed to conquer enough territory around Judea to run a fully independent Jewish Kingdom from 110 to 63 BCE keeping Hellenic influence away from Jewish culture and practices. This again reinforces the primordial nature of Jewish nationalist thought. Almost 2,000 years before the birth of modern nationalism, the Maccabees were protective of their culture as a *nation* and were concurrently trying to build a sovereign Jewish *state*. Jews today celebrate the festival of *Hanukkah* to mark the short-lived triumph of the Maccabees over their Seleucid rulers and Hellenised Jews.

In 63 BCE, the Romans invaded Jerusalem annexing the region and made it a part of the Roman Republic. Spolsky notes that around this time: "...Greek and Latin became important, but Aramaic remained the vernacular of many Jews (and Hebrew of some) and was used in inscriptions and legal documents."[137] The political landscape of Roman rule in Judea was fragmented at best. By this stage, there had emerged three distinct sects of Jews: the Pharisees, the Sadducees, and the Essenes. All three groups were divided by competing religious beliefs and political attitudes towards the question of Jewish emancipation from perpetual *Galut*. The Pharisees believed in strict adherence to the Torah and devoted much time debating how to interpret scripture while rejecting the Jewish leadership of the day. The Sadducees believed in worshipping at the Temple and took a literal approach to reading the Torah while supporting the Jewish leadership of the day. The Essenes were a socially withdrawn monastic community of political zealots who saw the other two groups as sellouts that had abandoned the quest for Jewish independence from Roman rule. Not all, but a considerable number of politically active Essenes saw it as their duty to carry forwards the short-lived legacy of the Maccabeans and to continue to engage in guerilla warfare against both the Romans and against the Jews who collaborated with the Romans.

It was amid this political turmoil that Jesus Christ surfaces within the Essenes community. Some believed him to be the long-awaited Messiah. While Jesus had followers, he was largely seen as a troublemaker by both the Romans and the Jews. He was executed while Judea remained under Roman rule. Most Jews did not accept Jesus as their Messiah because he did not fulfil the prophecy of setting them free from Galut. Yet Jesus attracted many followers, especially from the downtrodden and neglected underclasses. His earliest followers saw themselves as another sect of Second Temple Judaism but, as differences grew apart over time, this breakaway movement evolved into Christianity - a separate religion. The reasons why most Jews did not accept Jesus as their Messiah were numerous.[138] Yet the most fundamental factor was that Jews interpreted their Messianic prophecies in the Tanakh (or the Old Testament) as promising emancipation from Galut. In other words the Messiah, by Jewish expectations, was supposed to be a God-sent *nationalist* who would make the Jews sovereign in the land promised to their forefather Abraham. This would have meant ending Roman occupation which Jesus evidently did not achieve. Besides, he was actively critical of the Jewish establishment at the time. So, it is hardly surprising that Jewish nationalist struggles for independence from Rome continued on with other Jewish rebels carrying the mantle. Under Emperor Vespasian's rule, the Romans retaliated harshly by destroying the Second Temple in the year 70 of the common era. Far from putting an end to Jewish insurgency, the destruction of their temple inflamed the Jews even more, turning them ever more militant. The insurrections against Rome continued with more rigour and force. Bar Kokhba's Revolt (132 to 136 CE) went on for several years at the end of which, Roman Emperor Hadrian changed the region's name from *Provencia Judea* to *Provencia Syria-Palestina* banning the Jews from entering Jerusalem and sent them into yet another exile. Spolsky points out that according to an account of Rome's history written by Cassius Dio around 220 CE, some half a million Jews were killed in the process, and many of those who survived ended up leaving by choice.[139]

This not only ushered in the latest wave of the Jewish diaspora, it was one that would continue on until only a century ago with the birth of the political Zionist movement in the late 1800s. Grounded in the narrative of bondage in ancient Egypt featuring Moses as the saviour, the idea of exile and emancipation have been central to multiple strands of Jewish thought through the ages. The same is true of the destruction, reconstruction, and second destruction of the Jewish Temple, first in 586 BCE by the Babylonians and then by the Romans in 70 CE. Yehudit Henshke notes that by: "...the second century,

Hebrew began declining as a spoken language and gradually became confined to the realms of religious worship and study. It remained in this status for centuries, until its revival as a living language at the close of the 19th century." In the last centuries BCE and first centuries CE "...a state of Hebrew-Aramaic diglossia existed in the land of Israel. Aramaic gradually replaced Hebrew as the dominant vernacular."[140]

This period saw the completion of some seminal Jewish texts such as the Jerusalem Talmud in 200 CE, the *Midreshei Haggadah* written in Galilean Aramaic mixed with Hebrew and the Babylonian Talmud completed in 500 CE, written in Babylonian Aramaic mixed with Hebrew.[141] Note that the Talmud has two components: the Mishnah itself and the accompanying Gemara that explains it. The Mishnah is almost exclusively in Hebrew, while the Gemara, often referred to generically as 'the Talmud', is largely in Aramaic. The Assyrians in 721 BCE, the Babylonians in 597 BCE and the Romans in 135 CE all sent the Jews into exile centuries apart from each other for similar reasons: failure to respect foreign authority, standing up for their religious practices, refusal to worship foreign deities like other more subservient conquered people had one, and perhaps most important of all their nationalist persistence in seeking self-determination in their ancestral homeland. This perpetual state of *Galut* across the centuries often meant it was one day in Jerusalem and by the banks of the Tigris and the Euphrates the next. Yet one thing that has continued to remain constant through these various upheavals and exile was the liturgical use of the Hebrew language. No matter where the Jews lived, they faced Jerusalem when praying three times a day reciting their daily prayers in Hebrew, even when Aramaic was the language spoken at home and on the street.

As the last major exile came about in 135 CE with Roman Emperor Hadrian's expulsion of Jews following the Bar Kokhba Revolt, the Jews came to be scattered around all ends of the known world at the time. Some went northbound into Europe and Russia. Others went westwards into North Africa, as far west as Morocco and eventually into Spain. Yet others went eastwards into Arabia, Iran and India. Some even made it so far as China. In his 2017 publication *Globalisation, Translation and Transmission: Sino-Judaic Cultural Identity in Kaifeng*, Jewish academic Moshe Bernstein has extensively researched the history of China's Jewish community in the city of Kaifeng.[142] The existence of this fascinating community in the most improbable of geographical locations shows how far and wide the Jewish diaspora came to manifest itself through centuries of Galut. Chinese Jews often adopted some local customs from Chinese culture, but *still* continued to use Hebrew as a language of liturgy and worship and through it, managed to preserve their Jewish identities.

With the Second Temple destroyed, the challenge for the Jews was to ensure cultural continuity away from the theological centre of gravity, Jerusalem. Judaism, an otherwise *central* religion based around worship at a specific territory was left with no choice but to *decentralise* its practices and ensure its survival. As a result, the diaspora beginning in 135 CE gave birth to the *Rabbinic* model of Judaism grounded in instructions inscribed in religious scriptures, called the two Talmuds, the Jerusalem Talmud completed in 200 CE, and the Babylonian Talmud in 500 CE. Although these Talmuds are written in Aramaic, Hebrew remained the language of prayer and worship in Synagogues right around the world. The Gemara states that Rabbi Yehuda HaNasi (or Judah the Prince, 135–220 CE) in this period instructed his household to speak only Hebrew.

The 7th century saw Islam emerge as a religious and political movement in the Arabian peninsula. Islam saw itself as a continuation of the Jewish and Christian religious traditions. The diaspora had seen large numbers of Jews moving southbound and settling in the Hejaz region, today part of Saudi Arabia. Islam's founder Prophet Muhammad came in close contact with the Jews of Medina and had a complex political relationship with them. At first he had a peace treaty with them in 622 CE called *al-Meethaq al-Madinah* or the Constitution of Medina. Later as the pact was broken, relations turned sour. By the time of his death in 632 CE, all of Arabia had fallen into the hands of the emerging Islamic Empire. Shortly after his passing, his successors

Abu Bakr, Omar, Uthman and Ali managed to spread the faith to all ends of the known world. It was under Caliph Omar Ibn Al-Khattab that Jerusalem was conquered by Muslim Arabs in the year 637 CE. Since the Jews and the Christians are viewed in Islam as *Ahl al-Kitab* or the 'People of the Book' meaning not necessarily *false* religions, but more so *obsolete* religions, they were to be granted special status as protected minorities under an Islamic government, provided they agreed to pay a *dhimmi* tax and wear a yellow armband as a mark of social distinction.[143] From this point on, Jews around the world would go on to seek their survival either as a minority under Islamic rule in North Africa and the Middle East, or under Christian rule in Europe and Russia. The Romans persecuted the early Christians for the initial three centuries following the emergence of the newfound religion, until Roman Emperor Constantine issued his Edict of Milan in 313 CE following a mysterious vision at the Battle of Milvian Bridge.[144]

Eventually in the year 381 CE Roman Emperor Theodosius I adopted Christianity as the state religion of the then Roman Empire.[145] Since the Christians had traditionally blamed the Jews for the crucifixion of Jesus Christ, for centuries to come, Jewish communities in Christian lands would be subjected to harsh discrimination, mass expulsions, and hostility. During the Middle Ages, Christian European antisemitism towards the Jews was further compounded by the fact that Christianity had forbidden the practice of usury, and Jews over time came to be the money lending class. This was because Judaism only forbade Jews from charging other Jews interest, but they were permitted to loan money to non-Jews with interest. The allegation that they had murdered Christ combined with the resentment that came from the practice of usury, the Jews were collectively blamed by Christian authorities in Europe and expelled from England in 1290 under the 'Edict of Expulsion' issued by King Edward I[146] and from Spain and Portugal in 1492 under the 'Alhambra Decree' issued by Queen Isabella I of Castile and King Ferdinand II of Aragon.[147] J. Gordon Melton notes that:

> In response to the Spanish expulsion of Jews and Muslims, Ottoman sultan Bayezid II sends the Ottoman navy to Spain to facilitate

their evacuation and provide transport to Ottoman territory. Simultaneously, he issues a set of proclamations calling upon his subjects and especially government officials to welcome the refugees while granting the refugees permission to establish their residence and become Ottoman citizens.[148]

As far as language was concerned, wherever the Jews went they spoke local languages and maintained a degree of integration into the host society. The Ashkenazi Jews of Europe predominantly spoke Yiddish, a dialect of German written in Hebrew script, or Russian. The Sephardic Jews of North Africa predominantly spoke Ladino or Arabic written in Hebrew script. The Mizrahi Jews of the Middle East spoke Arabic, Persian, or Gujarati depending on where they were. The Ethiopian Jews spoke Amharic. Despite these ethnic subdivisions and linguistic diversity, the liturgical use of Hebrew continued to be the source of a common consciousness among world Jewry. While the common Jew knew how to read Hebrew to understand the liturgy and religious texts over the centuries, the rabbis continued to produce countless volumes of Hebrew literature including commentary, legal tomes, ethical treatises, philosophical works, and responsa. Hebrew was also used as the language of communication among the rabbis of various European, North African and Levantine communities. Though it was not a spoken language for 2,000 years, it continued to serve as a mode of interpersonal communication for the literate class as well as for poetry, prose and letter writing in general.

Between the Roman expulsion of the Jews from Jerusalem in 135 CE and the Islamic conquest of Jerusalem in 637 CE, the region's population turned into a Christian demographic majority with Aramaic as the dominant language under Byzantine rule. This landscape again began to gradually alter following the Muslim Arab conquest. Caliph Omar had a peace treaty with the then Christian patriarch of Jerusalem, Sophronius. Over time Arabic began to replace Aramaic as the spoken language, although Islam did not immediately replace Christianity as the dominant religion until many centuries later. The Muslim Arab conquest of this sliver of land between the Jordan River and the Mediterranean Sea did not bother the Jews at the time, so much as it bothered the Christian rulers in Europe. In fact, under

Islamic rule the Jews were permitted to return to Jerusalem after five centuries of being barred by the Romans and later the Byzantines, both before and after Rome's embrace of Christianity in 381 CE. This was a tough time to be Jewish anywhere in the world, and especially within historic Palestine. At a time when attacks on Jewish Synagogues by Christians were commonplace, Spolsky observes that:

> The Muslim conquest was probably welcomed by these Jews, who modified the mosaic [from Synagogues] by removing human and animal images, as required by Muslim iconoclasm. There were other influences of Islam: rabbinic literary work, which flourished in Tiberias, Jerusalem, Cairo, and Baghdad, was produced in codices rather than in the scroll form that had previously been followed. As Aramaic was replaced by Arabic, new versions were produced, and books began to be written in a variety of Biblical Hebrew and later in Arabic. Jews and Samaritans began to use Arabic for secular and religious works.[149]

Between the years 1095 and 1291, a series of wars were fought between European Christian and Muslim Arab forces over who would rule Jerusalem. These are called the Crusades and there were nine of them during this period. The Jews fought alongside the Muslims during the Crusades given the antisemitism towards them in Christian Europe.[150] From 1517, the Ottoman Empire took control over Jerusalem. Jews under Ottoman Turkish rule had a considerable degree of political and religious autonomy. The Ottoman Empire had established an ecclesiastical court known as the Office of *Hakham Bashi* that would enable Jews to govern themselves.[151] Jews under Ottoman rule were a demographic minority in Palestine while Arabic-speaking Christians, Druze, and Muslims had over time become the demographic majority.[152]

The Golden Age of Jewish literature and learning coincided with the Islamic Golden Age in Al-Andalus, that was Spain under Umayyad rule. The liturgical use of Hebrew continued to serve as the glue that bound practising Jews together despite great geographical distance. Given the sanctity of Hebrew, Jewish grammarians continued to write prose, poetry, and philosophical treatises in the ancestral language throughout the Middle Ages. The examples of Medieval Jewish scholars from the Islamic world are numerous. It was 10th century Jewish scholar Saadiah Ben Yosef Al-Fayyumi, often known as Saadiah Gaon, who led the rabbinic academy called *Sura* in Medieval Iraq. He is known for his works on Hebrew grammar and philology. He also translated the Bible into Arabic. His most remarkable achievement was his strong stance against the emerging *Karaite* movement that came to reject the Talmud and promoted a 'Torah only' version of Judaism.[153]

Likewise, 10th century Jewish poet and polyglot Menahem Ben Saruq composed a Hebrew dictionary. His contemporary and rival Dunash Halevi Ben Labrat developed a theory about Hebrew verbs. Jewish linguists Judah Ben David Hayyuj and Jonah Ibn Janah's works on Hebrew roots and grammar are from the same period and equally well known. Originally in Arabic, some of these works were later translated by 11th century Bible exegete Moses Ibn Gikatilla into Hebrew.[154] As is evident, even without native speakers, these remarkable developments in the grammar and lexicography of the Hebrew language, often produced in Arabic, ensured the survival and preservation of the ancestral tongue across generations of diaspora. The treatment of Jewish minorities under Islamic rule in North Africa and the Middle East was far less hostile than the treatment of Jewish minorities under Christian rule in Europe and Russia. This is a fact recognised by the overwhelming majority of learned Jewish scholars and rabbis who know their history. Yet it would surprise many in our own times because modern observers tend to view Jewish-Muslim relations through the prism of the on-going Israel-Palestine conflict, which dates just over a century and stems from competing nationalist claims between the Jews and the Palestinian Arabs of the so-called promised land.

As Jews were scattered around the world during the 2,000 year long diaspora, speaking many different tongues,[155] the hope or *HaTikvah* to return to Jerusalem continued to remain a key feature in Jewish thought. No matter where in the world Jews met, at the conclusion of their Passover meals, they would recite "L'Shana Haba'ah

B'Yerushalayim" which means "Next year in Jerusalem". They would pray three times daily for the restoration of Jerusalem. A similar prayer is repeated in the Grace after meals:

> Return in mercy to Jerusalem Your city and dwell therein as You have promised; speedily establish therein the throne of David Your servant, and rebuild it, soon in our days, as an everlasting edifice. Blessed are You L-rd, who rebuilds Jerusalem. (Amidah)

> Have mercy, L-rd our G-d, upon Israel Your people, upon Jerusalem Your city, upon Zion the abode of Your glory, upon the kingship of the house of David Your anointed, and upon the great and holy House over which Your Name was proclaimed.

> ... And rebuild Jerusalem the holy city speedily in our days. Blessed are You, L-rd, Who in His mercy rebuilds Jerusalem. Amen. (Birkat HaMazon, Grace after Meals)

The traditionally held view among learned Jews was that the re-establishment of a Jewish state and in-gathering of the exiles could only happen through *divine* intervention with the return of the promised Messiah. This was the dominant belief among Jewish rabbis, scholars and community leaders all over the world. Unlike the Maccabean revolt before the common era and the Bar Kokhba revolt in the common era, there were no significant instances of Jewish insurgency attempting to achieve Jewish statehood during the Middle Ages nor in the early modern period. The matter had been left in the hands of God.

Yet Jewish history takes a new turn in the late 1800s. After centuries of antisemitism, mass expulsions and pogroms, and throughout all of this, an endless waiting for emancipation through divine help, a generation of secular Jewish intellectuals emerged with the conclusion that the Jewish people could no longer afford to keep waiting for the Messiah to come and emancipate them. They were not driven by a religious motivation and felt the matter needed to be dealt with through human effort. Their idea of a Jewish nation was not entirely dissimilar from some of the existing nationalist ideas that had begun surfacing across Europe following the Revolutions of 1848. This was the new European belief in the secular ideas of nationalism and self-determination that made popular the idea of the sovereignty of *man* over the sovereignty of *God*. These two concepts are differentiated within Jewish nationalist thought. The Hebrew expression "ribono shel olam" refers to the sovereign of the universe while "ribonut" is sovereignty and the sovereign is the "ribon".

Hungarian-born secular Jewish intellectual Theodor Herzl is generally seen as the founder of Jewish nationalism, otherwise known as political Zionism. Yet Herzl's seminal treatise *Der Judenstaat* or *The Jewish State* was only published in 1896 with the First Zionist Congress taking place in 1897. Another Jewish intellectual Leon Pinsker had already beaten Herzl to the call for a Jewish state a decade and a half earlier with his seminal treatise *Auto-Emancipation* published in 1882. That was also the year of the First *Aliyah* marking the inaugural wave of European Jews migrating into Ottoman-ruled Palestine. All of this occurred over a decade and a half before Herzl. Zionism had begun to transform from being an esoteric discussion among Jewish intellectuals to a recognised nationalist movement on the stage of global affairs.

During the diaspora, Jews had for the most part been free to visit and live in Ottoman Palestine, and many did so, through the centuries. They were afforded a considerable degree of religious and political autonomy, and often served in high ranking positions in the bureaucracy. There were ecclesiastical Jewish courts and an official rabbinate in Jerusalem under Ottoman rule. Yet the yearning to be sovereign within the ancestral homeland continued to permeate the minds of Jewish thinkers and leaders through the ages. The contemporary critics of the State of Israel often blame political Zionism for its "occupation" of the Palestinian territories. In so doing, they attempt to isolate Zionism from Judaism claiming that their criticism is not aimed at Jews or Judaism, but at Zionism alone, which critics view as a colonial expansionist ideology designed to usurp land from the Palestinian Arab population whom critics consider to be indigenous to the region. It is crucial to note that returning to the hills of Zion and Jerusalem has been central to Jewish thought long before the efforts of nineteenth century Jewish intellectuals Pinsker and Herzl. The Zionist perspective is that the Jews are the indigenous people of historic Palestine (originally called Judea), or what they would call *Eretz Yisrael*. They are not like the British settlers who came to grow tobacco in Rhodesia or Kenya, or the Europeans who settled the Americas and Australia on behalf of European Imperial powers. The Zionists sought to represent a nation of the Jews or *Am Yisrael* that was the downtrodden of the earth, *itself* escaping persecution.

As early as 1160, we find that David Alroy had started a Jewish movement in the Kurdish regions of Iraq aspiring to retake historic Palestine for the Jews. The self-proclaimed messiah Sabbatai Zevi from Ottoman-ruled Turkey tried to do the same in 1648 claiming he wanted to see the Jewish exiles returned to their promised land. In 1868, another called Judah Ben Shalom led a movement of Mizrahi Jews from Yemen into Ottoman Palestine with the same motivations. It is clear that while most diaspora Jews had settled for the belief that only the Messiah could come and rescue them, there were still efforts made by enthusiasts like Alroy, Zevi and Ben Shalom to seek an early return to the Jewish ancestral home across three entirely separate timeframes, centuries apart from each other.

Even as Jews awaited their Messianic emancipation, many other noteworthy figures had begun encouraging Jews to start moving to Palestine. Yehuda Alkalai, Moshe Hess, Zvi Kalischer and Yehuda Bibas remain notable examples of nineteenth century Jewish leaders and intellectuals to have tackled the question of Jewish emancipation encouraging mass aliyah even before the likes of secular thinkers Leon Pinsker and Theodor Herzl picked up the mantle. From the hardline approach of Alroy to the pacifistic approach of Hess, if one thing is clear, it is the centrality of establishing a Jewish national home in the hills of Zion and Jerusalem.

As the secular Zionist movement began to gain momentum, a few different options were considered for where the Jewish state would be. This is because Herzl's Zionism was not religious by its nature.

He was more interested in having a state where the Jews could be free, rather than the specific land of their ancient Israelite ancestors. Although in the end, Ottoman Palestine became the most desirable option due to the Biblical and ancestral narrative. The argument was that if there is to be a Jewish state re-established at all for the first time since the short lived Hasmonean Kingdom (140 BCE to 37 BCE) more than two millennia earlier, it may as well be in the ancestral homeland promised to the Prophet Abraham 4,000 years earlier in Genesis 12:1 in the Bible.[156] No other place made much sense to many early Zionist thinkers. There was, of course, a pre-existing sentimental and historical attachment to the land of the Bible. To most Ashkenazi Jews from Europe and Russia, the options to create a Jewish state in remote places like Argentina or Uganda were ridiculous. While liturgical use of Hebrew had done well enough to preserve Jewish identity and kept alive the hopes of returning to Jerusalem, could the Zionist enterprise have succeeded without a common language? Oddly enough, this was not a question that necessarily concerned Theodor Herzl. In his *Der Judenstaat* (The Jewish State) published in 1896, Herzl says the following on language:

> It might be suggested that our want of a common current language would present difficulties. We cannot converse with one another in Hebrew. Who amongst us has a sufficient acquaintance with Hebrew to ask for a railway ticket in that language! Such a thing cannot be done. Yet the difficulty is very easily circumvented. Every man can preserve the language in which his thoughts are at home. Switzerland affords a conclusive proof of the possibility of a federation of tongues. We shall remain in the new country what we now are here, and we shall never cease to cherish with sadness the memory of the native land out of which we have been driven.
>
> We shall give up using those miserable stunted jargons, those Ghetto languages which we still employ, for these were the stealthy tongues of prisoners. Our national teachers will give due attention to this matter; and the language which proves itself to be of greatest utility for general intercourse will be adopted without compulsion as our national tongue. Our community of race is peculiar and unique, for we are bound together only by the faith of our fathers.[157]

As can be seen from this passage, Herzl acknowledges that most Jews could not, at that stage, converse with each other in Hebrew. Yet he goes on to downplay the significance of a common language, using the example of Switzerland which was and still is a multilingual society. Neither did Herzl know Hebrew himself nor was he necessarily particularly fond of ever learning it. He writes in a diary entry in September 1897:

> In deference to religious considerations, I went to the synagogue on Saturday before the Congress. The head of the congregation called me up to the Torah. I had the brother in law of my Paris friend Beer, Mr Markus of Merau, drill the brokhe (benediction) into me. And then I climbed the steps to the altar, I was more excited than on all the Congress days. The few Hebrew words of the brokhe caused me more anxiety than my welcoming and closing address and the whole direction of my proceedings.[158]

Herzl did not grow up as a religious Jew. His personal indifference to the Hebrew language as captured in the above passage may account for his failure to realise its value in building a modern Jewish nation-state. Besides, 19th century political Zionism was a distinctly *European* Jewish nationalist movement based on the concerns of Ashkenazi Jews from Europe and Russia. Herzl, for instance, was deeply moved by the Dreyfus Affair in 1894 when French Jewish artillery officer Alfred Dreyfus was accused of leaking French military secrets to the German Embassy in Paris and sentenced to life imprisonment as a result. European Zionists were concerned about the wave of antisemitism that had swept across Tsarist Russia around the same timeframe. There does not appear to be much evidence that the European Zionists were actively thinking about the Sephardic, Mizrahi or Ethiopian Jews of the East. They do not generally feature in the writings of the early Zionist pioneers. Yet once the Jewish state was established, it was inevitable that it would not simply go on to being a Yiddish-speaking country for European Jews. The yearning to return to Jerusalem and the hills of Zion is not exclusive to the Ashkenazi Jews, it is in fact a Jewish belief shared by any mainstream Jew, including the anti-Zionist Neturei Karta. The difference is about how statehood is to be achieved, not whether or not it should be achieved at all. So if a Jewish state were to be created, it would have been one that was open for migration by all Jews from all over the world, including the eastern Jews from North Africa and the Middle East or for that matter, from India and China.

It follows that if the Zionist enterprise was to succeed in its objective, what it would end up creating in Palestine would not have been a country comparable to Switzerland where a linguistically diverse population of German, Italian, French and Romansch speakers could unite under a common Swiss national identity. Instead, it would have been a hodgepodge of conflicting identities in an ethnically and linguistically fragmented society. Herzl's comparison with Switzerland was overly simplistic and short-sighted. The linguistic borders within Switzerland are clearly defined. Most people who live in French speaking villages, for instance, do not come into close contact with people in the German speaking parts of the country on an on-going basis. Since the population of Switzerland is entirely *culturally* European, industrialised, literate and enjoys a similar diet, on balance, the country has been able to function with *considerable* degrees of harmony. Yet there did emerge a political movement in Switzerland's north-western French-speaking region of Canton Berne that caused ethnic strife comparable in nature to those in Belgium and Quebec. A separatist movement called '*Le Rassemblement Jurassien*' surfaced in 1947 that had aimed to split the French-speaking areas in the country's Jura mountains.[159]

Herzl died in 1904 and did not live long enough to witness those linguistically motivated ethnic tensions in Switzerland. By contrast, the Sephardic Jews of North Africa and the Mizrahi Jews of the Middle East were culturally more like the Arabs with whom they had shared a geography and a diet for over a millennia and a half. They ate hummus, falafel, rice, flat bread, couscous, with meat dishes on the side cooked with strong spices. They were not generally educated, industrialised nor entrepreneurial like the Ashkenazi Jews of Europe and Russia. Many Mizrahi males wore turbans, females wore headscarves, both genders wore robes just like Arab men and women. As an *Oriental* people, they shared little else besides a religious identity or shared past with their *Occidental* counterparts from Europe and Russia.

If a Jewish state was to be established in historic Palestine bringing together Yiddish, Polish, Russian, Ukrainian or Lithuanian speaking European Jews with culturally exotic Arabic, Persian or Turkish speaking Oriental Jews, such an experiment would have resulted in a divided society torn along linguistic lines. Unlike Switzerland's case, there would have been no clear regional boundaries separating native speakers of more than a dozen European and Oriental languages from each other. Without a doubt, the requirement of a shared national language was a key necessity for the success of a Jewish state in Palestine. Praying in Hebrew and reading the Torah had done well enough to keep alive the Jewish sense of nationhood in the diaspora. To go from nation to nation-state, a shared language was needed. It would enable Jewish settlers in historic Palestine to be able to form sociable communities, to function as one volk, to be able to read and respond to the same language on state documents and currency as one other. Realising as much, the other Zionist intellectual Leon Pinsker in his treatise *Auto-Emancipation* published in 1882 wrote:

> An equality of this kind did exist in the now long forgotten past, but unfortunately, under present conditions, the prospect that will readmit the Jewish people to the status of nationhood is so remote as to seem illusory. It lacks most of the essential attributes by which a nation is recognised. It lacks that autochthonous life which is inconceivable *without a common language a*nd customs and without cohesion in space. The Jewish people has no fatherland of its own, though many motherlands; no center of focus or gravity, no government of its own, no official representation. They are home everywhere, but are nowhere at home. The nations have never to deal with a Jewish nation but always with mere Jews. The Jews are not a nation because they lack a certain distinctive national character, inherent in all other nations, which is formed by common residence in a single state. It was clearly impossible for this national character to be developed in the Diaspora; the Jews seem rather to have lost all remembrance of their former home. Thanks to their ready adaptability, they have all the more easily acquired characteristics, not inborn, of the people among whom fate has thrown them. Often to please their protectors, they recommend their traditional individuality entirely. They acquired or persuaded themselves into certain cosmopolitan tendencies which could no more appeal to others than bring satisfaction to themselves.[160]

Pinsker's account reflects the cynicism we find inherent in the writings of other Zionist thinkers of the time. Yet his description of what life was like for Jews in the diaspora is not invalid. Pinsker was swift in noticing the rise of various national identities and nationalisms that had swept across Europe during the mid to late 1800s. He goes on to remark that:

> In a few decades we have seen rising into new life nations which at an earlier time would not have dared to dream of a resurrection. The dawn is already breaking through the darkness of traditional statecraft. The governments already incline their ears – where it cannot be avoided – to the clamor of the awakening of self-consciousness of nationalities. It is true that those happy ones who attained their national independence were not Jews. They lived upon their own soil *and spoke one language*, and therein they certainly had the advantage over us.[161]

We can see how Pinsker was more sympathetic to the need for a shared language compared to Herzl who downplayed its relevance and would have settled for German. As waves of Jewish migrants began pouring into Ottoman-ruled Palestine from the 1880s onwards, the time had come for the dead ancestral language to be brought back to life. And the man who would do this job for his people was a Russian-born Jewish lexicographer whose own Zionist vision *predated* both the conventional fathers of Zionism, Pinsker and Herzl. This was Eliezer Ben Yehuda. Within decades, his revival of Hebrew literally transformed what it meant to be a Jew in the modern age. His achievement adds a fascinating twist to the story of the Jewish identity and its quest for statehood.[162] Describing his own vision for Jewish emancipation seven years earlier than Leon Pinsker's *Auto-Emancipation (1882)* and nineteen years earlier than Theodor Herzl's *The Jewish State (1896)*, Eliezer Ben Yehuda writes in 1875:

> Suddenly as if lightning struck, an incandescent light radiated before my eyes, and my conscious thought flew from Shifka Pass in the Balkans to the Jordan River Crossing in the Land of Israel, and I heard a strange inner voice calling to me: *'The revival of Israel and its language on the land of the forefathers!* This was the dream!'[163]

It was during his visit to Paris in October 1881 that Ben Yehuda engaged in what scholars have since recognised as being possibly the first conversation in revived Hebrew in modern times. Within a year of that experience, he ended up making aliyah and settled in Jerusalem. He found that Jewish settlers that had come from Poland only dealt with Jews who spoke Polish, Jews who came from Romania only associated with others from Romania. Ben Yehuda realised this needed to change and the way to do this was through the revival of Hebrew. The same year that the First Aliyah began in 1882, Ben Yehuda started his mission by becoming a teacher at Jerusalem's Alliance Israelite Universelle School. Until that point in time, the literary centre of the Hebrew language rested with two societies the *Tehiyat Yisrael* or 'The Revival of Israel' and *Safah Berurah* or 'Clear Language'. Ben Yehuda's planned revival of Hebrew took various forms. He started his own newspaper Hatzvi in 1884. Two years later he was known for declaring that:

> The Hebrew language will go from the synagogue to the house of study, and from the house of study to the school, and from the school it will come into the home and become a living language.

In 1890 Ben Yehuda joined the Hebrew Language Committee. As a relevant aside, this body was eventually renamed in 1953 after the creation of Israel and called the Academy of the Hebrew Language. The institution continues to operate as the Hebrew language regulatory body in Israel to date. Ben Yehuda's strategy was to get as many Jewish migrants in Palestine to engage with the Hebrew language as he could and to teach it to their children. He took on the role of editor with several other newspapers such as *Havatzelet*, *Hashkafa* and *Haor*. Far from appreciating his efforts, he faced stern opposition from two directions. In the first instance, there were those European Jewish settlers in Palestine who wanted to retain Yiddish as the language of the upcoming Jewish state. In the second instance, there were the ultra-orthodox Jews who believed that Hebrew was a sacred language and reviving it for conversational use would be an unholy act. Determined as ever, Eliezer Ben Yehuda remained unperturbed by the frequent criticisms aimed at him. It was no secret, he was to take Hebrew from a liturgical language to one spoken by all on the street. He would respond to his critics saying:

> If a language which has stopped being spoken with nothing remaining of it save what remains of our language can return and be the spoken tongue of an individual for all necessities of his life, there is no room for doubt that it can become the spoken language of a community.[164]

Ben Yehuda's first wife Davora could speak Russian, French and German, but he had imposed a strict 'Hebrew only' rule around the house. His son Ben Zion was often kept at home as a baby so that he would not be exposed to other languages. Ben Yehuda once scolded his wife when he discovered that she had been singing their son a lullaby in Russian. The story goes that the child opened his mouth in Hebrew and said "enough already, dad!" Several years later, Davora contracted Eliezer's tuberculosis and died. Within 90 days of her death, 3 out of 5 children died. Ben Yehuda ended up marrying his deceased wife's sister Hemda, who then continued to assist him with the revival of Hebrew. As the new city of Tel Aviv was beginning to be settled in the outskirts of the old city of Yaffo, placards were placed in the streets that said "Yehudi! Daber Ivrit" which meant "Jew! Speak Hebrew!"[165] Scholars have understood Itamar, his young son, to be the first native born speaker of revived Hebrew. He also became the face of the public campaign for revival. The Jews who would respond in any other language were to be ignored as part of this campaign.

Often working as many as 18 hours a day, Ben Yehuda began building the first ever 17 volume *A Complete Dictionary of Ancient and Modern Hebrew*. After his passing, the project was taken over and completed by Hemda, his second wife, as well as his son. One of the great challenges of revival was the obvious lack of modern terminology. The last time Hebrew had existed as a spoken vernacular, there were no words for such things as towel, pistol, jelly, newspaper, handkerchief, doll, bicycle, typewriter, goggles, ice cream, omelette, and dictionary. While these modern words did not pre-exist in any other language, as modern industrial inventions had begun to surface, languages were updated over time. What makes the Hebrew case unique is that Hebrew skipped the *in-between* stage of the natural course of linguistic development. It was an ancient language at the time of its death and it had to immediately adapt and become a modern language, in an industrial age, at the time of its resurrection. The transition was rapid in a few short decades. Before Ben Yehuda's time, Jewish intellectual Mendele Mokher Sfarim had attempted to modernise Hebrew with some neologisms, which too ended up being incorporated into the revival process, but his efforts were incomparable to the far more comprehensive efforts by Ben Yehuda. When he went on to create a new word, he did his best to stay consistent with the Semitic roots of Hebrew grammar. In ancient Hebrew, the word for time was "et" so he called newspaper "iton" which tells readers about news in real or current time. The word "mila" meant word, so dictionary became "milon" as a collection of words. He also created a committee to review his lexical innovations. Where words could not simply be invented, Arabic became a big source in the revival of Hebrew. Joshua Blau describes the work of the committee as insisted upon by Ben Yehuda and writes that:

> In order to supplement the deficiencies of the Hebrew language, the Committee coins words according to the rules of grammar and linguistic analogy from Semitic roots: Aramaic, Canaanite, Egyptian [...] ones and especially from Arabic roots.

Ben Yehuda maintained that Arabic roots: "...were once a part of the Hebrew language . . . lost, and now we have found them again!".[166] He goes on to note that:

> Arabic, in particular, was a kind of source of salvation for me in the linguistic research of our language. First, because it lives at this moment, we are standing on solid ground when explaining the meaning of its words. Second, as I have already proved in one of my papers at once of the Language Council meetings [...] very ancient grammatical forms of all the Semitic languages have been preserved for us in Arabic, and its very expansive and rich vocabulary is the joint treasury of all the Semitic languages. The deeper I went into Arabic language research, the wider the gates of understanding of the Hebrew language opened before me, the Arabic vocabulary enabled me to discover the authentic explanation of many biblical words.[167]

Ben Yehuda's indulgence in Arabic was often met with resistance from colleagues at the Hebrew Language Council. He went on to incorporate many Arabic root stems into revived Hebrew regardless. Although his colleagues Israel Eitan and E. M. Lifshitz are known for opposing this idea, arguing that most Arabic root stems had been created in distant desert life, not modern city culture of the kind of society the Zionist enterprise was in the process of building in Palestine. Critics often went on to suggest Aramaic as an alternative.[168] Still, there was agreement that the revival process should not rely on non-Semitic roots. The obvious exceptions were the Greek and Roman terms incorporated into Hebrew during antiquity. Although Joshua Blau in *The Renaissance of Modern Hebrew and Modern Standard Arabic: Parallels and Differences in the Revival of Two Semitic Languages* and Avihai Shivtiel in *Languages in Contact: The Contribution of the Arabic language to the Revival of Hebrew* note that where Aramaic was of little help, the revivalist did tend to turn to roots from other Semitic languages. It remains intriguing that when Theodor Herzl eventually met Ben Yehuda in Jerusalem in 1898, he described the encounter in his diary entry with the following remark:

> I met the young fanatic who tried to convince me that what our movement needs is to adopt Hebrew as our national language. It is, of course, ridiculous!

Yet due to Ben Yehuda's sustained campaign, the number of native Hebrew speakers in Palestine kept growing. Founded in 1904, the *Va'ad HaLashon HaIvrit* or the Hebrew Language Council was to support the revival process with a nationalist attitude. Even by this stage, some continued to share Herzl's pessimism about the prospects of revival. German orientalist Theodor Noldeke is a case in point. In 1911, he said:

> The dream of some Zionists, that Hebrew - a would be Hebrew, that is to say – will again become a living, popular language in Palestine, has still less prospect of realisation than their vision of a restored Jewish empire in the Holy land.[169]

Noldeke died in Karlsruhe, Germany in 1930. Had he lived another 18 years, he would have seen how far off the mark his assertion was. As Ben Yehuda's project began to gain substantial influence, Ultra-

Orthodox Jews in Jerusalem declared him a heretic, insisting that it was sacreligious to turn the holy language *Lashon HaKodesh* into one spoken on the streets. Growing resistance soured relations between the Hebrew Language Council and other Zionist institutions. As discussed in both the first and second chapters, the use of a shared language for nation-building as well as state-building is neither new, nor unique. What makes the Hebrew case *exceptional* is that its revival and imposition were not part of any *official* nation-building process as has been the case with other nationalist movements.[170] The revival of Hebrew began as a privately initiated enterprise. Far from supporting the project, both the secular Zionist as well as the religious orthodox Jewish establishments were opposed to the project for their own reasons. The secularists preferred a European language such as Yiddish as the national language. The religious orthodox thought Hebrew was too holy to be brought back to life.

Yet in the end, the revival succeeded as a grassroots project almost single-handedly masterminded by Ben Yehuda. As Turkish academic İlker Aytürk observes, the Hebrew Language Council was to have a three-pronged approach: First, transform Hebrew across all walks of life, at home, in schools, public sector, trade, industry, the arts, philosophy, and the sciences. Second, the council was to safeguard oriental quality of the Hebrew language and determine precise pronunciation of its letters. Third, the council was to provide modern Hebrew with required flexibility to make possible the expression of every known aspect of human thought.[171] Attempts by secular Zionists to inculcate their secular version of Jewish identity often alarmed non-Zionists and the anti-Zionist orthodox establishment. The *Hibbat Tziyon* spoke for Russian Zionists. It was under Ahad Ha'am's spiritual guidance that the *Hovevei Tziyon* or 'Lovers of Zion' committed themselves to a *cultural* revival of the Jews, rather than political independence. The two had clashed from the beginning.

Aytürk goes on to note that in order to maintain unity, Theodor Herzl, and later David Wolffsohn, tried to remove cultural questions from the Zionist congress agenda. At last, Eliezer Ben Yehuda's longstanding efforts paid off and the resistance from religious Zionists subsided by the 11th World Zionist Congress in 1913 at which Menachem Ussishkin recommended supporting what became known as *Am Ekhad ve Safah Akhat* or 'One Nation and One Language' policy.[172] This was a major turning point in the history of the establishment of the Jewish state. After decades of no language policy, the World Zionist Organisation was now on board supporting Hebrew as the national language.

The Ottoman Empire collapsed by the end of World War I and the region fell under British rule. In less than a decade, by 29th November 1922, Hebrew had been recognised as an official language of the British Mandate for Palestine alongside Arabic and English. Eventually when the State of Israel was established on 14th May 1948, Hebrew was adopted as its national language. As a modern nation-state requires a shared sense of history and language, the Zionist movement provided a timeless borderless narrative of Jewish suffering in the diaspora which all Jews could relate to, regardless of ethnic or sectarian differences, and Ben Yehuda provided the shared language. To date, Hebrew continues to be the glue that binds together modern Israelis as one *volk* despite stark ethnic diversity. Revived modern Hebrew is based on ancient Hebrew, the language of what the Jews call the Tanakh and Christians call the Old Testament. There are grammatical similarities between the two, even though ancient Biblical Hebrew is a Verb-Subject-Object (VSO) language while revived modern Hebrew is a Subject-Verb-Object (SVO) language. As far as pronunciation is concerned, modern Israeli Hebrew is spoken with a Yiddish-influenced accent where certain epiglottal and pharyngeal sounds are pronounced with a harsh tone.

Israeli linguist Ghil'ad Zuckermann has argued that: "Yiddish is a primary contributor to Israeli Hebrew because it was the mother tongue of the vast majority of language revivalists and first pioneers in Eretz Yisrael at the crucial period of the beginning of Israeli Hebrew." He argues that Zionist revivers of Hebrew could not divorce themselves from their Ashkenazi European mindset. Their attempts to erase their European diaspora influences and avoid hybridity did not work. Zuckermann argues that if: "...the language revivalists had been Arabic-speaking Jews from Morocco, Israeli Hebrew would have been a totally different language - both genetically and typologically, much more Semitic. The impact of the founder population on Israeli Hebrew is incomparable with that of later immigrants".[173] Still, the unique Yiddish-influenced Israeli accent has now become a marker of the modern Israeli identity. Arab Israelis do not generally speak Hebrew with the same Yiddish-influenced accent, except for those who tend to work in the entertainment industry as they are often required to play the role of Jewish Israeli characters in film and television. The Arab Israeli pronunciation of Hebrew is more like ancient Hebrew on the consonants 'r' and certain variations of 'a' and 'h'. As with the story of the Gileadites and Ephraimites in Judges 12, the distinct Israeli accent and pronunciation have now become the marker of the Israeli national identity. Robert McColl Millar reminds us that:

> The revival of Hebrew as a spoken living language must be placed in the context of the intellectual and political history of European Jewry. During the eighteenth century, two intellectual streams flowed through the intellectual life of (primarily) Ashkenazi Jews. In rural districts of central and eastern Europe, a considerable, often heated, rebirth in orthodox Jewish life took place. The disputes which reflected this renaissance were regularly conducted in Hebrew. Many within the movements encouraged the pious return to the 'land of Israel', and especially Jerusalem, so that a growing Ashkenazi community was present in the ancestral homeland. Since there was already a considerable Sephardic and Oriental Jewish population present, speaking a variety of Jewish vernaculars, the oral use of Hebrew became prevalent under certain conditions.[174]

For too long, the success of the Zionist project has been attributed to the conventional founding fathers whose names are echoed in the hallowed halls of university campuses. As a case in point, Israeli Prime Minister Benjamin Netanyahu's father and renowned Jewish historian Benzion Netanyahu in his 2012 bestseller *The Founding Fathers of Zionism* profiles the Zionist intellectuals he believes have made the greatest contributions to Jewish emancipation. In so doing, he lists Leon Pinsker, Theodor Herzl, Max Nordau, Israel Zangwill and Ze'ev Jabotinsky in *that* order.[175] For whatever reason, Eliezer Ben Yehuda is nowhere to be seen. This is only symptomatic of a larger problem. When it comes to the study of political Zionism, the tendency to overplay the significance of other mainstream nationalist thinkers (like the ones Benzion Netanyahu lists) over the linguistic genius of Ben Yehuda seems to have become the norm. Yet as this case study has shown, without the resurrection of Hebrew, the resurrection of the Jewish state would have struggled to develop and maintain a coherent national identity and culture. In a documentary titled *The Hope: Eliezer Ben Yehuda* his grandson points out:

> ...Imagine if there had not been an Eliezer Ben Yehuda, in 1948 you would have Jews living in Israel, 70 to 80 languages! it would have never worked.[176]

He goes on to say that:

> The language was absolutely part of the rebirth, it was necessary just as breathing is necessary to survival and Ben Yehuda is the man God appointed to make that possible.[177]

> Until he started talking Hebrew in Jerusalem, the Jews that came from Poland only dealt with other people who came from Poland because they spoke the same language and the people who came from Romania only spoke with other people who came from Romania.[178]

Indeed, the revival of Hebrew has breathed life into an ancient cultural identity. It was because the likes of David Ben Gurion and Chaim Weizmann shared Ben Yehuda's vision of "The revival of Israel and its language on the land of the forefathers" that modern Israeli society was made possible. Some may argue that the mere fact that Jewish identity managed to survive for 2,000 years without common geography or language contradicts some nationalist scholars like Ernest Gellner and Benedict Anderson, both of whom, as seen in the first chapter, think of nationalism as the result of actual sociability between members of an imagined community. While such an expectation is both reasonable and central to my argument, at the same time, as outlined in the second chapter, the use of language for worship and liturgy can also be a powerful marker in binding together religiously based imagined communities. As this chapter has shown, wherever Jews were in the world, they continued to pray in Hebrew and maintained their sense of belonging to *Am Yisrael* or the 'Nation of Israel' through the diaspora. What *revived* modern Hebrew did was that it gave the ethnically diverse Jewish settlers a common lingua franca, a spoken vernacular to be able to form sociable communities. As a result, the Yiddish-speaking Ashkenazi, Arabic-speaking Sephardic and Mizrahi and Amharic-speaking Ethiopian Jews were able to come together as *Israelis*. God promises the Jews in Zephaniah 3:9 in the Bible:

> I will restore to the people a pure language, that they may all call on the name of the Lord, to serve him with one accord.[179]

Far from opposing the idea of revival as the ultra-orthodox Jews of Ben Yehuda's days had done previously, contemporary orthodox Jewry tends to see the resurrection of their dead ancestral language as a modern miracle and a fulfilment of the aforementioned prophecy in Zephaniah. The same is true of the very idea of Zionism itself. Many religious Jews in Leon Pinsker and Theodor Herzl's days thought that Jews were not supposed to create a Jewish state and must keep waiting for the Messiah to arrive and lead the emancipation through divine help. This view is still shared by the small minority of Neturei Karta Jews. As the Zionist project began to look more imminent, Chief Ashkenazi Rabbi of Jerusalem Avraham Isaac Kook became a central figure in binding political Zionism together with mainstream Judaism. He argued against the anti-Zionist Jews and pointed out that the Zionist settlement of Palestine was part of God's plan towards laying down the foundation for the ultimate redemption that was to come through the arrival of the Messiah. Otherwise known as Rav Kook, he is often seen as the founding figure of *religious* Zionism.

Dr Uri Harel, Director of the Center for Hebrew notes that Hebrew is the only language to be revived. Diana Bregman Feld, the daughter of Yiddish language poet Edith Kaplan Bregman described the contempt for Yiddish she saw first hand when she visited Israel literally only a year after its creation. Yiddish essentially reminded people of Galut and the Diaspora. Paul Berg, Yiddish activist notes that there is no conflict in supporting Yiddish and being a proud Jew, but still acknowledges that Yiddish would have continued to remind the Jews of the Holocaust. Avi Hoffmann, actor, says Yiddish was not encouraged in Israel. Frances Schlitt has also discussed the lack of Yiddish education and media in Israel. The reasons for this are the success of Ben Yehuda's Hebrew revival project. Gabriel Bernbaum of the Hebrew Academy says that Ben Yehuda is the reason why Israelis speak Hebrew today. He goes so far as to argue that if modern day Jewish Israelis had not spoken Hebrew, they may not have been there at all. Leanne Hinton explains the general attitude towards the Hebrew revival when she says: "This revitalisation of a language that had not been spoken in daily life for over 2,000 years is an inspirational model for others whose languages are no longer spoken." As this chapter has shown, sustained use of Hebrew for liturgical purposes did well enough to preserve the Jewish identity in diaspora, but to put a Jewish state back on the world map, it needed to be revived as a spoken vernacular. Ilker Aytürk remarks that the success of Hebrew revival in fact: "opens new vistas of theoretical inquiry to students of nationalism".[180]

As seen in the first chapter, nationalist scholars Herder, Kohn, Berlin, Gellner, Hobsbawm, Lewis, Kedourie, Seton-Watson, and Smith *all* emphasised the need for a shared past in nationalism. This was provided by the Zionist movement with its narrative of centuries old Jewish persecution and antisemitism. Lexicographer Ben Yehuda provided the ideal language solution that helped create sociability and became a marker of the modern Israeli identity. Kohn also said that: "the spoken language was accepted as a natural fact" before the age of nationalism and: "it was in no way regarded as a political or cultural factor, still less as an object of political and cultural struggle".[181] The triumph of Hebrew challenges this assumption. Languages indeed come and go, but they do not all return to life after more than 2,000 years of slumber. People and their identities too come and go. Nobody today, for instance, still identifies as a *Canaanite* or an

Assyrian or *Babylonian* or a *Viking* or a *Norman* or a *Visigoth*. Yet these were all valid ethnic groups with *national* characteristics that existed in the distant past. Today these identities would be considered extinct as their descendants have morphed and hybridised into *other* identity constructs through the natural course of history. The case of modern Jewry as both an ethnic and a religious imagined community, and as a nation, is exceptional. It is the tale of the world's oldest continuing form of nationalism, as seen in the cases of the Maccabean Revolt (167 to 160 BCE) and Bar Kokhba's Revolt (132 to 136 CE). This would make the Jews the world's oldest *continuous* nationalist cause - a *primordial* sense of nationhood, brought together as a *modern* nation-state through the Zionist movement.[182] The Jewish story of survival and self-preservation across 4,000 years, half of which were spent in diaspora is intriguing. Eliezer Ben Yehuda's achievement shows that when a powerful and inclusive narrative about shared history is properly brought together with a shared language, with the proper policies in place to impose that language on the masses, the end result is the successful integration into a common cultural-political form. The revival of Hebrew is and should continue to be of interest to the shared study of language and nationalism. Indeed as Cecil Roth famously said: "Before Ben Yehuda, Jews *could* speak Hebrew, after him they *did*."[183]

4

CASE STUDY 2

HOW URDU TURNED EAST PAKISTAN INTO BANGLADESH

The last chapter saw the example of a bottom-up nationalist effort to revive and create a shared vernacular language for the purposes of nation-building. The Israeli case with the revival of Hebrew could be fairly described as successful. This is because the Zionist movement and Lexicographer Eliezer Ben Yehuda together gave the ethnically diverse Ashkenazi, Sephardic, Mizrahi, and Ethiopian Jewish settlers in historic Palestine both a shared history and a shared language. This chapter discusses a different approach to the use of language by nationalists. In August 1947, British rule in the Subcontinent came to an end after three centuries. What was left behind on the map was not one, but two newly created nation-states: Muslim majority Pakistan and Hindu majority India. During British rule, Muslim nationalists had hoped to mobilise Muslim ethnicities of the Subcontinent under a common national identity as *Pakistanis*. As far as they were concerned, the most efficient tool for achieving this was through the deliberate, planned and top-down institutionalised use of the Urdu language. Yet the accompanying historical narrative was *reactionary*. It assumed the right-to-left Arabic script to be the marker of Muslim identity, while the left-to-right Brahmi script was seen as the marker of the Hindu identity. East Bengal had emerged as a province of Pakistan. The Bengali people were religiously divided, had a distinct sense of history and theirs was the only ethnic language in Pakistan

THE LINGUISTIC ROOTS OF NATIONALISM

that was written in the Brahmi script. In 1971, East Bengal seceded to become Bangladesh, the independent nation-state of the ethnic Bengali people. Pakistan was home to over a dozen ethnicities from the start. Seven decades later, they are still around as *Pakistanis* much like the ethnically diverse Jews are still around *Israelis*. What went wrong in the Bengali case? As this chapter shows, there were multiple factors behind the secession. Yet the story began on a familiar note: Language.

From the beginning, the national borders of India and Pakistan had not reflected the theoretical considerations that had formed the basis for their partition in the first place. Some blame this on the fact that the borders were drawn up by an Englishman that had never been east of Paris and possessed no awareness of the Subcontinent's geography, history or demographics, let alone its religious complexities. As historian William Dalrymple observes:

> Cyril Radcliffe, a British judge assigned to draw the borders of the two new states, was given barely forty days to remake the map of South Asia. The borders were finally announced two days *after* India's Independence.[184]

This was intended to be a partition along religious lines. That was always going to be a challenging task. Provinces with mixed religious populations like Punjab and Bengal were split in half. Millions of Hindus and Sikhs were left on the Pakistani side and many million Muslims still on the Indian side. The case with Kashmir was unique. Its King *Maharaja* Harilal Singh was a Hindu who wanted to join India, but the local population was predominantly Muslim. Still unresolved, the conflict over Kashmir has led India and Pakistan to wars in 1947, 1965 and 1999 and many border skirmishes across the years. After seven decades, it continues to be an obstacle to peace between the two countries underpinning a rivalry that is often manifest across wide ranging arenas, from the floor of the United Nations General Assembly to the cricket field.

The case with Hyderabad was the inverse of Kashmir. Its King, *Nizam* Osman Ali Khan Asif Jah VII, was a Muslim who ruled over a Hindu majority population, but refused to join India. Hyderabad originally reached a standstill agreement with India, but following civil unrest the Indian military led an invasion in September 1948 compelling the ruling *Nizam* to surrender. Hyderabad was ceded to India. The partition of India and Pakistan led to the greatest population swap in world history. A total of some 14 million people, roughly 7 million from each side, fled their homes to go and live on the other side. But not everyone did that. Many Hindus remained as a minority in Pakistan. Even more Muslims remained as a minority in India. Radcliffe has often been unjustly criticised for his role in the creation of a geographic landscape that left families torn apart in the best case, and full blown wars, in the worst. British American poet W. H. Auden wrote a scathing review of Radcliffe's role in the carve up in a famously sarcastic poem called *Partition* published in 1966.

Yet it was not Radcliffe's decision to divide India and Pakistan. The partition was what Hindu and Muslim nationalist elites had demanded for decades. Radcliffe happened to be the man employed by the Last Viceroy of India Lord Mountbatten in July 1947 to come up with a map that would bring these demands to reality. While Radcliffe did lack expertise on the Subcontinent, an actual expert in his shoes would have struggled nearly as much, if not more. Critics often assume that there were clear geographic divides between the Subcontinent's Hindu and Muslim populations. It was not as easy as that. Hindu and Muslim populations in too many areas were completely interwoven into each other. Often within the same village, in the same district of the same province, there were as many Hindus as there were Muslims. These demographic overlaps were more pronounced in some areas than in others. Without mass population transfers, it was impossible to create *exclusively* contiguous Muslim or Hindu communities on such heterogeneous landscape. Another challenge Radcliffe faced was that of ethnic groups where the ratio of Muslims and Hindus, or Sikhs, was relatively even. This explains why today there is a province of Punjab in Pakistan and another by the same name in India. For the same reason, there is today a province for the Bengali people in India called West Bengal, as well as an independent nation-state called

Bangladesh, which seceded from Pakistan in 1971.

There were nearly as many Hindu Bengalis as there were Muslim Bengalis. Realising as much, the British Empire had previously partitioned the province of Bengal in October 1905. This was an administrative decision by India's Viceroy at the time, Lord George Nathaniel Curzon. The Hindu majority areas became West Bengal and the Muslim majority areas became East Bengal. Many Bengalis protested this decision accusing their British rulers of trying to divide and rule the Bengali people. The backlash was so strong that in 1911 Lord Hardinge ended up ordering for the reunification of Bengal. This is the timeframe within which Bengali intellectual Rabindranath Tagore wrote many patriotic songs celebrating the Bengali identity, such as *Amar Shonar Bangla* that went on to be adopted as Bangladesh's national anthem after independence in 1971. These early displays of ethnic patriotism help us understand how the Bengali people, from very early on, saw themselves as a distinct *nation* that went beyond mere religious identities.

Radcliffe's map inherited the borders of the 1905 partition of Bengal. East Bengal was absorbed into Pakistan while West Bengal remained with India. Radcliffe did the best job he could based on the demands of nationalists on both sides. Although the Bengalis had protested the British Empire's 1905 partition of their province, the relationship between Hindus and Muslims had since deteriorated in the dying days of British rule. With the rise of the nationalist Pakistan Movement demanding a separate state for Muslims, the leaders of various ethnic communities had to make a choice whether or not to join the initiative. For ethnic groups such as the Pashtuns and Balochis that were almost exclusively Muslim, the choice was not difficult. They were also largely unaffected by the Hindu-Muslim tensions given their remoteness from the usual centres of civil unrest. Punjab, Sindh, Gujarat, Maharashtra, Delhi, Uttar Pradesh, Bihar, Hyderabad, and Bengal had become hotbeds of violent clashes between Muslim and Hindu nationalists on a regular basis.

As the Bengalis did not have an exclusively Muslim population, this made the choice more difficult. Yet there were three key factors that brought Bengali Muslim intellectuals on side with the Pakistan Movement. One, as Nasir Islam notes, was that in pre-partition times: "Bengali Muslims were alienated from Bengali Hindus" and argues that this "...alienation resulted from a natural sentiment of resentment against the Hindu landlords who had exploited the Muslim peasants all through the British occupation of Bengal."[185] Two, there was an internal class divide within the Bengali Muslim community that worked to the advantage of the nationalist Pakistan Movement. As Tariq Rehman points out:

> Before the advent of the British, the upper class Muslims in Bengal (ashraf), in common with Muslims throughout India, identified with Urdu and spurned Bengal's regional cultural and linguistic identity. The ashraf considered Bengali identity to be basically Hindu, and Muslim peasants who could speak only Bengali were despised and learned to despise themselves.[186]

Three, a major talking point of the nationalist Pakistan Movement was that democratic elections in an undivided India would be dominated by Hindus, and Muslims would become a disadvantaged minority. So, it was argued that Muslim self-determination was the only answer. These three factors resonated with many Bengali leaders.[187] Bengali Muslim intellectuals not only played key roles in the Pakistan Movement, the Muslim League was itself established in Dhaka, East Bengal in 1906.[188] In fact, three Bengali Muslim pioneers went on to becoming Prime Ministers of Pakistan after independence: Khawaja Nazimuddin, Huseyn Shaheed Suhrawardy and Nurul Amin. The idea of an independent state for the Bengalis had been considered in passing by Suhrawardy, but there was no formal proposal and it never progressed.[189] The Rohingya Muslims of western Burma also spoke the Bengali language. During the 1940s, Rohingya leaders had expressed a desire to be a part of the up and coming Muslim state.[190] This did not happen due to lack of support from the leader of the Pakistan Movement, Muhammad Ali Jinnah.[191]

The partition happened over two days in 1947. Pakistan declared its independence on 14th August and India followed the next day on

15th August. In line with Radcliffe's map, East Bengal was in Pakistan and West Bengal in India. Critics sometimes claim that it was always going to be difficult for Pakistan to administer East Bengal because it was non-contiguous territory situated on the other side of India. This view is simplistic. There are many cases of non-contiguous territories that are administered without civil unrest, let alone secession. Alaska and Hawaii in the United States are the best example. Tasmania does not have a border that touches Australia. The north and south islands of New Zealand are geographically apart from each other. Thousands of scattered islands make up Indonesia. Japan and Greece both comprise over many different islands that are not geographically connected.

Suffice it to say, the mere fact that a nation-state might have some of its territory situated away from its mainland borders is not, of itself, a reason for struggling to administer the territory. The fact that Pakistan would go on to struggle with East Bengal for 24 years and eventually end up losing it in 1971 has *other* explanations. It began with tensions over the status of Urdu and Bengali languages. Until partition, Islam had played a crucial role in defining Muslim nationalism embodied in the Pakistan Movement. The so-called 'Two Nation Theory' had assumed that the Muslims of the Subcontinent were a single nation, different religiously and culturally from their Hindu counterparts. The Urdu language was seen by Muslim nationalists as the ultimate means to mobilise the ethnically diverse Muslim populations of the Subcontinent with a common lingua franca. After achieving independence, the challenge now was to test to see if this combination of 'Islam and Urdu' would be sufficient to hold the newborn Muslim state of Pakistan together beyond independence. Alyssa Ayres points out that:

> The year of independence, 1947, thus marked the beginning not only of a new political formation – a homeland founded on the basis of religion – but also of a new belief about the linguistic medium of a unitary culture in a large bounded territorial homeland. On this basis, Urdu was presented as a spiritual muse by the heads of state of this new Pakistan.[192]

Pakistan had five provinces to start with: East Bengal, Sindh, Punjab, Balochistan and what was then called the North West Frontier Province (NWFP) but has, since 2010, been renamed Khyber Pakhtunkhwa. Each province not only had its own dominant ethnic group: Bengali, Sindhi, Punjabi, Baloch and Pashtun, but also contained other ethnic minorities. In addition, there were seven million Muslims that had come across from Delhi, Uttar Pradesh, Bihar and Hyderabad among other regions to live in the newborn Muslim state. These were *native* speakers of Urdu. Punjab was home to many Seraiki speakers in the south. Khyber Pakhtunkhwa or NWFP as it was back then, had many Hindko speakers and other minority groups, like the Kalash people in the north (who are often believed to be the descendants of Alexander the Great's armies from his invasion in the fourth century Before Common Era).

Like the newborn Jewish state of Israel in 1948, where Judaism alone seemed insufficient to hold the ethnically diverse Ashkenazi, Sephardic, and Mizrahi Jews together as one nation without the imposition of the Hebrew language, Pakistan's case was similar, though two differences should be noticed: One, Hebrew had been a dead language for 2,000 years and had to be revived by lexicographer Eliezer Ben Yehuda, while Urdu had been a living spoken vernacular for eight centuries. Two, Hebrew's role in creating the modern Israeli national identity began as a bottom-up movement. Its revival was orchestrated privately by Ben Yehuda and originally faced resistance from both secular and religious Jews. As seen in the previous chapter, the Zionist nationalist elites had to be convinced about the utility of a common language in nation building. Urdu's role in creating the modern Pakistani national identity was top-down from the beginning. Its use was *institutionalised* as a distinct marker of Muslim identity in the Subcontinent by Muslim nationalist elites. Founder Muhammad Ali Jinnah made this explicit in his famous public address:

> Let me make it very clear to you that *the state language of Pakistan is going to be Urdu and no other language*. Anyone who tries to mislead you is really *the enemy of Pakistan*. Without one state language, no nation can

> remain tied up solidly together and function. Look at the history of other countries. Therefore, so far as the state language is concerned, Pakistan's language shall be Urdu.[193]

In mainland Pakistan the ethnic groups had a shared geography, with many villages and major cities connected through road and rail. Members of these imagined communities had long traded with each other and featured in each other's literature and poetry. Long before its adoption by the Muslim nationalist movement, Urdu had already emerged as the natural lingua franca for the different ethnic groups to communicate in and form quasi-religious sociable communities. So, developing a *confederated* national identity through the Urdu language was not as challenging a task within West Pakistan as its attempted extension for use across East Bengal. It is not surprising that following independence, Urdu became the dominant language of Pakistani film, television, journalism, and education curriculum. There was *negligible* resistance from the provincial language groups within what was then *West* Pakistan. On balance, Sindhis, Punjabis, Pashtuns, and Balochis managed to adapt to Urdu literacy. As the Bengalis were resistant to Urdu from the beginning, Pakistan's *Dawn* newspaper on 16th December 1947 ran an editorial that said:

> ...we do not hear of a Punjabi-Urdu controversy, a Pashto-Urdu controversy or a Sindhi-Urdu controversy. Why must there be a Bengali-Urdu controversy?[194]

The Bengalis had a distinct national mindset from the beginning. Imposing Urdu on them was set to be a challenge for the Pakistani government. Bengali literature had existed as early as the 11th century. Bengali authors had official patronage under the Pala dynasty from the 8th to 12th centuries, under the Senas from 11th to 12th centuries and under the Mughals from 16th to the mid-18th centuries.[195] This rich literary and poetic tradition set the tone for the Bengali Renaissance during the mid-1800s headed by the likes of Ram Mohan Roy and Rabindranath Tagore (the composer of the national anthems of both India and Bangladesh, and the recipient of a Nobel Prize for Literature in 1913). This renaissance essentially put Bengali history on a separate trajectory to that of other Muslim ethnic groups in the

Subcontinent. It injected aspects of modernity and secular thought into Bengali consciousness.

This period saw an intellectual awakening in Bengal similar to the renaissance movements that had swept across Europe centuries earlier. The movement grew increasingly skeptical of established tradition, orthodox beliefs, parochial values, the subordination of women, and the caste system and the dowry system. Although not necessarily devout Hindus by faith, almost all the pioneers of the Bengali Renaissance had been Hindus by religious identity.[196] It was in this period that Bengali philosopher Ishwar Chandra Vidyasagar standardised a version of the Brahmi script for written Bengali, making it the only language in the Subcontinent to be shared by substantial numbers of Muslims that was not written in a version of the Arabic script. After Roy and Tagore, the mantle of Bengali intellectual tradition was carried forward by Satyajit Ray. By the 1930s, Bengali cinema had become popular. From early on, Bengalis preferred watching films in their native tongue as opposed to conventional Hindi movies made by Bollywood.

With the exception of the upper class Bengali Muslim *ashraf* that were assimilated into Urdu high culture and preferred to identify as 'Muslims' rather than 'Bengalis' we can see why common Bengalis would see themselves as a distinct nation and resist efforts to have another language imposed on them. Yet the partition had left Bengalis of Hindu and Muslim varieties separated across two different countries. Now that independence had been achieved, Muslims no longer feared becoming a disadvantaged minority. Political unrest between Hindus and Muslims had subsided. There was no longer a reason for Muslim Bengalis to resent Hindu Bengalis. Many Bengalis went back to seeing Bengalis as a single unified nation regardless of the Muslim-Hindu distinction. Even during the independence phase, when Bengali leaders were at the forefront of the Pakistan Movement, many were still protective of their linguistic identity. As Nasir Islam notes:

> The Muslim League made great efforts to promote the Urdu language

in the congress, but failed because of stiff resistance from the Bengali delegates.[197]

The lack of religious plurality and secular thought made it easier for other ethnic groups in Pakistan to seek shelter under the umbrella of an Urdu speaking Pakistani identity. Since there were no Hindu, Sikh, or Christian Pashtuns, it was *more likely* that a Pashtun or a Balochi would naturally presume that being a Pashtun or Balochi was synonymous with being a Muslim. This, in turn, bound them together as one imagined community with *any* other ethnic group that had similar identity configurations. Islam again notes that:

> Various Muslim groups in the Subcontinent were able to suspend their regional, ethnic and linguistic identities. Religion - as a way of life - had become the predominant force as a basis for future nationalism, other ethnic factors being temporarily pushed aside.[198]

The Bengalis had been largely on board with this, except they maintained an assertive degree of resistance to the imposition of Urdu from the beginning. When Aligarh Muslim University Vice-Chancellor Dr Ziauddin Ahmad had declared that Urdu would be the national language of Pakistan, Bengali linguist Dr Shahidullah famously responded saying that: "...would be tantamount to political slavery."[199] The fact that the Urdu versus Bengali language tensions had been brewing even *before* the birth of Pakistan would go on to threaten national unity after independence.

Typical nationalist movements not only tell their followers who they *are* supposed to be, but also who they *are not* supposed to be.[200] The nationalist Pakistan Movement was no exception. During British rule, it had mobilised its support base by highlighting both the Hindus and the British colonists as the enemies of Islam. They often accused the two of collaborating with each other to undermine the interests of the Muslims *ummah*, both within and outside the Subcontinent. Yet once independence was achieved, those enemies were no longer part of the picture. Nasir Islam notes that the "external enemies of the Muslim nation - the Hindus and the Colonial regime - were removed from the domestic political scene."[201] The challenge *now* was to figure out how to keep a heterogeneous nation together in one piece. The biggest obstacle to that became the demands from Bengali leaders to grant their language official status. As Tariq Rahman notes:

> Pakistan was barely a year old when its central government was first challenged by an ethnic group - Bengali ethnicity expressed through the Bengali language movements *Bhasha Andolan* of 1948 and 1952.[202]

Yet Pakistan's founder and then Governor-General Muhammad Ali Jinnah had made it very clear that only Urdu would be the state language and anyone who disagreed was an enemy of the state. As Nasir Islam notes:

> [The] Pakistani government wanted to have *Urdu as the only state language of Pakistan*. Jinnah, the father of the nation, and the first two Prime Ministers, one of whom was a Bengali, openly declared their support for this policy. It sparked a controversy in the National Assembly and led to a strong language movement in East Pakistan in favour of Bengali as one of the state languages of Pakistan.[203]

In line with Jinnah's vision, the Pakistani government began to implement its Urdu only policy. At the first National Education Conference in November 1947, the institutionalisation of Urdu as the language of education faced resistance from Bengali delegates.[204] Bengali did not feature anywhere on the national imagery such as postage stamps or currency.[205] This was so *despite* the Bengalis being the single largest ethnic group in Pakistan, accounting for more than half the country's population.

These measures helped mobilise Bengali intellectuals. Next, Professor Abul Kashem founded the Bengali Language Movement. It barely took four months following independence for Bengali students to start gathering on campus at Dhaka University in December 1947, hold up placards, and chant slogans demanding that Bengali be made one of the state languages of Pakistan. The same month, the first *Rashtrabhasha Sangram Parishad* or Language Action Committee was formed with the help of Bengali Professor Nurul Huq Bhuiyan. This movement was a major distraction for Pakistan in its early years. Now threatened, the Pakistani government in February 1948 responded by proposing that Members of Pakistan's National Assembly be required to either speak Urdu or English during parliamentary proceedings. A Bengali MP from the Congress Party moved an amendment to have Bengali included, but the leadership denied the motion. The Premier of East Bengal at the time, Khawaja Nazimuddin (later, Governor-General and Prime Minister of Pakistan) and from the Bengali ashraf class, responded by pointing out:

> There is only one state of Pakistan and that *can have only one language and that can only be Urdu*. This means that the language of the Central Government and the language used for communication with the provinces will be Urdu, when it is decided to replace the English language by the national language [...] Urdu has already been virtually recognised as the language of the Muslim nation since before the Partition of India, and it cannot be substituted by any other language now.[206]

As the news became public, Bengali activists went on a general strike on 11th March 1948 to protest. The government launched a major witch hunt, arresting many Bengali leaders and activists, including rising Bengali stalwart Sheikh Mujibur Rahman, who would go on to become the Pakistani government's greatest threat. To calm the unrest, Pakistan's founder and then Governor-General, Muhammad Ali Jinnah, paid a visit to Dhaka in East Bengal the same month, but only ended up instigating further resentment by again declaring in public that Urdu was to be the only official language of Pakistan.

As a result, the original Muslim League party lost credibility with many Bengalis. The Awami Muslim League was formed in 1949 to represent the interests of the Bengali people, with Maulana Abdul Hamid Khan Bhasani as its leader. Another representative of the Pakistani government, this time Khawaja Nazimuddin, himself an ethnic Bengali from the pro-Urdu *ashraf* class, addressed an audience in Dhaka in January 1952 and ended up restating the government's existing position on language. Two days later there was another big strike.

Maulana Bhasani formed an *All Party Central Language Action Committee* with Kazi Golam Mahboob as its convenor. The committee called for another major rally on 21st February 1952. The Pakistani government decided to crack down hard on protesters under Section 144 of its Constitution, but the rally went ahead regardless.[207] Bengali activists chanted slogans, and the police responded with tear gas and bullets, killing unarmed protesters. Among those dead were the prominent Bengali activists, Abdul Jabbar, Abdul Barkat Abdus Salam, and Rafiquddin. Today *Shaheed Minar* or the Tower of Martyrs stands as a national monument at the Dhaka University in their honour, and February 21 has since become a national day of commemoration in Bangladesh.[208] Every February the *Omar Ekushe Granta Mela* is held in Dhaka to celebrate the Bengali language, culture and literature. The festivities generally last a month. February 21 has also been declared by the United Nations to be its Language Day.

As a proud nation, the Bengalis were not prepared to give up so easily and to begin assimilating. They had their own contiguous province that was ethnically homogeneous and carried all the features of a modern nation, *except* autonomy itself. It was ironic that Pakistan had become a *state* but was struggling to be a *nation*, while the idea of 'Bangladesh' was a *nation* struggling to become a *state*. The Pakistani government's persistent refusal to accept Bengali had a paradoxical effect. It awoke from their slumbers many Bengali intellectuals, triggering a second Bengali Renaissance. Not ready to let their language and its rich legacy be replaced by Urdu, this second wave of Bengali thinkers began producing mass literature. They adopted enlightenment approaches to liberal social orders and rational thought. They reinterpreted the history of the partition. The Muslim league was seen as elitist. The Two Nation Theory had become obsolete in their eyes. They opted for a secular, as opposed to Islamic, cultural identity.

Nasir Islam observes that Kamruddin Ahmad and Hasan Murshid produced works to reinterpret many scholarly works in India. Mufazzal Haider Chaudhri, Abul Fazl, Abul Mansoor Ahmad, M. Shahidullah, Abdul Mannan, Hasimuddin, Sufia Kamal and Hamida Rehman, were prominent writers, artists and journalists from this period, and became vanguard members of the cultural awakening of East Bengal in the early 1950s.[209] University students, professors, authors and artists, all played major roles in reviving Bengali culture in defiance to the Pakistani state policy to enforce Urdu, or to 'Islamise' the Bengali language. The nationalist rallying cry of 'Joy Bangla' also emerged during this time. While Bengalis were becoming more assertive, secession was still not what Bengali leaders and activists had in mind. Up until then, their preference was to have Bengali recognised, while remaining part of Pakistan. After all, what was the point of so many Bengali intellectuals helping pioneer the Pakistan Movement? When it first began, the Bengali Language Movement was exactly that, a *language* movement. It was not a separatist movement.

Yet the government had gone out of its way to prevent Bengali from being used for official purposes. What the language movement had demanded in turn was a reversal of this policy. Far from carrying secessionist dreams, many Bengalis actually remained loyal to Pakistan despite the Urdu only policy. The fact that Bangladesh eventually ended up seceding in 1971 after Pakistan's humiliating defeat in the Bangladesh Liberation War, has other explanations. The secession was the result of a complex chain of events that began with Pakistani refusal to give Bengali official status, and which, when eventually granted in 1956, came as too little, too late. Mutual mistrusts were deeply entrenched by this stage. Pakistani refusal to accept democratically elected Bengali Presidents and Prime Ministers would be the undoing of national unity between West Pakistan and East Pakistan.

Meanwhile in West Pakistan, though Urdu had developed the reputation of a rich literary language, those who spoke it as a native tongue were few and far in between. Urdu was the spoken vernacular in Delhi, Uttar Pradesh, Bihar, and Hyderabad. Many of the Muslim settlers from these regions indeed spoke Urdu as their native tongue, but they accounted for less than 4% of Pakistan's population at the time. As we can see, Urdu in the early years was not simply imposed on the Bengalis alone. It was in fact imposed on every Muslim ethnic group in Pakistan. This included Pashtuns, Balochis, Punjabis,

Sindhis, Seraikis, Brahuis, Hindkos, Makranis, Chitralis, and other linguistic minorities. There were also many Memons, Marathis, Tamils, Malayalis, and Gujaratis that had come across to Pakistan to live in a Muslim state. Most of these settled in Karachi alongside the native Urdu speaking settlers, and daily interaction accelerated their assimilation into the state sanctioned national language.

Pashto, Balochi, Sindhi and Punjabi were languages written using a variety of the left-to-write Arabic script, exactly like Urdu. Sindhi had previously been written using the Hatvanki or Khojki scripts and Punjabi using the Gurmukhi script. Both languages had eventually made the transition to modified Arabic. This gave their written form a distinctly recognisable Muslim character. The Arabic script had come to be a marker of Muslim identity in the Subcontinent long before the Pakistan Movement had started. No local language spoken by Hindu majority ethnic groups was written in the right-to-left Arabic script. Hatvanki, Khojki, and Gurmukhi along with Devanagari (used for Hindi) are all variants of the left-to-right Brahmi family of scripts.

These scripts have come to be a marker of Hindu identity in the Subcontinent. In rare cases, where there were Muslim minority populations within Hindu majority ethnic groups, those minorities would use the Brahmi script. Doing so neither resulted in an identity crisis nor stigmatisation by other Muslim groups comparable in scale to the Bengali experience. Gujarati Muslims are a case in point. They do not use an Arabic script to write Gujarati yet this does not see Gujarati Muslims being accused of being too Hindu influenced. This is for two reasons: One, it is understood that Gujarati Muslims were in the minority within their own ethnic group and were not seen to have much control over the literary destiny of their native tongue. And two, Gujaratis did not end up with a contiguous province within Pakistan, let alone demand that their language be given official status. As a relevant aside, Pakistan's Muslim founder Muhammad Ali Jinnah and India's Hindu founder Mahatma Gandhi were *both* ethnically Gujarati.

Unlike Sindhi and Punjabi, Bengali had not transitioned to an Arabic script. This made its appearance resemble other languages associated with the Hindu identity.[210] In response to growing pressure from Bengali activists, at one point the Pakistani government almost decided to belatedly declare it as a second national language on the condition that it be reformed. In 1949, the East Bengal Language Committee was set up with the task to reform Bengali and cleanse it from its Sanskrit heritage. Saadia Toor tells us that the committee recommended that: "...the Arabic script be adopted for Bangla in order to make it more of an 'Islamic' language."[211] She notes too that Bengali activists argued that the change in script would leave Bengali people:

> ...cut off from their cultural heritage of literature, enshrined in Bengali characters. Not to speak of the contribution of any other literati, even poets and literati like Ahmad Saghir of the past, and Rabindranath Tagore, Nazrul Islam [...] of the present age, will at once become unreadable and unintelligible to us.[212]

There are two observations to be made from this. One, this tells us about the reactionary nature of Muslim nationalism, the extent to which its narrative had sanctified the status of Arabic as a symbolic marker of Muslim identity, and saw the Brahmi script, even when it was being used by Muslims, as a marker of the Hindu identity. Two, this also tells us about the extent to which the Bengalis were self-conscious of how much that Brahmi script meant to them. Apart from the literary elite, neither were Muslims usually taught the Brahmi script, nor were Hindus usually taught the Arabic script. Yet each knew how to identify the other's language by mere sight. Unlike the Gujarati case, the Bengalis *did* end up with their own province in Pakistan, and began fighting for official status for what in Pakistani eyes was a language associated with Hindus. As Nisar Islam points out:

> In spite of the fact that Bengali was recognised later (1956) as one of the official languages, the central government from time to time kept proposing to Islamise the language by changing its script or eliminating certain letters, with a view to bringing it closer to Urdu. A large number of non-Bengali civil servants who came to administer the province tended to use either English or Urdu. This was perceived

by the Bengali population as some sort of conspiracy to impose Urdu upon them.²¹³

Other ethnicities in Pakistan had historically interacted with each other, featured in each other's poetry and literature, traded with each other, fought with each other, yet over time learnt to identify each other as Muslims of the Subcontinent. Given their lack of geographical proximity, West Pakistan's ethnic groups had little historical contact with the Bengali people from the East Bengal province. The West Pakistani ethnic groups - Pashtuns, Balochis, Punjabis, Sindhis, and native Urdu-speakers - had existed alongside the ethnic Bengalis on opposite ends of the Subcontinent the same way that Scandinavian ethnic groups - Norwegians, Swedes, Finns, and Danes - exist alongside the ethnic Maltese on opposite ends of the European continent. Yet the two categories had little to do with each other historically.

When Muslims of other ethnic varieties saw *written* Bengali featured in newspapers or billboards, it would have been impossible to identify it at first sight as a language spoken by Muslims. In their minds, any regional written script other than the Arabic one represented Hindus. As Zillur R. Khan writes: "many West Pakistanis nurtured the belief that the Bengalis were culturally linked with Bengali Hindus of India and therefore their ideological tie with West Pakistan was very loose."²¹⁴ Saadia Toor makes a similar observation. In the eyes of West Pakistanis:

> ...East Bengal was constructed as a veritable hotbed of seditious elements such as Hindus and communists who were bent on destroying Pakistan [...] East Bengali culture was projected as one that was hopelessly under the influence of Hinduism and therefore not Pakistani enough.²¹⁵

These perceptions came to form the basis for rejecting Bengali demands to give their language official status. Pakistan had achieved *statehood* in the political sense, it was now time to achieve *nationhood* in the cultural sense. A vital part of Pakistan's nation-building process was for its citizens to differentiate themselves from Indians and Hindus. As Saadia Toor writes: "no cultural overlap between the two states could be conceded, because according to the dictates of cultural nationalism, that was previously what distinguished one nation from another." She goes on to say that: "...a shared culture with India would not only undermine (retrospectively) the very *raison d'être* of the demand for Pakistan, but also throw Pakistan's status as a legitimate nation-state into question."[216]

Other than Bengali having the *appearance* of a Hindu language, was there another reason why the Pakistani establishment was threatened by Bengali? Saadia Toor makes a fascinating observation. In demanding a separate state, for decades, Muslim nationalist elites had long argued that the Muslims of the Subcontinent constituted a *separate nation* of their own, with a distinct set of values, history, and culture. Except most of *that* Islamic legacy, cultural history and its architectural masterpieces ironically all found themselves trapped in what became India, not Pakistan. Indeed, as Toor observes:

> Partition had cast a wrench into the neat division between Hindu and Muslim culture and civilisation that had been contained within the 'two-nation theory'. The clearest manifestations of the Indo-Muslim culture and history (such as the Taj Mahal, Fatehpur Sikri, Delhi's Jama Masjid, and so on) on whose basis claims to Muslim nationhood had so persuasively been made over the preceding decades, had not fallen within the newly constituted borders of Pakistan.[217]

This was a *strange* predicament at best. Yet there was *one* eternal artefact of Islamic civilisation in the Subcontinent which, despite *itself* originating on the other side of the border, was *not* bound by geography: the Urdu language. Saadia Toor picks up on this point, arguing that:

> The Urdu language became imbued with even more meaning as the one aspect of Indo-Muslim culture which was not at the mercy of arbitrary borders. The proposal that Bengali be considered Pakistan's second national language therefore posed a challenge to the very idea of a shared Muslim nationhood, premised on a unitary (national) culture of which the Urdu language was understood to be a crucial part. In the eyes of Muslim nationalists in East and West Pakistan, Urdu was the 'natural' choice as the national language of Pakistan.[218]

Given this, the government's stern response in the early days was not surprising. It was inevitable that the Pakistanis would do whatever it took to preserve the one artefact of their Muslim identity that was within reach. In their eyes, giving equal status to another language would violate Urdu's sanctity. So, the response from the Pakistani government, as Saadia Toor, notes was "...far from conciliatory."[219] Yet by the mid-1950s the Pakistani government's attitude begins to soften. To maintain national unity, in 1954 the then Prime Minister of Pakistan, Muhammad Ali Bogra, himself an ethnic Bengali, launched what became known as his One Unit policy. Its main objective was to create unity and progressive integration between the two separated regions.[220] In an announcement on 22nd November that year, Bogra claimed that by having a single province:

> There will be no Bengalis, no Punjabis, no Sindhis, no Pathans, no Balochis, no Bahawalpuris, no Khairpuris. The disappearance of these groups will strengthen the integrity of Pakistan.[221]

The implementation of this idealistic vision began under Prime Minister Chaudhry Muhammad Ali in late 1955. In September 1955, the Pakistani Parliament voted to amalgamate all of West Pakistan into a single province. In October that year, East Bengal was renamed East Pakistan. The following year, on 23rd March 1956, Pakistan ditched the Commonwealth to become a Republic. The name changed from the 'Dominion of Pakistan' to the 'Islamic Republic of Pakistan.'

Having taken 'Bengal' out of the province's name the previous year, the Pakistani government did not want Bengali leaders thinking that was part of an effort to erode their national identity again. To offset that, Pakistan acceded to the demands of the Bengali Language Movement. So, in 1956, Bengali was at last given official recognition. This should have been the end of Pakistan's on-going tensions with its Bengali citizens. Badruddin Umar argues that achieving constitutional recognition in 1956 "...soon became a matter of no concern for the Bengali bourgeoisie, even under Pakistan. They just sought satisfaction in recalling and ruminating the struggles and achievements of the 1952 language movement, but did little or nothing to work for the development of the Bengali language."²²² On the contrary, Bengali national consciousness grew stronger in the decades that followed. Umar underestimates the extent to which Bengali national identity had kept growing apart from Pakistani identity. As all the leading scholars of nationalism, Hobsbawm, Anderson, Gellner and Smith have observed, the premise of a national identity lies in shared and shareable perceptions of history. As far as the Bengalis were concerned, not only did they have a proud history of secular thought and renaissance, their struggles for linguistic autonomy against the Pakistani government had now become an entrenched part of their story. Thinking of themselves as mere 'Pakistanis' would confound the difference between an aggressor and a victim.

In short, all that stood between the Bengalis and their demands for a separate state was one more Pakistani government policy that subjected them to differential treatment compared to that of other ethnic groups. As far as the Pakistani establishment was concerned, to say that by this stage their political anxieties about Bengalis had reached an all time high is an understatement. There were three factors for this: one, there was a genuine fear that the Bengali Language Movement's success would open up a political wishlist with further demands for Bengalis to assert greater influence over Pakistan.²²³ The second factor lay in the fact that despite the language tensions, many prominent Bengalis had already served in the highest possible roles in Pakistan: 2nd Governor-General and 2nd Prime Minister Khawaja Nazimuddin (r. 1951-1953), 3rd Prime Minister Mohammad Ali Bogra (r. 1953-1955) who introduced the One Unit policy, 5th Prime Minister Huseyn Shaheed Suhrawardy (r. 1956-1957), and the 4th Governor-General and 1st President Iskander Mirza (r. 1956-1958). Eventually there would be a short lived 8th Prime Minister, Nurul Amin (r. 1971-1971). Many in the Pakistani establishment had long felt uneasy about what they saw as Bengali over-representation in Pakistani politics. The third factor was that since there were more Bengalis than Pakistanis of any other ethnic variety, there were genuine fears that non-discriminatory democratic elections would perpetually keep on delivering Bengali Presidents and Prime Ministers.

When Pakistan became a Republic on the 23rd of March 1956, it adopted a new constitution. The office of the Governor-General was abolished, and the 9 year old country's first democratically elected President by a direct vote was an ethnic Bengali, former Governor-General and now 1st President, Iskander Mirza. His time in office was dogged by controversy as he dismissed four Prime Ministers in a mere two years. The population of West Pakistan was smaller than that of East Pakistan. As long as the Bengali citizens of Pakistan voted along ethnic lines, as they had done in Mirza's case in 1956, Pakistani leadership would forever remain in the hands of Bengali leaders. Fearing such a scenario, General Ayub Khan had Iskander Mirza ousted in 1958. A new Constitution of Pakistan was enacted in 1962 that ended the election of a President by popular vote. Bengali leaders knew the motives behind this move was to limit their influence over Pakistani politics. Yet many average Bengalis had still not developed separatist sentiments. A survey in 1964 in a sample of 1,001 factory workers and peasants in East Pakistan showed 48% considered themselves Pakistanis while only 11% identified as Bengalis. The rest identified with their village or district. Another survey revealed 74% regarded themselves as Pakistanis, only 24% as Bengalis.[224] Schumann goes so far as to argue that there was no awareness by the man-in-the-street in East Pakistan of any conflict between his identity as a 'Bengali' and his identity as 'Pakistani.'[225] But in the minds of Bengali leaders, the end of universal suffrage in Presidential elections was a turning point in Pakistani-Bengali relations. It was clear by this stage that the Pakistani establishment was nervous that true democratisation of its electoral system would hand power over to the Bengalis.

For a nation founded on the premise that the Muslims of the Subcontinent were a single nation, to make its system undemocratic in order to curtail Bengali ethnic dominance was neither Islamic nor democratic. Every Bengali leader that had become a President or Prime Minister of Pakistan was a Muslim, and that was the premise behind Pakistan's creation after all. Yet as Zillur R. Khan has observed: "many West Pakistanis regard the Bengalis as inferior beings, unfit to rule themselves and therefore must be ruled by the 'superior' West Pakistanis."[226] Nasir Islam similarly explains the gradual shift in Bengali attitudes:

> The effort of the Central Government to impose Urdu as the national language and the denial of representation on the basis of population by the West led the Bengalis toward a complete distrust of the central government. Thus, the Bengalis began to make demands for a weaker center and for stronger provinces in the future constitutional setup of the country.[227]

From this point on, the tensions were no longer over language recognition. They were about greater autonomy for the Bengali people.[228] So in 1966, Bengali nationalist and Awami League leader Sheikh Mujibur Rahman came up with a Six Point plan demanding from the Pakistani government the following:

1. Elections through universal adult franchise. Meaning every adult citizen regardless of caste or creed gets a full vote.

2. Federal government could only deal with foreign affairs and defence while every other portfolio would be handled by regional units in the federation.

3. Separate currencies for West Pakistan and East Pakistan.

4. Powers of taxation and revenue collection relegated to regional units in the federation with federal government to be provided with a share of the taxes through levies of a certain percentage from all states.

5. Separate accounts for foreign exchange, free trade across West and East, autonomy to deal directly with overseas trade partners.

6. Separate paramilitary force for the defence of East Pakistan.

This proposal was unanimously rejected by the Pakistani government and all political parties, including secular and Islamic ones, though the Six Point Plan remained popular in East Pakistan. Nasir Islam observes that: "Bengali nationalism grew in response to the changing nature of ethnic-group inter-relations in Pakistan." And that: "It began as demands for language rights and economic equality as a reaction to the central government's policies to impose Urdu on Bengalis, to reduce Bengali representation (both political and administrative) in the central government, and to increase economic disparity."[229]

As part of a major crackdown, Pakistani President Ayub Khan, in 1968 accused Sheikh Mujibur Rehman of conspiring with India to destabilise Pakistan, and had him charged with sedition.[230] Yet this was only the beginning. While the election of the President had been brought under restraints to prevent the election of a Bengali, the voting in general elections was still a strategic risk to the Pakistani establishment. There were 300 seats in its unicameral National Assembly. As with other Westminster systems, the distribution of seats in Parliament was based on population.

At the time of the distribution, there were 60 million people in West Pakistan, which left it with 128 seats, and 68 million in East Pakistan, which gave it 162 seats. In a general election, the winning party would require 151 seats to form government. Given all that Pakistan had been through, the reluctant recognition of Bengali as an official language, the election of a Bengali inaugural President Iskander Mirza, followed by his impeachment, and now Sheikh Mujibur Rehman's Six Point plan demanding greater autonomy, the last thing the Pakistani establishment wanted to see was another Bengali Prime Minister. Yet that is exactly what the next general election would go on to deliver.

Undoing the One Unit policy, President Yahya Khan dissolved the province of West Pakistan on July 1st 1970 with a vision to conduct general elections. An interesting turn of events followed. In November that year, East Pakistan was struck with Cyclone Bhola and a tidal wave that left 300,000 dead.[231] General Yahya Khan deployed one helicopter in response to the calamity. Offers of assistance from the international community, including India, were turned down. As Sarah Glynn reminds us: "The inaction of the West Pakistan-based authorities in the face of this calamity drove a further wedge between them and the Bengalis."[232] The Bengali citizens of Pakistan were rightfully fed up with the way they had been treated.

The general elections were held on the 7th of December, 1970. The Islam-centric political parties that had gone to the polls promising to unite all ethnicities as one Muslim *ummah* performed miserably. In East Pakistan, Sheikh Mujibur Rahman's Awami League went to the poll promising regional autonomy, and ended up winning an impressive 160 out of 162 seats. Meanwhile in West Pakistan, Zulfiqar Ali Bhutto's Pakistan People's Party had managed to secure 81 out of the 138 seats.[233] The Awami League's landslide win was an unprecedented feat in any democracy. The Awami League also won 298 out of 310 seats in the Provincial Assembly of East Pakistan. These results were a clear indication that the Bengali people had made up their minds about regional autonomy.

If the election results had been honoured, Mujibur Rehman would have been sworn in as the Prime Minister of Pakistan. Yet neither the President Yahya Khan nor would-be Opposition Leader Zulfiqar Ali Bhutto were prepared to accept an Awami League government.[234] It is interesting to note that Zulfiqar Ali Bhutto's Pakistan People's Party and Mujibur Rehman's Awami League were both centre-left socialist parties that had run on very similar economic platforms. Their only major policy difference was over the Six Point plan which concerned the autonomy of East Pakistan. As was the case with the election of ethnically Bengali President Iskander Mirza in the direct vote of 1956, the election of the ethnically Bengali Prime Minister-elect Sheikh Mujibur Rehman was an indication that the Bengali citizens of Pakistan would vote along ethnic lines. This fact also validates the anxieties of the Pakistani establishment.

Realising that Pakistan was not prepared to honour the election results, Mujibur Rehman called for a general strike. Many Bengalis took to the streets to protest, and were fired at by Pakistani troops. After 24 years of a turbulent relationship, it was at this point that Bengali secession seemed like the only logical solution. On the 7th of March 1971, Mujibur Rehman responded to public outcries by addressing a crowd of one million Bengalis and declaring that:

> This time, our struggle is a struggle for freedom. This time, our

struggle is a struggle for independence.²³⁵

The date of 23rd March, previously Pakistan Day, was dubbed Resistance Day by Bengali separatists. The new Bangladeshi flag was flown in both public and private settings in East Pakistan. On 26th March 1971, the Pakistani government responded by launching Operation Searchlight as part of a major military crackdown on Bengali separatists.²³⁶ According to Indian and Bangladeshi sources, this was a campaign of systematic persecution and ethnic cleansing. It left up to 3 million dead and an estimated 200,000 plus Bengali women raped. Many were evicted from their homes.²³⁷ Sheikh Mujibur Rehman was never sworn in as Prime Minister. President Yahya Khan kept delaying the National Assembly's inauguration, despite the Awami League having a clear democratic mandate to govern after its landslide win. When the Pakistan People's Party's Zulfiqar Ali Bhutto and the Awami League's Mujibur Rehman began negotiating, President Yahya Khan had both men arrested. The civil unrest continued on.

The Awami League meanwhile began operating as a quasi-government in March 1971. India had to date remained neutral in the Pakistani-Bengali conflict. At least, that was its public position. The ensuing crisis left 10 million Bengali refugees pouring into India. As Pakistan became suspicious that India might help liberate the Bengali people, Pakistan Air Force launched pre-emptive strikes on Indian air bases on the western front on 3rd December 1971. India in turn launched a full blown attack on both the western and eastern fronts. After nine months of combat, Commander of the Pakistan Army in the east Lt Gen A. A. K. Niazi surrendered to India's Lt Gen J. S. Aurora with 90,000 Prisoners of War. The war ended. Bangladesh was born.

Sheikh Mujibur Rehman was hailed *Bangbandhu* or 'friend of the Bengali people.' He became the inaugural President of Bangladesh. He was assassinated in a coup in 1975. Meanwhile, Yahya Khan resigned and left power in the hands of Zulfiqar Ali Bhutto. Pakistan and India went on to sign a peace treaty known as the Shimla Agreement on 2nd July 1972 in a process headed by Zulfiqar Ali Bhutto and Indira Gandhi.

India returned lands it occupied during the war back to Pakistan. The Prisoners of War were released and bilateral negotiations on Kashmir resumed. Neville Maxwell perceptively used an analogy to describe the fate of West and East Pakistan when he observed that:

> Pakistan was pregnant with Bangladesh from the moment of its own birth. Labor was brought on unexpectedly by the decline of Ayub [...] and birth was achieved by Caesarian section with India acting as the scalpel.[238]

On reflection, the issues arising from the demands of the Bengali Language Movement tell only half the story. The fact that Pakistan was so threatened by the election of a Bengali President, Iskander Mirza in 1956, that it had to amend its constitution and take universal suffrage away making the electoral system less democratic is telling. The fact that Pakistan was equally threatened by the election of a Bengali Prime Minister, Sheikh Mujibur Rehman, in 1970 that it would ignore the outcome of a democratically conducted election and deliberately delay the inauguration of the newly elected National Assembly and use military force to suppress dissenters is even more telling. In a properly defined constitutional framework such abuse of power would be, at the very minimum, unwelcome. Pakistan lacked that from the beginning.

Nasir Islam writes that in Pakistan: "it seems that it was taken for granted that the religious national identity of being Muslim would always prevail in all situations." It is not merely the secession of Bangladesh in 1971, but the entire 24 years of the turbulent history of West and East Pakistan that challenges this assumption of Muslim unity. There is a difference between an *Islamic* State and a State for *Muslims*. This difference is substantial, not semantic. An Islamic State by definition is a state based on Islamic values. Pakistan was never imagined by its pioneers as that kind of a state. Myron Weiner correctly observes that:

> The Westernised, largely non-religious leadership which led the pre-independence movement was primarily concerned with creating a state with a Muslim majority, free from what they said would be the

domination of the Hindu majority in India. They had no desire for an Islamic State.[239]

Muslim nationalist elites were no different from the secular Zionists that had created Israel in the same timeframe. As an ethnic Gujarati, Muhammad Ali Jinnah was not himself a native speaker of Urdu - the very language he went out of his way to enforce on all ethnic groups including the highly resistant Bengalis. Jinnah was neither well-versed in Arabic nor the Quran. Muslim nationalist elites basically saw the Muslims of the Subcontinent as a distinct *nation*, the same way that Theodor Herzl, who was neither a practising Jew nor spoke Hebrew, saw the Jewish people as a *nation* for whom he wished to secure a Jewish state. The parallels between Herzl and Jinnah are strikingly similar.

This symbolic use of Islam had many limitations. Pioneers of the Pakistan Movement made no effort to draft a workable constitution that would lay down the framework for governance after independence. Was Pakistan to be an Islamic or democratic state, or a synthesis of both? If so, would it accommodate ethnic and linguistic diversity as many earlier Islamic empires had done? What would be the appropriate status of religious minorities? These questions were left unanswered, with no consensus. Many nation-states around the world practice a form of ethnic nationalism. Israel is the best example. It unapologetically proclaims itself as a nation for the Jewish people while providing democratic rights to its one fifth Arab minority. Nation-states of the English-speaking world tend to opt for civic nationalism. Anyone can opt-out or opt-in through the naturalisation process to become American, British, Canadian, Australian, or New Zealander. Where was Pakistan to fit in on the nationalist spectrum? No one had exactly thought that far ahead.

Before partition, the fact that Urdu would be sanctioned by the state after achieving independence was common knowledge. The Pakistan Movement had never made any secrets of that. Bengali leaders were aware of this yet chose to remain on side. They simply resisted Urdu before partition and continued to resist it after partition. But let us suppose, if in those days the Muslim nationalist elites driving the Pakistan Movement had declared from the beginning that Pakistan would be somewhat of a *quasi-ethnic nationalist* state where more or less any Muslim ethnic group was welcome, so long as its identity configurations were not fraught with Hindu overtones, perhaps the Bengali intellectuals *ashraf* and commoners alike may have chosen to opt-out of the Pakistan Movement altogether. Instead, they were given idealistic promises about Muslim unity as one *ummah*.

Who could have predicted the extent to which Pakistan would be vehemently opposed to the democratic election of a Bengali President Iskander Mirza in 1956 and that of a Bengali Prime Minister Sheikh Mujibur Rehman in 1970? The details of the Islamic ideology that was to define the fabric of Pakistani society would remain vague at best.[240] Nasir Islam observes that after independence: "...there was no modern interpretation of Sharia to provide a basis for a Pakistani constitution that could be largely accepted by all political groups."[241] If Pakistan had been based on Islam as a *religion* as opposed to Islam as a *national identity* its pioneers would have had a real chance to build consensus on a constitutional framework within which all citizens would have representation.

Yet at the time, it was all about stressing the *commonality* of every Muslim in the Subcontinent while dismissing the ruling British and Hindus as enemies of Islam and the chief threat to Muslims. The thought of one Muslim ethnicity being singled out as a threat by another collection of Muslim ethnicities would have been unthinkable. There were many factors that set the Bengalis apart from the Punjabi, Pashtun, Sindhi, Balochi, and other Pakistani ethnicities. The Bengalis were conscious of their renaissance history and embrace of secularism. Even more so, the fact that there were so many Hindu Bengalis was a constant reminder that the idea of a *Bengali* is not synonymous with being a Muslim as was the case for the Pashtun or the Balochi. The Bengali language was, and still is, a living embodiment of their national uniqueness. For Pakistan to attempt to brush this aside and enforce Urdu was a costly move.

Pakistan's inability to accept the Bengali language from 1947 to 1956 as a valid Muslim language despite its lack of Arabic script deepened the cost. The suspension of the constitution and using the military to undermine a Bengali President in 1958 and a Bengali Prime Minister-elect in 1971, was the final icing on the cake.

The people of what was once East Bengal, and later Bangladesh, would look back at those turbulent 24 years when they were a part of Pakistan. From their standpoint, there would not be too many memories to cherish. On 17th November 1999, UNESCO announced that 21st February would become an International Language Day due to the eventual success of the Bengali Language Movement's 1952 demonstrations. Bengali has no doubt come a long way. In 2009, Bangladeshi Prime Minister Sheikh Hasina proposed Bengali be adopted as an official language at the United Nations.[242] While this has not happened, Bengali continues to be the spoken vernacular of 250 million speakers around the world. Its story is no less fascinating than that of Ben Yehuda's revival of Hebrew. The fact that this entire Pakistani-Bengali conflict began over language again reinforces the view that national identities are primarily linguistic constructs. But language isn't enough to bind a people together. The narrative or what some might describe as the national mythology that accompanies any linguistic efforts to mobilise a nation is equally important. By contrast, there was nothing inherent within the Zionist narrative that differentiated between a Yiddish-speaking Ashkenazi Jew from Poland, or an Arabic-speaking Mizrahi Jew from Yemen. A Jew was a Jew. The narrative, based primarily on mainstream Jewish beliefs about exile and the yearning to return to Zion, was an inclusive one. This set the perfect conditions in place for modern Hebrew after its revival to end up becoming the basis for binding modern Israelis together. As this chapter has shown, the Muslim nationalist movement of the Subcontinent did not have an inclusive narrative to accompany its efforts to mobilise the ethnically diverse Muslims of the Subcontinent through the enforcement of the Urdu language. That narrative was based on differentiation to the extent that it almost came across as saying what is Muslimesque cannot concurrently be Hinduesque and vice versa. Naturally, the end result was that the ethnic groups of West Pakistan managed to come together as a nation while East Pakistan broke away to become Bangladesh.

5

CASE STUDY 3

HOW RUSSIAN ENDED THE SOVIET EXPERIMENT

The previous two chapters dealt with forms of *cultural* nationalisms. In other words, both the Zionist pioneers and the Muslim nationalist elites in the Subcontinent were trying to unite their target audiences by telling them they were part of the same cultural grouping, with a shared past and, in turn, a shared language. One fully worked, the other partly. What makes the Soviet case different is that it was a form of *ideological* nationalism. In that sense, the Soviet Union, as we will soon see, neither had a shared past nor a shared language from the beginning. During Tsarist rule, the Russian Empire went through large scale eastward expansion across the continent of Asia. Its territorial possessions stretched far beyond the Ural Mountains, reaching the Sea of Japan. This colossal landmass was home to many different ethnic and religious communities, now under Russian control. The Tsardom fell in 1917. After an initial civil war,[243] the Union of Soviet Socialist Republics (USSR) emerged in its place in 1922. That diverse population now found itself under Soviet rule. Early Soviet pioneers had assumed that communist ideals and the promise of liberation from class struggles would provide sufficient basis to mobilise their diverse subjects under a shared national identity. By 1991, this assumption had been invalidated. USSR broke up into 15 distinct nation-states. What went wrong? Traditional historians have either attributed this collapse to the supposed "intrinsic nature" of communist ideology or to bad economic leadership. Yet if that was the case then it seems plausible that, a change of ideology or leadership could have sufficed. Why did the Soviet state *itself* collapse and fracture into 15 *ethnic* nation-states? This chapter argues that the patchwork for eventual disintegration was to a crucial degree an unintended consequence of the Soviet Union's contradictory language policies over the decades.

The rise and fall of USSR can neither be understood in isolation from the historical context that brought about Russian eastward expansion, nor outside the Soviet Union's rivalry with the United States during the Cold War. This chapter examines both these historiographical approaches. In the aftermath of World War II, the Soviet Union and the United States emerged as competitors for global hegemony.[244] The Soviet Union aspired to sponsor various communist regimes around the world. While the United States aspired to contain the spread of communism at any cost. In an age of nuclear weapons, neither party had officially declared war on the other for fear of mutually assured destruction. This rivalry assumed many implicit forms ranging from a space race to an arms race and, especially on the American side of the conflict, propaganda wars through its film and television. From the early 1950s to the late 1980s, the two superpowers backed different sides in various proxy wars on the international stage.

The Korean War (1950-1953), the Vietnam War (1955-1975) and the Soviet-Afghan War (1979-1989) are prime examples. In one instance, the Cold War had left members of the same ethnic group *with* a common language torn apart by arbitrarily drawn national borders, based purely on the political alignments of the regimes in power. *West* Germany, *South* Korea, *North* Yemen, and *South* Vietnam were aligned with capitalist United States. While *East* Germany, *North* Korea, *South* Yemen, and *North* Vietnam were aligned with communist Soviet Union. In another instance, the Cold War brought members of different ethnic groups *without* a common language together within the same national borders. The Czechs and Slovaks formed Czechoslovakia. The Serbs, Croats, Slovenians, Bosnians, Kosovars,

Montenegrins, and Macedonians formed Yugoslavia. The Armenians, Azeris, Belarusians, Estonians, Georgians, Kazakh, Kyrgyz, Latvians, Lithuanians, Moldovans, Russians, Tajiks, Turkmen, Ukrainians, and Uzbek formed the Soviet Union. These are the *major* ethnic groups in the Soviet case, there were hundreds more.

North and South Vietnam reunified as one when the Soviet-backed Viet Cong captured Saigon in 1975 marking an end to the two decade long Vietnam War.[245] Under US Presidents Jimmy Carter and Ronald Reagan, the United States began isolating the Soviet economy through international pressure applied via trade embargoes and sanctions. Oil prices skyrocketed as a result, adversely impacting on Soviet production capacity. The outcome of the Soviet-Afghan War was a major turning point in 20th century history. The American backed *Mujahideen* rebels managed to force the invading Soviet troops to withdraw from Afghanistan in 1988.[246] Within months, the Soviet Union itself began to crumble, as did the Soviet-backed communist regimes across eastern Europe. This signalled an end to the Cold War, or the 'end of history' as ambitiously characterised by American political scientist Francis Fukuyama.[247] The world map was once again altered. In 1990, West and East Germany reunified.[248] As did North and South Yemen, the same year.[249] In 1992, Czechoslovakia split up into the Czech Republic and Slovakia.[250] Between 1991 and 1992, Yugoslavia broke up into Slovenia, Croatia, Serbia, Macedonia, and Bosnia-Herzegovina.[251]

During the Cold War decades, people's ethnic identities within the Soviet sphere of influence had been overridden by state-sanctioned appeals to communist ideology, class struggle and incompetently imposed national languages. These experiments ultimately failed. The lessons from the aftermath were clear: Where a *single nation* had been scattered across multiple states such as (West and East) Germany and (North and South) Yemen, the end result was *reunification* into a single state. The inverse case was equally revealing. Where *multiple nations* had been lumped together in a single state such as Czechoslovakia, Yugoslavia, and the Soviet Union, the end result was *disintegration* into multiple states. To date, North and South Korea remain the last surviving remnants of the arbitrary divides brought on by the Cold War. The Korean case is the exception, rather than the rule. Besides, experts have not ruled out the prospects of their potential reunification in the near future.[252]

This pattern of reunification and disintegration is crucial in understanding why the Soviet Union resulted in the 15 national configurations that emerged from its spoils. Often called the *Post-Soviet* states, these were: Armenia, Azerbaijan, Belarus, Estonia, Georgia, Kazakhstan, Kyrgyzstan, Latvia, Lithuania, Moldova, Russia, Tajikistan, Turkmenistan, Ukraine, and Uzbekistan. These 15 countries could be re-categorised by their shared *regional* identities. The *Caucasus* states: Armenia, Azerbaijan, and Georgia. The *Baltic* states: Latvia, Lithuania, and Estonia. The *Eastern Slavic* states: Ukraine, Moldova, Belarus, and Russia. And the *Turkic* states: Tajikistan, Turkmenistan, Uzbekistan, Kazakhstan, and Kyrgyzstan. In an alternative case scenario, the collapse could have resulted in 4 confederated nation-states instead of 15. There could have been a Baltic state, an Eastern Slavic state, a Caucasus state, and a Turkic state. After all, strong arguments *can* be made in favour of such national configurations. Bear in mind that British decolonisation from the Subcontinent only resulted in 2 confederated multiethnic nation-states: a Muslim majority Pakistan and a Hindu majority India. Yet this did not happen in USSR's case because no government policy implicitly or explicitly allowed for regionally based national identities to develop. Contradictory language policies by successive Soviet governments paved the way for various *ethnic* nationalisms to grow within its federal structures. This in turn sowed the seeds for USSR's eventual fracturing. As this chapter shows, emphasis on the failure of language policies seems largely absent from the existing scholarship that tries to explain the collapse of the Soviet Union.

There are two approaches to investigating the scholarship on the Soviet experience. They can be categorised as the *Cold War historians* and *Soviet Union historians*. The Cold War historians examine the *external* dynamics between the United States and the Soviet Union. The Soviet Union historians examine *internal* processes and policies within the Soviet regime from 1917 to 1991. Within each approach, there are wide ranging theories to account for the Soviet collapse. Many of these theories share considerable common ground. Still, some starkly contradict the others. This chapter examines both historiographical approaches. Within the Cold War historians, there are four main schools of thought. These could be categorised as follows: 1) Orthodox view: blame Soviet communism, 2) Revisionist view: blame American capitalism, 3) Hybrid view: blame both and 4) Retrospective view: Amalgamate all previous theories and blame bad economic leadership. The 4th category overlaps significantly with the other approach of Soviet Union historians.

Arthur M. Schlesinger Jr. remains the lead historian in the orthodox camp. This view argues that the USSR was an expansionist state from the beginning. That all that the United States was trying to do was be the global peacemaker because it did not want the atrocities of World Wars I and II repeated ever again. The international community needed a strong global leader and, having won World War II, the United States was the best fit for the job. That the Truman Doctrine was only a defensive measure to curtail Soviet sponsorship of communist regimes around the world.[253] That the Marshall Plan was a defensive measure to circumvent Soviet sponsorship of communist political parties in Europe. That NATO too was a defensive measure to counter-balance the rising threat of the Soviet Union.[254]

Most historians and political scientists in American universities during the 1940s and 1950s shared this view. Some might argue there was no alternative. One could often be blacklisted as a communist sympathiser or a spy if one did not share this orthodox view. During the 1960s, more people began to question the establishment narrative, resulting in a diversity of viewpoints. Many from the baby boomer generation began enrolling at universities learning about the evils of communism while their government was still engaged in the Vietnam War, the centre stage of the Cold War at the time. Many from that generation began questioning the orthodox narratives taught in American universities. William Appleman "Bill" Williams remains the lead historian within the revisionist camp. This view regarded America as the expansionist state wanting to spread capitalism and build military bases around the world. It held that the rhetoric used against communism had been grossly exaggerated to advance American foreign policy interests.[255] By the 1980s, there began to emerge a hybrid between the two views. Historian John Lewis Gaddis is the lead historian in this hybrid camp.[256] He and several others put forward arguments that overlap with both the orthodox and the revisionists. Those views were not mutually exclusive.

Following the collapse of USSR in the 1990s, there emerged a generation of retrospective views now that the Cold War had ended. The task for these historians was easier since they knew how the Cold War story ends. They were not making predictions about the future. Rather, they were analysing the past with the obvious benefit of hindsight. The Soviet archives had opened up by this period. Scholars had more material to examine and to draw conclusions from. Arthur Schlesinger Jr, William A. Williams and John Lewis Gaddis would have had limited access to most of this content. This new generation of revisionist historians merged many of the previous theories together and began drawing new conclusions. These are discussed later on in this chapter. Joseph Stalin was dubbed the main villain responsible for starting the Cold War. The same process occurred in Russia in reverse. There, the orthodox view was that the Americans started the Cold War. Their revisionists began to acknowledge the Soviet Union's role in contributing towards prolonging the conflict. This leads into the next approach as many of the thinkers from this category overlap with the other camp.

Within the Soviet Union historians who look at internal factors, there are three main schools of thought. These can be categorised as: 1) those who blame authoritarian communism, 2) those who blame ethnic nationalism, and 3) those who blame bad economic leadership. The first camp which blames authoritarian communism argues that the Soviet Union was destined to fail from the beginning *because* it was an authoritarian communist state. It assumes that Soviet political configurations were an inherent recipe for disaster. This view is generally more common among traditional Western scholars who saw USSR through capitalist American lens. In his 1994 publication *The Soviet Tragedy: A History of Socialism in Russia, 1917-1991*, historian Martin Malia argued that USSR was doomed from the beginning because it was at odds with human nature.[257] The vision of communism that inspired the Bolshevik revolutionaries to create the Soviet Union was a utopian vision of heaven on earth embodied in Marx's famous statement: "from each according to his ability to each according to his needs."[258] Malia suggested that it was impossible for a society to be naturally based on such a maxim. From his vantage point, it made perfect sense that the Bolsheviks would go out of their way to artificially create the perfect utopia through tyranny and fail in the end. There is no mention of contradictory Soviet language policies, or the manner in which ethnic tensions had shaped up. Instead, Malia sums up the collapse of the Soviet Union by stressing that:

> One might think that the great crash of 1989-1991 would have settled these questions once and for all with the conclusion that Communism was irreformable, since it in fact failed to reform itself. But no: the objection is raised that because something did not happen, this does not mean it could never have happened. And as a matter of abstract logic, this is true. But we are not dealing with abstract logic. We are dealing with concrete historical events, and the cascade of Communist collapses in 1989-1991 ought surely to tell us something about the logic of that particular system.[259]

Former Moscow correspondent and Pulitzer Prize winner David Remnick in his 1993 publication *Lenin's Tomb: The Last Days of the Soviet Empire* describes the structural flaws inherent within USSR's government since its birth. His account is based on personal anecdotes from his time in Moscow as a journalist. The crux of Remnick's narrative is that the collapse resulted from the cruelty of authoritarian rule and corrupt leadership. He cites the Katyn Massacre, the Red Terror under Lenin, and the purges under Stalin to explain how the Communist Party ruined itself in the end.[260] There is no mention of the language policies that created the mosaic of division within Soviet society.

Malia and Remnick's arguments are more alike than meets the eye. Both argue that the Soviet Union was structurally doomed, except Malia blames communist ideology while Remnick blames authoritarianism. Not only were these the causes for the collapse of the Soviet Union, for a generation raised in the heydey of the Cold War accustomed to seeing the world through capitalist American lens, the *inverse case* was an even more exciting proposition. In their eyes, the collapse of the Soviet Union was *proof* that communism and authoritarian rule never work. The problem with this line of reasoning is that it is based on hindsight. If it was so inevitable that communist and authoritarian societies were necessarily destined to collapse, these theories would have emerged in advance as *predictions* as opposed to being published as 'after thoughts' carefully crafted with the benefit of hindsight.

There are occasions when scholars are able to do this. American political scientist Samuel P. Huntington remains one of the best examples yet. In his *Clash of Civilisations and the Remaking of World Order* which first appeared as an essay in 1993 and was later published as a book in 1996, Huntington argued that after the Cold War, the next pattern of global conflict would be based on cultural and religious identities. Out of the 9 civilisations he identifies on the world map, he goes on to argue that Western and Islamic civilisations were at the greatest risk of a clash.[261] Many observers see the attacks on New York's World Trade Centre on 11th September, 2001 and President George W. Bush's consequent 'War on Terror' in Afghanistan as a fulfilment of Huntington's prediction.[262]

In the Soviet case, as William Taubman has often pointed out, nobody foresaw the collapse. The closest would be Andrei Amalrik who wrote an essay in 1981 called *Will USSR survive 1984?* which was a play on words referring to George Orwell's *Nineteen Eighty-Four* dystopian novel in which Amalrik poses a question, rather than making a serious case forecasting the collapse.[263] French scholar Emmanuel Todd in his *The Final Fall: An essay on the decomposition of the Soviet sphere* in 1976 vaguely hints at the possibility.²⁶⁴ In a similar vein, Indian economist Raveendra N. Batra in his *The Downfall of Capitalism and Communism* in 1978 speculates on more general terms, as the title itself suggests, the possibility of a world without capitalism and communism. No one in the American intellectual establishment saw it early.

Malia and Remnick overlook that China also began as an authoritarian communist state under Chairman Mao Zedong following the revolution of 1949. Yet from 1978 onwards under Deng Xiaoping, it began undergoing major economic reforms. It liberalised many of its institutions while still maintaining a fundamentally authoritarian method of governance, and survived. There was no 'collapse of China' so to speak. This is precisely what General-Secretary Mikhail Gorbachev had hoped to achieve in the Soviet Union through his *glasnost* and *perestroika* policies during the late 1980s, except his reforms stagnated and failed. Chris Miller argues that there are competing interpretations to account for the economic stagnation that the Soviet Union went through. On the left, it is often argued that rapid privatisation does not work and that USSR should have followed China's path of *gradual* reforms. On the right, it is often argued that political reform complicates policymaking and USSR should have followed China's more *hardline* stance. These are diametrically opposed suggestions. Miller argues that Gorbachev's Soviet Union did in fact learn from China, except he was too weak to implement his reforms correctly.²⁶⁵ Either way, the question remains, if China managed to undergo economic and institutional reforms despite its own authoritarian communist origins, why did the Soviet Union fail? It follows that there is more to the story than to say that authoritarian communist states are inherently beyond reform.

The second camp which blames ethnic nationalism argues that the Soviet Union was destined to fail from the beginning because it was multiethnic and multireligious. It assumes that those demographic configurations were an inherent recipe for disaster. This view is often common among Western and Russian scholars alike. Vladislav M. Zubok, Serhii Plokhy, and Ronald Suny acknowledge these factors among others. Ronald Grigor Suny in his 1993 publication *The Revenge of the Past: Nationalism, Revolution and the Collapse of the Soviet Union* notes that the development of competing nationalisms within the Soviet Union was a contributing factor to its collapse. Suny is on the right track as he observes that the: "...Soviet Union had created territorial nations, with their own state apparatuses and ruling elites. Each had the trappings of any sovereign state, from the national opera house to a national flag and seal but without real sovereignty".[266] This is a valid assessment, but Suny overlooks the role of Soviet language policies in reinforcing these competing nationalisms.

An inverse angle within this line of thinking argues that certain ethnic elites decided to appeal to nationalist separatism because it was more incentivising for them to become the ruling class in an independent ethnic nation-state without being beholden to a parent federal structure. This view has been argued by Fred Weir, David Kotz and Stephen Kotkin. It makes the ethnic separatist elites in the Soviet case sound comparable to those in the United Kingdom who supported Brexit from the European Union in 2016. Milanovic does not disagree with the premise of Weir and Kotz's views. Rather, he explains it by pointing out that:

> Communist economic failure predisposed people to look for scapegoats in order to vent frustration and anger over their declining living standards. The people needed to blame their failure on somebody else. In multinational states, that somebody else was somebody of a different nationality. Every ethnic group began to believe that, had they been left alone, they would have done better. Everyone felt cheated and exploited – even the nationalities that were demonstrably better off in a common state.[267]

Milanovic argues that: "Had these countries been economically successful extreme nationalist views would have been contained at the margins of society – where they belong in developed capitalist countries".[268] These theories rest on the assumption that the Soviet Union and other countries within its communist sphere were artificial constructs engineered by the Bolshevik revolutionaries. So, the end of communism meant the end of the states. Milanovic calls this the 'pressure cooker' theory, which is frequently cited in print media. It holds that nationalist sentiments were suppressed by communism and once the structure collapsed, these nations emerged through an explosion. Milanovic claims this is a simplistic theory which presumes that the more you constrain a thing, the greater the ferocity that it will spring back with once the source of the pressure is no longer present. He argues this theory is false because communist federations overemphasised the nationality issue. "No national group in the three communist federations was nearly as oppressed as Basques and Catalans in Franco's Spain, or as Kurds, until recently, in Turkey, or as Native Americans in the nineteenth-century United States, or even as Corsicans in France".[269] The pressure cooker theory has failed in Spain. If pressure cooker only applies in communist-controlled states, it then necessarily follows that there are special factors regarding those countries which it fails to address. What Milanovic himself and Weir, Kotz and Kotkin whom he criticises collectively fail to address is that the Soviet Union was not simply sitting atop these national fractures until the pressure cooker whistle blew, rather these fractures were created by the state itself as this chapter soon explains. Besides, even if this was true, it does not explain why China, India and Brazil are still in one piece. Historically each of those have been both multiethnic as well as communist. Yet they are still on the world map.

Milanovic points to Samuel Huntington's statement as an example of this: "In Yugoslavia and the Soviet Union, communist ideology provided the ideological legitimacy for multinational states. If the ideology were rejected, the basis for the state would disappear and each nationality could legitimately claim its own state". Milanovic argues that neither Yugoslavia nor Czechoslovakia, both founded in 1918, was created by communists. He argues that: "Communists played no role whatsoever in the formation of these two countries, and were, moreover (in the case of Yugoslavia, at least), opposed to it."[270] It is true that both countries owe their existence to 19th century pan-Slavic movements. They were not *created* by communist revolutions of the sort that brought down the Russian Empire in 1917, but ethnic and linguistic differences that were rife from the beginning in each case. Soon after the rise of the USSR, each foreign country that has fallen within the Soviet sphere of influence ultimately collapsed when the parent state did.

The question remains, why are China, India and Brazil still in one piece despite being *even* more multiethnic and multireligious than former USSR? It follows that there is more to the story than to say that states with ethnic and religious diversity are always doomed to collapse. This contrast between the *now fractured* Soviet Union and the *still united* India remains intriguing. Two multireligious, multiethnic societies, one collapsed, the other did not. No doubt, successful nation-building requires a common cultural core as seen in previous chapters. India had more of a cultural core and shared history rooted in its Vedic tradition. The Soviet Union was an ideological experiment, it neither had a shared history nor a shared language. From the very beginning, the Bolshevik Party had a virtual monopoly over means of artistic production and communication. It could have achieved a shared cultural-political form to make the Soviet identity work, but it did not. There was neither a cultural, nor a linguistic blueprint, and despite all the state power, the Soviets were unable to build one.

The third camp which blames bad economic leadership argues that it was the wrong decision at the wrong time that led to the collapse. This line of reasoning has been pursued by historians William Taubman,[271] George Breslauer,[272] and Archie Brown.[273] They place the blame on General-Secretary Mikhail Gorbachev's economic and social reforms which seem to have backfired. The ethnic public used the newly granted freedoms to ironically criticise the Soviet regime and ended up breaking it apart in the process. Branko Milanovic agrees with this view. He points out that:

> By banning all independent political activity, communism did not allow any groupings based on shared economic or social interests to emerge; workers could not assemble in trade unions or a labor party; small business owners could not form a conservative party; environmentalists could not organise an independent organisation or a Green party; and the like. The only accepted form of political organisation was territorial.[274]

In a similar vein, Stephen Kotkin in his 2009 publication *Armageddon Averted: The Soviet Collapse 1970-2000* has put forward a view that synthesises the views from earlier camps. He acknowledges that it was Gorbachev's romantic idealism and his belief that his policies of *glasnost* and *perestroika* would help reform the Soviet Union that contributed to the collapse.[275] Kotkin argues that Gorbachev's reforms ended up imploding the power structures that had been built to suppress free thought and press.[276] As a result, once the lid was removed, ethnic elites manipulated nationalism to seize power.[277] This again follows the same logic as Branko Milanovic's argument. Both fail to take into account that this situation could have been avoided with proper linguistic integration from the beginning as fully done by Ben Yehuda in the Israeli case and partly done by the Muslim nationalists in the Pakistani case.

Besides, if bad economic leadership was the case, then one wonders why collapsing the regime did not suffice instead of collapsing the state? Bad leadership decisions occur everywhere in the world. At the most, they are remedied by a change of government, not a change of international borders. Taubman, Breslauer, and Brown's view also presupposes that the kind of economic reforms Gorbachev tried to implement were destined to prove difficult to begin with. Yet this does not explain how Deng managed to implement the same reforms in China. It follows that there is more to the story than to say the collapse was the result of bad leadership decisions at the wrong time.

During the Cold War, it was not uncommon for Westerners to look at communism with deep suspicion. Many laymen and scholars alike saw the collapse of the USSR as a self-fulfilling prophecy. On balance, Russian scholarship has taken a more empathetic approach to account for the Soviet collapse. Many prominent Russian scholars appeared relatively late on the international scene. This was due to the gradual extension of academic freedoms in post-Soviet Russia. Publishing in 2009, Vladislav M. Zubok's *A Failed Empire: The Soviet Union in the Cold War from Stalin to Gorbachev* not only argues that Western intellectuals have exaggerated the Soviet collapse, he goes so far as to point out that many continue to fear that post-Soviet Russia might itself turn into another Soviet Empire.[278] His account is also far more detailed and sophisticated than conventional scholars. Zubok argues that the American policy to contain the spread of communism reinforced xenophobic sentiments in the Russian consciousness towards the US-led West.

From the Soviet vantage point, there was nothing wrong with developing an ideological alternative to American capitalism. The exaggerated degree to which the Americans invested in chasing after and isolating the Soviet Union for its commitment to spreading communism was, in Zubok's eyes, problematic. Despite emphasising external pressures of the Cold War, Zubok argues that ultimately the Soviet Union was not killed by the United States, rather it committed suicide. Serhii Plokhy in his 2014 publication *The Last Empire: The Final Days of the Soviet Union* makes the argument that the Soviet Union was the world's last remaining empire, that its democratic resurgence, economic struggles, imperial foundations, multiethnic population, and rigid totalitarian structures were the prime reasons for its collapse.[279]

There are significant overlaps across these theories. The combination of economic factors and bad leadership seem to be the common denominator. No doubt, the highly centralised nature of the economic system did conflict with the demands of a modern economy. Soviet researchers and scientists working in one institute could not exchange ideas with their counterparts in other institutes, let alone abroad. Economic growth stagnated, Soviet research and development slowed down despite its initial breakthroughs in science at the start of the Cold War. It overextended itself geographically in trying to compete. It placed sizeable proportions of its resources into surpassing the United States in the space and arms races, but still lagged behind. Soviet failures eventually bubbled up and not only did the regime collapse, the state itself did too. Yet the mystery remains. China was communist, it reformed and survived. India was multiethnic, it adapted and survived. Almost all countries experience bad economic leadership at some point, they simply change the regime, not the borders. What was different about the Soviet case? The seeds of the struggles that underpinned the nation building experience in the Soviet Union between 1917 and 1991 were sown much earlier. Russia conquered too much territory, absorbed too many different ethnicities within its borders and never had the right language policy in place to properly integrate its non-Russian subjects. This historical context is crucial to understand.

Much of what we know about the origins of Russia is derived from archaeological record and the writings of Medieval chronicler Nestor the Monk. He notes that Slavic tribes who spoke a shared Proto-Slavic language, the predecessor of Russian and Ukrainian, began to settle towards the east of the Ural Mountains in 862.[280] They established the city of Kiev and became known as the Kievan 'Rus'.[281] That was the Norse word for 'men who row'.[282] It was under the reign of Vladimir I in 988, that Orthodox Christianity was adopted as the state religion.[283] According to legend, the King had considered other religions but was put off by Islam's prohibition on alcohol and Judaism's diaspora due to expulsion from its holy land.[284] As the civilisational centre for Orthodox Christendom at the time, the Byzantine Empire modified the Greek alphabet to help create the first ever writing system for the Rus language. Called Cyrillic, this new script would go on to become the marker of Orthodox Christian identity across Europe and Russia in centuries to come. By 1054, Kievan Rus had broken up into smaller regions following the death of ruler Yaroslav the Wise.[285]

Four different rulers emerged to govern four different regions, they were: Rurik, Igor I, Sviatoslav I and Vladimir the Great. The Rus were at war with the Steppe peoples: Kipchaks, Khazars and Volga Bulgars for much of the 1100s. Conflict with other groups gave the Rus a sense of their own ethnic distinctness. Under Genghis Khan and later his grandson Batu Khan, the Mongols began invading Rus territories between 1223 and 1237.[286] They established a state called the Golden Horde and turned the Rus Kingdoms into their vassals, now required to pay taxes to their Mongol rulers.[287] The Swedes and the Lithuanians attempted to invade the Kievan Rus, but were unsuccessful. The Mongol Empire eventually fractured into smaller political units called Khanates. This allowed for the strengthening of regional powers such as Poland-Lithuania in 1264 and the Grand Duchy of Moscow in 1283. The two went on to acquire much of the territory of the Golden Horde and emerged as rivals to each other by the 1400s. This century was a period of great upheavals in European history and as a result, world history.

For centuries, the Byzantine Empire's capital Constantinople (now Istanbul in present-day Turkey) was seen as the 'Second Rome'. It projected itself as the civilisational centre of Orthodox Christendom. In 1492, Christopher Columbus discovered the New World ushering in an age of European maritime expansion. Most of the European empires that went on to explore, conquer and settle territories in North and South America were those with port cities on Europe's western shores: England, Holland, France, Spain and Portugal. They all became naval superpowers and colonial rivals to each other. This Age of Discovery, as it has been dubbed, was a fiercely competitive period in early modern history. The quest to acquire new territory and commodities for trade had become the single greatest priority for European imperial powers. Given Russia's geographic remoteness to the shores of western Europe, it was unable to keep up with its Western European naval counterparts in establishing colonies on the eastern shores of the Americas.

Yet this did not deter the Russians. A new political order emerged in 1547 under the notoriously named Ivan the Terrible, who referred to himself as 'Tsar', the Russian word for Caesar. Realising the difficulties in becoming a *maritime* superpower, Russia would soon emerge as a *continental* superpower. Going far beyond the Ural Mountains, the Russians soon conquered the Khanate of Siberia ushering in a period of eastward expansion. An increasing number of ethnic Russians began migrating east. Meanwhile, the vacuum left behind by the fall of Constantinople was filled by Moscow projecting itself as the

'Third Rome'.²⁸⁸ This was the new civilisational centre of Orthodox Christendom. Ivan drove what was left of the Mongols out and renamed the state 'Russia' after the Rus people that had inhabited it for centuries. Following a short-lived succession crises, Russia would soon survive multiple invasion attempts by the Poles between 1606 and 1613. A third of its population died. Once the instability came to an end, the Poles were driven out and a National Assembly elected Michael the new Tsar of Russia.²⁸⁹

Under the Romanov dynasty, Russia became a serfdom based feudal economy. Most of its peasant population lived as hereditary slaves. The campaigns for eastbound expansion continued on. By the 1650s, the Russian Empire's border was touching China and the Sea of Japan. It was in this period that hundreds of different ethnicities with their own languages and customs were absorbed as Russian subjects. Most were defenceless and could not resist Russian colonisation of their towns and villages. British linguist Bernard Comrie documents how the Tsars went about dealing with their diverse population demographics:

> There was no explicit plan envisaged or executed to enable non-Russians to learn Russian and assimilate, and of course no possibility was provided for them to develop within their own culture, in their own language. To the extent that there was any choice, it was between assimilating to the Russian population - and this could only be done by one's own efforts, since there was no widespread educational programme of instruction in Russian for non-Russians etc. – or remaining within one's own ethnic community and stagnating for lack of opportunity.²⁹⁰

Many of the colonised people saw benefit in pledging their allegiance to their colonial Russian rulers. The Steppes people from the Khanate of Cossack helped the Russians defeat arch rival Poland in the Russo-Polish wars from 1654 to 1667.²⁹¹ It was in this period that newly acquired territory was referred to as 'Ukrania', the Slavic word for 'borderland'. This would become Ukraine. The Tsars thought of themselves as the 'Great Russians' while Ukrainians were encouraged to think of themselves as a subdivision of Russians, or 'Little Russians'.²⁹² Tsar Peter the Great took to the throne in 1672.²⁹³

He turned out to be a great reformer. He went on to modernising the Russian army and introduced European style architecture, ship building, clothing and Western European Enlightenment ideas into Russian culture. As Bernard Comrie notes:

> If any member of one of the non-Russian ethnic groups wanted to advance himself, then effectively the only way to do this was by assimilating to the Russian population.[294]

Many Muslim nobles converted to Orthodox Christianity after the fall of the Kazan and took on important positions in the Tsarist administration. Russian coasts on the western front were in the extreme north or the Black Sea. As this was not conducive to maritime exploration, the Russians attempted to take more land and acquire ports on the western shores. Russia entered into a secret military alliance with the Polish-Lithuanian Commonwealth and Denmark. This Coalition first fought against the Swedish Empire in the Great Northern War from 1700 to 1721.[295] But from 1704 to 1709 the Polish-Lithuanian Commonwealth defected to join the Swedish side. The Ottoman Empire joined in from 1710 to 1714 and Great Britain from 1719. The result was a decisive victory for the Russian coalition. It projected the Tsardom of Russia as an emerging regional power in Europe. The process of further modernisation and integration into the European continent continued under the reign of Catherine the Great from 1762 on. She had killed her husband to seize the throne.

The French Revolution spelt bad news. The Russians were at first neutral to Napoleon Bonaparte's expansionist aspirations, then became an enemy, then an ally for a short while, only to go back and end up fighting him as enemy yet again in 1812. Napoleon's invasion of Russia proved disastrous for him. In 1815, Napoleon was defeated by Russian Tsar Alexander I (r. 1801-1825) who was in turn lauded as the saviour of Europe. Alexander was a key figure in redrawing the map of Europe at the Congress of Vienna (1814-1815).[296] The Russian Empire had become a major threat for the imperial powers of Western Europe. As a result, Britain and France forged an unholy alliance with the Ottoman Empire in the Crimean War

(1853-1856) and managed to defeat the Russians.[297] In 1861, Russia abolished serfdom in an event known as the emancipation reform.[298] Russia claimed Alaska as a colony in North America until the United States purchased it for $7.2 million in 1867.[299] The Ottomans and the Russians again clashed between 1877 and 1878 in the Russo-Turkish War.[300] This time, Russia won and managed to liberate Serbia, Romania, Montenegro, and Bulgaria from Ottoman rule.

In 1894, Tsar Nicholas II, who was believed to be under the influence of his mystic friend Rasputin, became the last Tsar of Russia.[301] The monarchy had been urged for decades to open up the economy. These pleas were met with refusal. The turn of the century proved to be a period of countless revolts against the House of Romanov. By this stage, the empire had grown so large and encompassed so many different religious and ethnic communities that revolts by ethnic and religious minorities had become increasingly frequent. Yet the Russian Empire had not paid much attention to appeasing its minorities. As Bernard Comrie observed:

> ...for most of the Russian Empire, *languages other than Russian had no rights* whatsoever. In some instances, *languages were actively discouraged* or even forbidden, as happened with Ukrainian between 1876 and 1905 as part of the government's policy to discourage Ukrainian separatism. And even where the use of languages other than Russian was not actively discouraged, the *languages were treated with official neglect*: they were not admissible for official purposes, and any encouragement given to their use was the work of private individuals.[302]

Likewise, John Myhill notes that:

> ...the Russians in building their empire *tended to deny the existence of ethnic differences* as a means of maintaining political control, and thus they adopted the official position that the spoken forms in the territories which are today Ukraine and Belarus were not distinct languages but rather dialects of Russian; such thinking is not normal for Slavs, who have rather typically constructed large numbers of small languages, each having relatively little dialectal variation.[303]

In the meantime, Japan had been relatively late in opening its doors to modernisation and willingness to trade. When it eventually did, it was at the dictate of US Commodore Matthew C. Perry through the use of gunboat diplomacy in 1854.[304] Soon after learning techniques of modern warfare from the Americans, Japan became an expansionist empire itself, with a vision to build colonies all over Far Eastern Asia. The Russian Empire's easternmost shores touched the Sea of Japan, home to the major Russian port city of Vladivostok. From 1904 to 1905, imperial Japan came to a head with the Russian Empire. Japan shocked the world by winning the Japanese-Russo War (1904-1905).[305] That was a decisive blow for the Russian Empire. As Japanese territorial expansion continued across the Far East, with colonies in Manchuria and China, imperial competitors in Europe and America became increasingly alarmed.

Political alignments underwent radical shifts. On one side, there were the Allied powers of the Russian Empire, French Empire, and British Empire. On the other side, there were the Central powers of the Austro-Hungarian Empire, German Empire, and Ottoman Empire. Following the murder of Austro-Hungarian Crown Prince, the archbishop Franz Ferdinand by a Serb nationalist, the Austro-Hungarian Empire began cracking down on Serbs. The Russian Empire came to Serbia's rescue. The rest of the allies were soon plunged into World War I (1914-1918). Intense battles occurred on land, at sea and in air for four years. Modern industrial weaponry was used for the first time on such large scale. The Allied powers won and borders were redrawn.

The Russian Empire went through two revolutions in 1917, in February and October, that brought an end to centuries of Tsarist rule. The Bolshevik revolutionaries took control under leader Vladimir Lenin. Russia became the Russian Soviet Federative Socialist Republic (RSFSR). Bernard Comrie notes that: "In the period before the Revolution, Russian was the official language for almost the whole of the Russian Empire. The only areas where a limited amount of local autonomy permitted the use of other languages were the Russian parts of Poland, Finland, and the Baltic provinces."[306] It is no surprise that the Baltics had a distinct sense of their own identities from the start. Between 1917 and 1922, civil war broke out resulting in the break away of Poland, Finland and the Baltic states.

What remained in 1922 became the Union of Soviet Socialist Republics (USSR). Nigora Azimova and Bill Johnston note that: "Russia is vast and hugely varied in demographic terms. Within the borders of the former Russian Empire there are peoples who differ significantly in language, religion, race and culture."[307] The ethnic and religious diversity that once fell within the Russian Empire's borders due to its eastbound continental expansion now fell within Soviet borders. Bernard Comrie also observes that at the outset, the USSR emerged as a: "...multinational state, containing some 130 different ethnic groups, speaking some 130 different languages".[308] Most of these can be categorised into different language families. The ones most prevalent in the Soviet Union at the time were: Slavonic, Baltic, Germanic, Romance, Hellenic, Iranian, Armenian, Caucasian, Uralic, Lapp, Permic, Volgaic, Ugric, Samoyedic, Altaic, Paleosiberian, Korean. For a single region, this was nearly as much linguistic diversity as found within the Subcontinent. Except, the Soviet Union would go on to manage its linguistic diversity far less efficiently.

Dealing with this level of diversity was certainly on the minds of the Bolsheviks even before the fall of the Tsardom. It was in 1913 that Bolshevik pioneers Vladimir Lenin and Joseph Stalin first began collaborating to devise a policy hoping to *neutralise* ethnic separatism once the Soviet Union was formed. Historian Terry Martin observes that:

> Lenin and Stalin worked together closely from 1913 to mid-1922 in formulating the Soviet nationalities policy and can properly be considered the co-authors of the distinctive Bolshevik strategy aimed at defusing separatist nationalism: the Affirmative Action Empire.[309]

From the beginning, it was Chairman Vladimir Lenin's vision to provide the non-Russian ethnicities a considerable degree of autonomy within their own republics, provinces, regions and districts. There would also be quotas to provide non-Russian ethnic minorities representation within the political and bureaucratic structures of the Soviet Union. These policies would be considered affirmative action in the West. In the same vein, the language policy of the Bolshevik party and the Soviet government took a radical shift away from the Tsarist period, both in its conception and execution. There was a general commitment to the equality of all peoples and languages. Russian was the majority language, but as Comrie notes:

> ...*everyone was to have the right to use his own language,* both in private and for public matters, such as addressing meetings, correspondence with officials, giving testimony in courts.[310]

Soviet subjects were essentially free to govern themselves as they saw fit. These measures were to ensure that the different ethnic groups did not see the USSR as an oppressive colonial occupier. While the USSR was to be the central state, its subordinate administrative subdivisions of autonomous republics, oblasts and autonomous oblasts would be granted considerable freedom. Martin notes that under these policies:

> *Each nationality would be given* its own territory, with its own ruling elite (promoted through affirmative action in education and hiring), and *its own language as official state language.*[311]

As a result, many of the ethnic and linguistic differences were eventually *defragmented* into 15 different autonomous republics. These were: Armenia, Azerbaijan, Belorussia, Estonia, Georgia, Kazakhstan, Kirghizia, Latvia, Lithuania, Moldavia, Russia, Tajikistan, Turkmenia, Ukraine, and Uzbekistan. Of these, Russia was the largest by area, the administrative centre was in Moscow and ethnic Russians formed the majority of the USSR's population. By this stage, it is clear how this would prove problematic when it came to governing. The memories of life under the Russian Empire were still fresh in the minds of the elder generations within ethnic minorities. Bolshevik leadership was aware of this. Since ethnic Russians constituted more than half of the Soviet population, they were at risk of being perceived by the non-Russian Soviet subjects as the ruling class. To offset this, the Russians were treated differently by the Soviet regime than other ethnic groups. The Russians were not given their own republic. Instead, they only had a multinational federal *Rossiiskii* republic.[312] As Terry Martin observes:

> Russians in national regions were required to learn local languages. Finally, traditional *Russian culture was stigmatised as a culture of oppression.* The goal of this strategy was to defuse non-Russian nationalism by granting the forms of nationhood and overcome non-Russian 'distrust' of their former oppressors by downplaying Russian nationhood.[313]

This approach was remarkably unconventional. It was a case of the ethnic majority discriminating against itself in order to keep the collection of minorities happy. The thought may have been noble, at least in theory, but it overstressed the fact that there was a demographic and linguistic imbalance within Soviet society. Non-Russian minorities could see that they were in fact living in a modern manifestation of the old Russian Empire. This helped sow the seeds for the 15 Soviet republics to consolidate their *separate* national identities from the very beginning of the Soviet experiment. Bernard Comrie acknowledges the difficulty with these policies:

> As often with an idealistic policy statement of this kind, there were immense practical difficulties in implementing this goal, leading in certain instances to partial abandonment of the goal.

And,

> Everyone was to have the right to education and availability of cultural materials in his own language.[314]

In the same vein, Jacob Ornstein has noted that: "The ethnic groups of the Soviet Union were to be given full opportunity *to develop their own languages* so as to equip them to express the concepts of a modern, industrialised society".[315] Non-Russian ethnicities were free to use Cyrillic, Latin, or Arabic scripts to write their native tongue. Russian orthography was also simplified slightly in 1918 to make it more accessible for the non-Russian minorities.[316] These policies were a radical shift away from previous Tsarist rule. In trying to differentiate themselves, Soviet pioneers went the opposite direction. Nationalist elites, in most cases, tend to administer ethnic differences by eroding the linguistic boundaries between the majority and the minority through the state's education system, mass media and active campaigns to encourage linguistic assimilation into a shared national identity. Early Soviet policies were the exact opposite of this. Yet the fact remained, in order for the citizens of the Soviet state to communicate with its citizens and for the citizens to be able to interact with each other, it was inevitable that a *lingua franca* would be required. Although Soviet rulers had gone out of their way to accommodate the non-Russian minorities, since Russian was the language of the Bolshevik elites as well as the native language of the majority of Soviet population, it became the obvious choice.[317] Most minority languages at the time did not have a written form. In his contributed chapter in Joshua A. Fishman's 1977 publication *Readings in the Sociology of Language*, Elliot R. Goodman makes the observation that:

> *The Soviet grand design for transforming the present nation-state system into a Soviet world state envisages a fundamental reshaping of national languages. A national language, as the nerve centre of a national memory, is probably the most important single medium through which national traditions are nurtured and transmitted.* Of all those ingredients producing a sense of national cohesion, *a national language is doubtless the fundamental element, although the existence of several multilingual nation-states would indicate that national languages need not be an insuperable barrier to the growth of broader loyalties.* Yet even here the continued use of national languages imparts a sense of national distinctiveness which cannot be obliterated, except through the destruction of the various national languages.[318]

Lenin and Stalin disagreed among themselves over laying down the formal constitutional structure of the Soviet state in 1922. The status of ethnic Russians became a focal point. Ornstein notes that: "Lenin [...] envisioned the *eventual* use of a single language as a means for achieving solidarity under socialism. At the same time, he opposed the idea of forcible coercion to impose Russian upon the peoples of the Soviet Union."[319] This is a clear indication that Lenin knew the importance of a single national language, but did not want to be coercive in enforcing it. He had hoped that Soviet subjects would eventually arrive at a single language through organic means. This attitude is the diametric opposite of Eliezer Ben Yehuda who tolerated no language other than Hebrew in the Israeli case[320] as well as Muhammad Ali Jinnah who tolerated no language other than Urdu in the Pakistani case.[321] Still, Stalin saw it differently, declaring:

> I have very little faith in this creation of a single universal language and the dying away of all other tongues in the period of socialism. *I have very little faith in this theory of a single, all-embracing language.* Experience in every case speaks not for, but against this theory".[322]

Stalin proposed that ethnic minorities within the Russian Soviet Federative Socialist Republic (RSFSR) be allowed to join RSFSR as autonomous republics. Although his plan was accepted, Lenin attacked him for compromising the status of the independent republics. Lenin's own proposal was to create a federal structure on top named the 'Union of Soviet Republics of Europe and Asia' and to have both the independent Soviet Republics and the RSFSR take part as equal members. Stalin was not in favour of this, but Lenin's proposal took precedence in the end.[323]

Terry Martin notes that: "Lenin's conflict with Stalin over the constitutional form of the Soviet state has often been portrayed as Lenin's defence of national minorities from Stalin's great power chauvinism."[324] There was resistance from ethnic minorities that ended up within RSFSR. Mirsaid Sultan-Galiev in October 1922 along with several Tatar colleagues proposed to separate his people from RSFSR and be allowed to enter the Soviet Union directly. Stalin dismissed his proposal remarking: "Such a proposal demands dissolving our federation into pieces".[325] Sultan-Galiev was arrested in May 1923. Terry Martin notes that the Soviet nationalities policy required:

> "...*downplaying Russian national culture* and limiting the institutionalisation of Russian nationhood. The onset of Stalin's cultural revolution in 1928, with its militant Bolshevik internationalism, greatly intensified this policy line. A striking symbolic expression of the contemporary attitude towards traditional Russian culture was a plan announced, though never implemented, to shift the Russian language from the Cyrillic to the Latin alphabet.[326]

In 1929, Stalin had stated: "It is well known that assimilation is categorically excluded from the arsenal of Marxism-Leninism as an anti-national, counter-revolutionary and fatal policy."[327] Yet attitudes within the Soviet Union remained torn between two absurd extremes. On one side, there were those in the Bolshevik ranks that had hoped that all ethnic distinctions, Russian and non-Russian alike, would eventually evaporate and one day be substituted with a common Soviet identity. But if this were to happen, the Soviet Union would need a common language for its education system, bureaucracy, government, media, and film. If Russian was to be the obvious choice, then the other non-Russian ethnic groups would inevitably end up being 'Russified'. Within a generation, their kids would grow up as Russians. Yet there was no linguistic apparatus to help make this happen. On the other side, there were those that feared that if ethnic identities were forcibly suppressed, that may lead to separatist sentiments. So they thought their best bet to create a homogeneous national consciousness was by stressing the communist ideals of liberation from class struggles while providing the non-Russian minorities maximum autonomy in their own space.

It remains ironic that this strategy only helped *reinforce* the very sentiments it had sought to neutralise. Granting maximum autonomy to ethnic minorities meant they felt a greater connection to their ethnic identity configurations rather than the federal Soviet one. The Soviet policy known as *korenizatsiia* had aimed to bring all the subjects of the Soviet Union as a single socialist 'imagined community' under the umbrella of a Soviet federal structure. Jacob Ornstein observes that: "...the process of what has been termed functional *korenizatsiia* was begun in the early 1920s. This meant the appointment of officials fluent in native languages to administrative positions in the non-Russian areas".[328] This would itself end up having consequences. The 1920s featured a resurgence of national cultures in socialist republics such as Belarus and Ukraine, with increasing importance placed on their native language. The Communist Party was blinded by its own idealism. Far from seeing this as a threat, Soviet leaders at the time saw it as successful *indigenisation* within Soviet society.[329] That is to say, people celebrating their autonomous identities while remaining loyal to the federal state. Convinced that this was a good idea, Stalin declared that:

> ...the national cultures of even the very smallest of peoples of the Soviet Union will develop and we will help them develop."[330]

It is visible by this stage how the patchwork of separate national identities was laid down early on in the Soviet experience. Languages within USSR that did not have their own writing systems were assisted by the Soviet regime to start receiving new scripts during the 1920s and 1930s. Terry Martin notes that: "Written languages were provided for populations numbering under one thousand."[331] This was to help create homogeneous national identities at the *local* level, within the socialist republics. Notable examples are the Nanay, Nivkh, Koryak, and Chukchi in the Far East, and the Khanty and Mansi languages in western Siberia.[332] Bilingualism in those days was seen as a *transitional stage* to eventual monolingualism, to be achieved once the small ethnic groups had assimilated into their corresponding nation. By some mysterious measure, some languages were revived while others were faded out. Bernard Comrie notes that: "In addition to phasing out languages with small numbers of speakers, there was one period in Soviet history when certain written languages were forcibly discouraged".[333] It was hoped that some minority languages would simply go extinct while others, through the use of new writing systems, would create a literate population that would blend in with the population of whichever one of the 15 socialist republics it called home. These policies were completely at odds with the way conventional nation-building occurs around the world.

The early Soviet vision of maximum autonomy followed by eventual Russification rested on the assumption that "Other languages did not influence Russian as much as Russian influenced them".[334] Under a more conventional nation-building process, the Soviet Union would have begun to assimilate its population into Russian culture and language as was expected under the Tsars. Lenin's idea of maximum cultural and linguistic autonomy laid down the heterogeneous framework for eventual fractures that were to come later in the century. This initial policy created 15 different national identities instead of a single

Soviet one. Terry Martin makes the crucial observation that the: "... cultural revolution resulted *not* in assimilation, but *ethnic* proliferation. The flowering of nations led to the discovery of new nations. The small Mari nation (200,000) splintered into 'meadow' (lugovoi) and 'mountain' (gornyi) Mari, with the latter smaller group (50,000) being given its own national *raion* within the Mari autonomous oblast. In Georgia, the Mingrelians (240,000) demanded the same status and were likewise granted their own national press and schools, though not a national *raion*".[335]

Anatolii Skachko observes: "the creation of new nationalities out of tribes which had earlier never dreamed of national existence [...] [and] their transition in just six years through all the stages of development, which for other peoples required thousands of years."[336] Another major cause for national disunity was the reduction of Russians into a minority status *within* the Soviet republics. As Canadian historian David R. Marples points out: "The Slavs tended to settle in the urban areas, embracing a separate culture and refusing to learn the native languages of their respective republics."[337] Terry Martin too observes that: "...an increasing number of Russians found themselves in the extremely unfamiliar status of being a national minority. They did not like it".[338] Martin goes on to note that: "Russian resentment of their perceived loss of status and the fact that every nationality except the Russians seemed to have a national homeland, began to concern Stalin."[339]

Notice here, how this was essentially an unprecedented case of the natural ruling class undermining *itself* to appease its minorities. It may be argued that this was a direct implementation of Marxist egalitarianism. The *bourgeoisie* practicing what they preached and acting as if they were the *proletariat*. Except, this was disastrous from a nation-building perspective. The dominant class is better off not denying that it is there to govern, that it would do so with justice and fairness, but still requires its subjects adapt to the national language. This is how Pakistan did it with Urdu,[340] Israel with Hebrew, India with Hindi, China with Mandarin, Brazil with Portuguese, and Britain with English. These are all multiethnic, multireligious nation-states, still in one piece.

When Stalin took over as the new leader, these policies gradually began to be abandoned. He started concentrating power in the centre of the state. He started favouring the ethnic Russians. As an interesting aside, he was an ethnic Georgian himself. In the case of the Eastern Slavic, the Baltic and the Caucasus states, the difference with their Soviet rulers were of an ethnic and linguistic nature. That was problematic enough as it was. Yet the tensions with the Muslim subjects of the Soviet Union across Central Asia were often more pronounced. In addition to ethnic and linguistic differences, this region was also *religiously* different, seeing itself as part of Islamic civilisation. For the Muslim intellectuals under Soviet rule, the cultural hangover from the Ottoman Empire's clashes with the Tsarist Russian Empire was still fresh. Often the greatest revolts against the Soviet Union came from these Turkic-speaking Muslims from Central Asia. The Muslim insurgent group Basmachi had staged a prolonged rebellion against the Soviet Union from 1918 to 1931.[341] This group was eventually crushed by the Soviet regime and its leaders were executed. In December 1933, the Chairman of the All-Russian Central Executive Committee's Nationalities Department, N. N. Nurmakov gave a remarkable statement warning that the process of preserving nationalities had gone too far:

> Some national minorities, fulfilling the task of bourgeois nationalist elements – whether consciously or not -- demanded the formation of special *raiony* for numerically insignificant groups of national minorities [...] the formation of such *raiony*, without necessary economic and financial conditions, does not at all further the rapid development of these national minorities; it creates purely Potemkin *raiony* without any future potential.[342]

This was a significant statement. Indeed, Terry Martin observes that by this stage the policy of ethnic proliferation had been *stigmatised* as bourgeois nationalist.[343] Nurmakov called for a change in language policy. He questioned the value of minority language schooling and stated that: "We open national schools not in order to provide mandatory instruction in native languages, but in order to give an education to national minorities."³⁴⁴ Martin points out that the Education Commissariat representative agreed that Russian must be given priority: "We must adapt to the language that has the higher culture".³⁴⁵ By this stage, it is clear how the earlier policies had failed to work and a gradual shift towards Russification was beginning to take shape. The Soviet Union unveiled its New Economic Plan (NEP) that contained an overhaul of languages for schooling, communications, and public life. "The new negative attitude towards ethnic proliferation was accompanied by a positive re-evaluation of the role of Russian culture."³⁴⁶ Martin goes on to differentiate between the old and new policies:

> This overall trend, and in particular *the new emphasis on Russian language education, opened up the formerly taboo topic of assimilation*. Prior to 1932, Soviet policy was unambiguously hostile to even voluntary assimilation.³⁴⁷

Many of the non-Russian ethnic elites had by this stage begun to realise the significance of assimilating into a common Russian-based Soviet culture. In 1934, the ethnic Uzbek Secretary of the Soviet of Nationalities A. Tadzhiev was giving his own children a Russian-language education.³⁴⁸ He makes a remarkable statement:

> *Local misunderstandings develop because we observe an opposition to assimilation.* One sometimes even observes this among communists. In fact, we should not oppose assimilation. Our nationalities policy is absolutely clear and we can never permit forced assimilation. We won't allow that, but *we should by all means welcome natural assimilation* [...] which takes place at its own pace. This is good as it leads to the formation of a *single nation, a single language.* ³⁴⁹

The interesting observation from that statement is that neither Lenin nor Stalin would have disagreed with it. With Lenin perhaps being the greater optimist. Still, this idea of *voluntary* assimilation was too much to ask for. As would soon become clear, the radical policy shift from preserving ethnic nationalities to instead assimilating them through Russification would not help consolidate a homogeneous Soviet national consciousness. As the policies began to shift in

1937, the policymaking unit of the Communist Party called *Politburo* issued a decree abolishing the schools and cultural institutions in USSR's diaspora nationalities: Germans, Poles, Finns, Estonians and Latvians.[350] It was expanded to include all "non-Russian schools in Russian regions", which meant the abolition of 4,598 national minority schools.[351] Within a year, "only Russian schools were functioning in the Russian regions of the RSFSR".[352] Around the same time, national minority newspapers in the Russian regions of the RSFSR had been reduced from 36 to 21.[353]

In an even more remarkable policy shift, from 1937 onwards all ethnic languages were required to start using the Cyrillic alphabet for writing. The underlying assumption was that abandoning the Latin and Arabic scripts would increase the likelihood of the Baltic and Turkic peoples, in that order, to improve their Russian literacy and fluency. These reforms eroded the sense of a regional Turkic identity by declaring mutually intelligible languages to be separated. Kazakh, Uzbek, Kyrgyz, and Uighur (spoken by people along the western China border) were treated as separate. Tajik which is a form of Persian was left in a category of its own. These languages had developed independently of each other in the lexical sense. Bernard Comrie writes:

> *The writing systems that caused most problems were those of the Islamic peoples of the USSR, which used the Arabic alphabet,* in general poorly adapted to indicate the range of phonemic differences that are found in such languages as Turkic languages (with a large number of vowels) quality distinctions, or Northeast Caucasian languages (with many consonants and vowel distincts that are not found in Arabic).[354]

The original attempt was to devise a simplified form of the Arabic script, but this idea was soon abandoned. Later they tried to impose Latin alphabets.[355] The Soviet regime tried to be careful from the beginning. As Comrie observes:

> One of the main reasons given for the choice of the Latin alphabet at this period was the need to avoid the impression, especially among traditionally Islamic peoples, that the replacement of their traditional script, with its religious connotations, was part of a policy of linguistic,

cultural, and religious Russification. The Latin alphabet was thus a compromise neutral between the conflicts of the Arabic and Cyrillic scripts.[356]

The process of *Russification* was now in full force. Russian would be the state language and a prerequisite for military conscription. The proliferation of the Cyrillic script enabled Russian loanwords to penetrate regional languages. Terry Martin notes that: "...by 1940 the Soviet Union had been divided into a Russian space (the RSFSR's oblasti/kraia), where institutional russification had been almost entirely completed, and a non-Russian space, where national minority status continued to be recognised."[357] He notes that: "This process led to the division of the Soviet Union into a central Russian core and a non-Russian 'national' periphery." and that in the 1920s: "... due to state support for ethnic proliferation, nationality permeated the entire Soviet Union and, in particular, the RSFSR. There was no purely Russian space. The creation of that Russian space took place in the 1930s and was the result of a conscious strategy of national consolidation and institutional russification".[358]

During this period, the Soviet Union was locked in a space race and an arms race with rival superpower, the United States. Much of the Soviet Union's scientific research and technological advances were published in the Russian language, which had full official status in the Soviet Union while other ethnic languages had territorial status only. The Soviet Union had gone from actively trying to suppress ethnic Russian dominance to embracing it as inevitable. No matter where ethnic Russians would settle across the colossal landmass, their linguistic rights were guaranteed. Street signs, shop signs, advertising billboards, newspapers, film, television, and radio were readily available in the Russian language.[359] The same was no longer the case for other ethnic groups. They had to learn, adapt and survive. This is after being told for decades during the phase of earlier policies that they could in fact celebrate and preserve their local identities and languages.

Describing an inevitable identity crisis resulting from these shifts in language policy, Terry Martin observes that: "For a substantial minority of the Soviet population, this revived the tension between the individual's passport and territorial nationality. On one hand, extra-territorial national minorities lost state support for the maintenance of their ethnic identity; on the other hand, the passport system implied that they should in any case preserve their national identity."[360] Soviet census too distinguished between *narodnost* (ethnicity) an *nacionalnost* (nationality). Ethnicity was determined by language spoken and nationality by what was declared. Chairman Stalin was now strongly in favour of eroding ethnic differences. He had opposed the degree of regional autonomy otherwise available to the different ethnic groups. He now preferred to promote ethnic Russians and the Russian language ahead of other ethnicities and their languages. Stalin went against the earlier affirmative action policies. He replaced the Secretary of the Communist Party of Kazakhstan with an ethnic Russian. This resulted in a public backlash from the Kazakh people.

In 1944, Stalin denounced the ethnic Meskhetian Turks from southwestern Georgia as "enemies of the people" and had them rounded and deported to the Central Asian region. Close to 155,000 Meskhetian Turks from 200 villages were moved to Uzbekistan, Kazakhstan and Kyrgyzstan. Many ended up seeking refuge in Turkey.[361] From the beginning, the Baltic states of Lithuania, Latvia and Estonia had a strong sense of their own national identities. This is because they were historically separate nations to begin with. They only ended up within the borders of the Soviet Union due to the Molotov-Ribbentrop Pact (1939) with Nazi Germany during World War II. According to its terms, the Soviet Union and Nazi Germany were to stay out of each other's ways. This was violated when the Germans invaded Poland and eventually came within 24 km range of Moscow. After Hitler's defeat in World War II, Stalin managed to retain control of the Soviet colonies in eastern Europe.

This so-called 'Iron Curtain' was seen with suspicion by the West. Other groups with strong national identities were the Ukrainians, Armenians, and Georgians. By this stage, the national configurations of the Soviet Union had already become what Lenin had actively tried to prevent. The Soviet Union had openly projected itself as *Russian* by ethnicity and *Russian* by language. As Nigora Azimova and Bill Johnston have noted: "One of the most effective tools of Russification was the Russian language itself. During the Soviet era, Russian became more than just a lingua franca - it also came to serve as a way to unite diverse nationalities and develop a Soviet identity. Russian was presented as *the language of the Soviet people* and *the second native language for non-Russians.*"[362] This policy would have had a higher chance of working if implemented from the beginning. The earlier policies had allowed for non-Russian ethnicities to develop their senses of separate national identities. By the time Russification began, it was too late. Non-Russian minorities had good reason to feel they were under a kind of Russian colonial rule. The end of Stalin's leadership in March 1953 resulted in demands for an overhaul of his hardline policies. Internal Affairs Minister Lavrentiy Beria demanded an end to what was, in many people's eyes, Russian chauvinism. As Nikita Khrushchev took power, he attempted to shift away from Stalin's nationalist rhetoric. In a secret speech to the 20th Communist Party Congress in 1956, he denounced Stalin's authoritarian rule and cult of personality. Yet as David R. Marples notes:

> ...*the elevation of Russian to the prevailing language in most republics continued. Moreover, the vast majority of publications were in Russian and education also was predominantly in that language.*[363]

Nigora Azimova and Bill Johnston also note that: "Education played a primary role in spreading the Russian language among non-Russian ethnic groups. The strong institutionalisation of Russian in the domain of education began in 1959 with reforms primarily centered on allowing parents to choose their child's school based on the language of instruction." This was contrary to earlier Leninist era policies where children were to receive education in their mother tongue. Due to these policy shifts from linguistic *autonomy* to linguistic *assimilation*, ethnic and national differences had become more deeply entrenched than ever before. As Leonid Brezhnev took control, he pursued a policy of 'merger of nations'. He thought that a 'New

Soviet Man' would emanate, with differences between the republics being absorbed into an overarching national identity. This was not dissimilar from Lenin's original vision of voluntary assimilation. Yet parents continued to make the practical choice "to enroll their children in Russian-language schools."[364] For the most part, the language policy had proven to be *relatively* successful. By the 1960s, Russian had begun to be the dominant language among the literate population in all ethnic groups. In pursuit of his New Soviet Man idea, as Nigora Azimova and Bill Johnston observe: "The use of Russian in the educational domain was further promoted during the Brezhnev period (1964-1982)."[365] In 1975 Brezhnev said that:

> ...under developed socialism, when the economies in our country have melted together in a coherent economic complex; when there is a new historical concept - the Soviet people - *it is an objective growth in the Russian language's role as the language of international communications when one builds Communism, in the education of the new man!* Together with one's own mother tongue one will speak fluent Russian, which the Soviet people have voluntarily accepted as a common historical heritage and contributes to a further stabilisation of the political, economic and spiritual unity of the Soviet people.[366]

Yet within a decade and a half since that statement, the Soviet Union was on the verge of collapse. By the 1980s, the Soviet experiment had proven difficult internally and externally. At home, ethnic nationalist sentiments had been brewing due to contradictory Soviet language policies which over the decades, had vacillated between the polar extremes of ethnic proliferation and Russification. Abroad, the Soviet Union had over-stretched itself in a difficult war with the US-backed *Mujahideen* following the Soviet invasion of Afghanistan in 1979. This war had become the final showdown between the two Cold War rivals. Meanwhile, Deng Xiaoping in China had begun leading great economic reforms from 1978 onwards. Like the Soviet Union, China had also started out as an authoritarian communist regime following the revolution of 1949. The pressure was on the Soviet Union to do the same.

It was against this tumultuous backdrop that Mikhail Gorbachev took control in 1985. He had a vision to reform the Soviet Union. He went about achieving this with his two signature policies of *perestroika* (restructuring) which was an overhaul of the political and economic system, and *glasnost* (transparency) which had aimed to provide greater freedom of thought and expression. There was an overarching acknowledgement of the errors of earlier Soviet history. Gorbachev's predecessors Lenin, Stalin and Khrushchev had kept the *Politburo* together. After them, disunity had emerged within this committee. There were competing streams of thought and Gorbachev found himself caught in the crossfire between hardliners and liberals. These fractures within the administration of the party made it vulnerable. The elite no longer thought the same way as before. Lack of common consensus and good will made running the country all the more difficult.

Gorbachev's reforms were well-intentioned, but the Soviet Union had by this stage become a megastructure sitting on top of conflicting national identities. These reforms removed the lid. As historian David R. Marples points out: "Gorbachev's most important mistake was his apparent failure to recognise how his policy of *glasnost* complicated and provoked the *nationalities question* in the Soviet Union."[367] By 1988 the Soviet Union had moved ahead to emulate a Western style market economy, multi-party political systems with elected legislators. Although Gorbachev did grow up in the ethnically fragmented Caucasus region of the Soviet Union, he somehow still came to assume that the national question was resolved. This could not be further from reality.

Marples observes that mass riots orchestrated by ethnic Kazakhs erupted in Alma-Ata (now Almaty, Kazakhstan) subsequent to the assignment of ethnic Russian Gennady Kolbin as leader of the party in the region, replacing of Dinmukhamed Kunayev on 16 December 1986. As it happened, in February 1988, Armenia and Azerbaijan faced each other off in a war over the Nagorno-Karabakh region.[368] Soviet withdrawal from Afghanistan had begun in 1988. The ensuing Revolutions of 1989 spelt further disaster for USSR. Soviet-imposed communist regimes across eastern Europe began collapsing one by one. Poland, Hungary, East Germany, Bulgaria, Czechoslovakia, and Romania all went through regime changes. Encouraged by the collapse of the Berlin Wall in November 1989, Baltic separatist leaders began pushing for independence from the USSR. Soviet government began cracking down on separatists across the country. Riots broke out in Georgia. Marples points out that Aleksandr Iakovlev, Eduard Shevardnadze, Stanislav Shatalin, Gavriil Popov and Anatolii Sobchak formed a Movement for Democratic Reform hoping to maintain order amid chaos. The Congress of People's Deputies of the Soviet Union (CCCP) was established in 1989 as the highest body of federal authority as part of these reforms.

In 1990, all three of the Baltic states declared independence. Gorbachev in turn declared their secession to be illegal. In January 1991, Soviet forces attacked TV stations in Vilnius, Lithuania. Yet Russian President Boris Yeltsin expressed sympathy with the independent republics. He sought foreign support for a separatist push. In March 1991, a referendum was held, in which nine republics endorsed Gorbachev's plan for a revised union attracting more than 76% of the vote.[369] It was too late. Marples observes that: "Republican leaders did not concur with the Soviet leader that the referendum results constitute an endorsement of his policies. In Ukraine, parliamentary leader Leonid Kravchuk commented that the referendum in his republic had demonstrated the striving of the population for independence."[370] Gorbachev continued to quote the referendum outcome to support his positions.[371] He did his best to keep the revised version of the Soviet Union together. By this stage, Russia (RSFSR) itself, had emerged as the leading force against the Soviet Union (USSR), competing to take it over. In a landmark declaration, Russian law came to take precedence over Soviet law. A separate Russian constitution was under preparation and negotiations between the Russians and other republics were underway to collectively *bypass* the Soviet administration.

In June 1991, Boris Yeltsin was elected President of Russia (RSFSR) with a kind of democratic legitimacy never pursued by Soviet leader

Mikhail Gorbachev, who had refused to subject his authority to any electoral approval. Yeltsin demanded businesses operating on Russian soil pay their taxes into the Russian Federation directly. Marples points out it was Yeltsin who began laying down the foundations for Russia to develop its own military. The fact that the Russian Federation would itself become the biggest rival to the Soviet Union amidst all the mayhem should surprise no one. Russia (RSFSR) was not only the largest territorial unit within the Soviet Union, it was also home to the dominant ethnic group with what had by this stage well and truly been projected as the dominant language, as observed earlier. It was only natural that Russia would lead the charge in putting the Soviet Union out of its misery. In August 1991, Defence Minister Dmitry Yazov and Vice President Gennady Yanayev led a coup and placed Mikhail Gorbachev under house arrest in his holiday home in Crimea. Three days later, Boris Yeltsin ordered their arrest and banned the Soviet Communist Party in Russia.

In September 1991, the Congress of People's Deputies of the Soviet Union (CCCP) voted for the dissolution of the Soviet Union. In December that year, leaders from Russia, Belarus, and Ukraine signed a pact to create the Commonwealth of Independent States, intended to be an alliance for Post-Soviet states. On 25 December 1991, Mikhail Gorbachev resigned as Soviet President. The Russian government took over the offices, military and bureaucratic structures and the Union of Soviet Socialist Republics was cast into the archives of history. The Bolshevik Revolution of 1917 had undone itself. As Branko Milanovic points out:

> ...in a single-party system, where no other type of political organisation was allowed, the only legitimate political base that existed was the regional one. 'Ethnically distinct political elites,' in power in each republic, had at their disposal all the essential accoutrements of state power. So long as communist discipline at the center held (until Gorbachev in the Soviet Union and until the death of Tito in Yugoslavia), regional bosses exercised their power only with caution.[372]

Milanovic goes on to explain that: "All of them enjoyed statehood, but as long as communists were at the helm in all such states, no problems, it was thought, would arise."[373] In his view, economic failure and consequent scapegoating with overemphasis on nationality issues as compensation for the ban on other political activities was what led to the Soviet collapse. Milanovic argues that if communism had been: "...economically successful, people would not have fallen so easily into the embrace of nationalist leaders".[374] This view overlooks two crucial points. First, contrary to popular misperception, the Soviet Union *did* manage to build an impressive economy *despite* the criticism and rhetoric from Western scholars. This was primarily achieved through collectivisation, rapid industrialisation, massive military expenditure, the willingness to sacrifice its own population to achieve the objectives of the state. So Milanovic's idea that if communism had worked the Soviet Union would have been less likely to collapse is weak at best.

Second, Milanovic overlooks the fact that the seeds for ethnic separatism were present in the Soviet Union from the *beginning* in 1917. Unlike the Subcontinent, where the different ethnic and religious communities had interacted and traded with each other for centuries as well as shared a common Vedic cultural heritage, in the Soviet case, its diverse communities had very little to do with each other historically and culturally. They only ended up inside the same borders by the happenstance of Russian eastward expansionism, orchestrated by Ivan the Terrible, in earlier centuries. Unlike the Subcontinent, where Urdu had been used to mobilise the Muslims and Hindi to mobilise the Hindus, in the Soviet case, the language policy was a contradictory mess. Milanovic and other observers have often downplayed these factors. L.A. Grenoble rightly observes that:

> The former Soviet Union provides an ideal case study for examining these relationships, in that it had one of the most deliberate language policies of any nation state. This is not to say that it was constant or well-conceived; in fact it was marked by contradictions, illogical decisions, and inconsistencies.[375]

Early Soviet pioneers were aware of the ethnic factor from the start. They simply did not know how to deal with it. When it came to creating a workable Soviet national identity, Bolshevik pioneers Lenin and Stalin actually had more in common with each other than most scholars seem to realise. Both of them knew, what they had inherited from the Tsarist Russian Empire was a colossal landmass impregnated with ethnic, linguistic and religious differences. They knew there was no single 'nation' to begin with, only a political structure, at first vested in the House of Romanov, later to be inherited by the Bolsheviks. Yet inspired by a utopian communist vision, Lenin and Stalin had both hoped that the ideology of liberation from class struggle that had *brought* the Soviet *state* together would be sufficient to *keep* the Soviet *nation* together.

Lenin and Stalin wanted the same outcome. Their method of implementation is where the difference lies. Lenin had hoped that by granting the Soviet Union's many administrative divisions maximum autonomy, he would be able to neutralise their senses of ethnic distinctness. He had hoped that over time, people would dissolve into a single Soviet nation. Yet he failed to implement a policy that could help deliver such an outcome. In fact, his policies were paradoxical. He ended up suppressing the ethnic Russian identity to ensure that non-Russian ethnicities did not view the Soviet Union as another oppressive extension of the old Russian Empire. He allowed them to have their own coat of arms, flags, anthems, regional governments as well as media, education system and bureaucratic structures in local languages. Far from helping bind non-Russians together as proud Soviet subjects, these policies only helped create a mosaic of satellite nations based on common ethnicity and language, operational *within* an arbitrarily imposed, ideologically motivated federal structure.

This was at complete odds with how nationalist elites in conventional cases tend to operate. By the time Stalin took over and began reversing some of Lenin's policies, the local identities were already set in stone. Martin Malia argued that the Soviet Union was doomed from the beginning because communism was beyond reform. Yet we know that Deng Xiaoping was able to achieve that in China, which also started out communist. The point is that China managed to implement the use of Mandarin as a lingua franca from the beginning.[376] David Remnick argued that Soviet Union was doomed due to corrupt leadership. The fact is that corrupt leadership can be remedied through a change of government. The absolute disintegration of the state itself into smaller pieces is not an exclusive consequence of corruption. Fred Weir, David Kotz, Stephen Kotkin, and Branko Milanovic argued that ethnic separatists exploited the turbulent economic and political landscape in the dying days of the Soviet Union to create ethnically distinct nation-states. The fact is that ethnic separatism has surfaced in many countries to varying degrees of intensity *irrespective* of the state of that country's economy. Britain had to deal with the Scottish independence referendum in 2014.[377] Spain had to deal with the Catalan independence referendum in 2017.[378]

Conventional scholarship has overlooked that the fundamental reason why the Soviet Union was always going to be a difficult experiment to begin with. Not necessarily for ideological reasons, or political reasons, or even ethnic reasons. But because Soviet leaders, with or without realising, had concentrated all their effort trying to build a *state*. What they ultimately failed to build was a *nation*. The Baltic states *never* wanted to be a part of the Soviet Union from the start. Latvia, Lithuania and Estonia each had its own language written in a variety of the Latin script, generally associated with Catholic and Protestant varieties of Christianity. These nations were *dragged* into the Soviet experiment due to the Molotov-Ribbentrop Pact (1939) between Stalin and Hitler. The Turkic states *never* wanted to be in either, as they were Muslim, spoke Persian and Turkic languages and wrote using a variant of the Arabic script. Mirsaid Sultan-Galiev's demands for greater autonomy in 1922 and the Basmachi rebellion from 1918 to 1931 are manifestations of Muslim resentment for the Soviet experiment. In short, the Soviet Union was an assorted mishmash of conflicting identities from the very beginning. In 1922, when Stalin feared that demands for regional autonomy would dissolve "...our federation into pieces",[379] little did he know that 69 years later, in 1991, his federation would fall into pieces.

If Soviet leaders had been cleverer, they would have pursued rigorous linguistic assimilation from the beginning. First, they only began shifting the language policy in 1937 when it was too late. Second, they started imposing the Cyrillic writing system, which was a distinct marker of the Orthodox Christian identity. This was never going to be well-received by non-Orthodox non-Russian minorities, without giving them the sense that they were living as subordinates under Russian colonial rule. It is more practical to enforce a new national language than to enforce a new script on an existing language. With a new national language, the new generation of youth gets taught the new language and grows up speaking it with native level proficiency. With only enforcing a new script, the youth learns two languages side by side and sees that his native language uses a script that represents a foreign religion.

All that these paradoxical language policy shifts did was that they ended up assimilating the ethnic elites in the end, as was evident from Nurmakov and Tadzhiev's statements. The Soviet Union went out of its way to create and preserve satellite nations that did not need reinforcement. It was strange that they first suppressed the Russian language only to later end up embracing it. It was not Mikhail Gorbachev's *glasnost* or *perestroika* that broke the Soviet Union into piece. The patchwork for eventual disintegration was present from the beginning. The observations from the aftermath of the Cold War are clear. Single nations with *one language* kept apart by Soviet-led communism such as (West and East) Germany and (North and South) Yemen ended up reunifying as one. Multiple nations with multiple languages kept together by the Soviet-led communism such as Czechoslovakia, Yugoslavia, and the Soviet Union itself broke up into smaller pieces. This pattern of *reunification* and *disintegration* is most revealing. Yet this point has been overlooked by both camps of historians, the Cold War historians and the Soviet Union historians. Ethnic diversity within a state's population is not an automatic reason for that state to collapse and disintegrate. Workable national identities can be - indeed *have been* - forged despite ethnic differences.

As evident from the case of Hebrew in Israel, when there is a shared historical narrative and a shared language, the nation works. In Pakistan's case, there was a shared historical narrative built on strong identification with the Arabic script, so that formula worked out well for most ethnic groups, yet by definition, precluded the ethnic Bengalis and they separated. No doubt, national integration is *best* achieved through a shared cultural basis, embodied in a shared history and the proper institutionalisation and promotion of a shared national language from the founding period of the nation-state. When implemented correctly, it is shared language that provides the most efficient means to articulate and harness national cohesion, sociability, and cultural homogeneity. Eliezer Ben Yehuda in the Israeli case and Muhammad Ali Jinnah in the Pakistani case knew this. The Soviet state, by contrast, never had the right policies in place to make this happen. Under Lenin, the idea was to provide the socialist republics maximum political and linguistic autonomy which ended up reinforcing their senses of national identities. Under Stalin, this policy of linguistic autonomy began to be reversed as Soviet subjects underwent a process of 'Russification'. This was a bad combination of policies. It is not surprising that when the USSR collapsed, the end result was 15 nation-states that were once 'socialist republics' under the former Soviet federal structure.

6

CONCLUSION

LINGUISTIC ROOTS OF NATIONALISM

Many great historians, sociologists, and political theorists have discussed at length the concept of nations and nationalism. Ernest Gellner, Benedict Anderson, Isaiah Berlin, Eric Hobsbawm, Anthony D. Smith, Ernest Renan, and Hugh Seton-Watson among others, are examples. Their ideas were discussed in the first chapter *Nationalism: Cavemen to Countrymen*. Many great linguists and cognitive scientists have discussed at length the uniqueness of human language and the sociability made possible by, and expressed in, linguistic communities. Noam Chomsky, Steven Pinker, John McWhorter, Michael C. Corballis, Michael Tomasello, and Daniel Everett among others, are examples. Their ideas were discussed in the second chapter, *Language: Armoury of the Mind*. The following three chapters drew on the themes articulated in these initial chapters to present a series of case studies concerned with the place and role of linguistic community – its conception, formulation, and implementation – in instances of successful, more or less successful, and ultimately failed, state-formation.

As this concluding chapter proceeds to summarise our findings and draws its conclusions, it is entirely appropriate to ask why the argument presented in this book should be of value. The point of any new historical or philosophical work is to evaluate the ideas put forward by other scholars, and to seek to fill any gaps that may exist within our shared areas of research. Renewed interpretation, after all, remains the backbone of advancing human understanding across all academic disciplines. In keeping with that tradition, this book (originally the subject of my PhD thesis) has been re-produced as a modest contribution to the combined study of language and nationalism. Its intent is to add new emphasis to the centrality of shared language in the human experience of identity and community. As such, it emphasises the conditions and content of various dimensions of group identity which nationalist movements have been known to evoke in their quest for statehood.

In reading its central claims (as with *any* theoretical work), it is as important to understand what this book *does not* argue, as it is to understand what it *does* argue. No serious author wants her or his argument to be misunderstood, misrepresented or taken out of context. To eliminate any ambiguity, it is crucial to note that this book does not argue that language is, or that it should be, the *exclusive* ingredient in the mobilisation of nations and the maintenance of national identities. On the contrary, as explored in chapter one, nations and national identities *can be*, and often *are*, premised upon a range of different cultural configurations. Their core ingredients can, and certainly do, vary from case to case, and may include one or more ethnicities, one or more religions, or a political ideology. Likewise, this book does not argue that each self-conscious nation has, or that it should have, a sovereign state of its own. On the contrary, as also explored in chapter one, nations *can*, and often *do*, exist without their own sovereign states. Inversely, states *can*, and often *do*, exist without constituting a single nation. Often states comprise of collections of multiple *sub*-national identities, with an overarching *supra*-national identity holding its citizens together. What this book *does* argue is that language, as explored in the second chapter is, in a *real* sense, the primary enabling condition of human identity and sociability. So, through the existence of various languages, it is central to the formation of *particular* communities and *particular* group identities.

CONCLUSION

This centrality finds one important expression in the possibility and progress of nationalist projects. This is especially so within context of the rise of the nation-state where it may be utilised to mobilise the masses into a common cultural form (nation) in order to integrate them into a common political form (state).

To that end, language remains the most viable tool for nationalists who aim to achieve that combined *cultural-political* form. The conceptual framework that underpins this book's argument is laid down in the initial two chapters. The first chapter discusses nationalism. It defines its key concepts and, in a general way, looks into the ways that political nationalists seek to mobilise the masses into a common cultural form *in order to* integrate them into a common political form. The second chapter deals with language. Again, by defining and elaborating those key concepts on which its unique features arise. In doing so, it shows the interconnection of language and sociable human community, allowing us to see how nationalism and a common language come together in a mutually complimentary fashion. Following on from that, the third, fourth and fifth chapters present case studies that provide robust support to the central claims that underpin this book's argument.

As shown in chapter one, a nation is a collection or "imagined community" of humans with a shared past. This point has, in different terms, been articulated by many scholars including Gellner, Anderson, Herder, Kohn, Berlin, Hobsbawm, Seton-Watson, Lewis, and Smith. Likewise, a state is a sovereign territory within which rulers have a monopoly over the legitimate use of force, as elegantly argued by Weber. Human identity is a *multitiered* phenomenon and can involve ethnicity, religion, sect, or culture. Nationalism, as a political concept, seeks to connect the nation with the state. As Ernest Gellner, Eric Hobsbawm, and Benedict Anderson have all argued, nationalism emerged in response to the transition of human societies from being primarily agrarian to complex industrial (and as such "modern") societies. The study of nationalism is divided into two main camps, primordialists and modernists, that have long been considered mutually exclusive, but are not.

The human tendency to identify with particular cultural in-groups is primordial. Yet the idea that the rulers of a given population must *also* be from the *same* cultural settings as their subjects is, in fact, a recent and modern phenomenon. Seeing nationalism as *either* primordial *or* modern overlooks this point. Many ancient to medieval people would in fact satisfy almost all of the criteria of a *nation* that Herder, Kohn, Berlin, Gellner, Hobsbawm, Seton-Watson, and Smith, put forward. Yet, with the exception of the Jewish people, *most* ancient nations were not necessarily nationalists and were not actively seeking to achieve sovereign statehood. This makes the Jewish case unique as arguably the world's oldest continuous form of nationalism. It sought territorial sovereignty in Jerusalem and had a scriptural mandate to achieve it. States too can be said to be primordial. Human societies have been organised in many ways, though in the western tradition that leads us into the era of modern nationalisms. It is common to speak of *ancient* city-states, *medieval* empires, and *modern* nation-states, as paradigmatic forms. But in the most general sense, both nations *and* states are ancient and primordial, while what is modern is the concept of the *nation-state* which seeks to bind the two together. This interpretation helps reconcile the primordialist and modernist camps of nationalism.

As shown in chapter two *Language: Armoury of the Mind*, Noam Chomsky has argued that the sudden emergence of language in humans less than 100,000 years ago resulted in the parallel emergence of rapid sophisticated cultural activity, otherwise absent or severely limited in earlier human ancestors. Whether or not this theory is correct, it is certain that we observe the advent of the writing systems, the print revolution, and in our own times the digital revolution. Each of these linguistic turning points has resulted in spectacular advances in our ability to record our experiences and convey them for use by future generations. This constant feedback loop remains the backbone of our evolution from cavemen, to countrymen. Language, as a concept, may be considered as simply human language, as a specific human language, or as a content-based domain of specialised terminology. Each of these senses is relevant to organising humans into sociable and political communities, and each can, and typically does, play a role in personal and group identity formation.

During the age of empires in the old world order, control over territory was ultimately maintained through force. Loyalty to the state was not simply *expected*, it was *demanded*. Territorial borders were not fixed, but instead, constantly shrank and expanded based on the outcomes of perpetual warfare. It did not always matter whether people spoke the same language or not, whether they had the same legal rights or not, whether they were of the same religion or cultural settings or not. They were brought together, and kept together, under the rule of whichever dynasty or regime conquered and subjugated them. Ancient empires like Egypt, Assyria, Babylon, Persia, Greece and Rome were by and large expansionist *states*, but not necessarily expansionist *nations*. The assimilation of conquered subjects was the exception, rather than the rule. When it did occur as state policy, it was generally of a *linguistic* nature, such as Aramaic replacing Hebrew as the language of the Jews under Babylonian captivity (597-539 BCE).

The religious beliefs of conquered people were often tolerated as long as those beliefs were not motivating the conquered subjects to rebel against their conquering rulers. When rebellions did occur, such as Carthage against Rome during the Punic Wars (264-146 BCE), or the Maccabean revolt against the Seleucids (167-160 BCE), or the Jewish zealots against Rome (66-136 CE), the imperial rulers cracked down harshly on the rebels. The Roman destruction of the Jewish Temple in 70 CE is a prime example. In ancient empires, the cultural assimilation of conquered people was not always a strict priority for several reasons: 1) In ideological terms, the rulers did not govern by popular consent, but by divine right, so it did not matter if the subjugated people were from the ruler's cultural in-group or not, 2) Literacy and education were not available to the commoner, so there was no medium through which to assimilate the populations *even if* the rulers wanted to, and 3) There was no mass media, so people living in one corner of an empire often had little or no clue about what people in another part of the same empire were like culturally. People's sense of community as something above and over a community of force was as such *local* and *actual,* as opposed to *translocal* and *imagined.*

From the early to high Middle Ages, the only form of cultural assimilation that did occur, was predominantly centred around religion. For instance, the Catholic Holy Roman Empire, the Orthodox Byzantine Empire, and the Islamic Umayyad and Abbasid Empires, are prime examples of imperial regimes that have left behind their religious footprints. It is no surprise that the present-day nation-states of Europe that happen to be predominantly Catholic are based on territories once under the rule of the Holy Roman Empire. Those that happen to be Orthodox were once part of the Byzantine Empire. Those that happen to be of a Protestant variety are the ones that broke apart from Catholicism following the advent of Protestant Reformation from 1517 onwards. The Muslim nation-states across North Africa and the Middle East were once part of many great Islamic empires of the past, of which the Umayyads and the Abbasids are two of the earliest examples. In Europe, following the Reformation, many regions were plunged into the Catholic-Protestant wars of religion that went on well past the Treaty of Westphalia (1648) which is often somewhat exaggeratedly thought of by contemporary historians as the major turning point that established territorial sovereignty in Europe.

That treaty certainly tried to do so, but was not at all successful in enforcing its intent. Early modern mercantile empires like Britain, France, Spain, Portugal, Russia, and the Ottomans were both empires as well as nations. Yet they all had different attitudes towards the assimilation of their diverse subjects. Britain established many settler colonies in its own cultural and linguistic image. The United States, Canada, Australia, New Zealand, and the Falkland Islands are examples of this. The English language was transferred to these regions as a result. France transferred the French language to its colonial possessions in North America, Sub-Saharan Africa, and places like

Mauritius. The same was true of the Spaniards and the Portuguese, who divided up most of South America among themselves with the Treaty of Tordesillas (1494) two years after the discovery of the New World by Christopher Columbus.

It was a *fundamentally* different world to the one we live in. Ours begins in the aftermath of World War II (1937-1945) that resulted in the United States and the Soviet Union emerging as competing superpowers. The rules-based world order that we often take for granted is based on the Kellogg-Briand Pact (1928) and United Nations Charter (1945) which sought to prohibit the acquisition of new territory by force. It sought to turn war into a measure of *last* resort, as opposed to first resort, as the case had been in the old world order. This argument has been well made by scholars of international law, Oona Hathaway and Scott Shapiro. Yet many wars have been fought since World War II despite this prohibition. The Arab-Israeli Wars (1948, 1956, 1967, 1973, 1982 and 2006), the Korean War (1950-1953), the Vietnam War (1955-1975), the India-Pakistan Wars (1947, 1965, 1971 and 1999), the Soviet-Afghan War (1979-1989), the Gulf War (1990-1991), the War on Terror in Afghanistan (2002), and the Iraq War (2003) are prime examples as, of course, are the various instances of US intervention in Latin America. Even the acquisition of territorial gains as the result of war have continued to happen despite the claimed rules-based world order. India's annexation of Goa from Portugal in 1961, Israel's conquest of East Jerusalem from Jordan in 1967 and its annexation in 1980, and Russia's plebiscite enfolded annexation of the Crimean Peninsula in 2014 are prime examples.

Critics would be within reason to ask if the rules-based world order has changed anything at all for the course of human history. Yet the fact remains, before the United Nations Charter, the world was more or less in a *perpetual* state of war. From the birth of human civilisation in Ancient Sumeria around 3,200 BCE until present-day, there has hardly been a period where wars were not being fought and territorial borders were not shrinking and expanding as a result. Warfare was not only frequent, it was also considered indisputably normal. At the very least this, arguably, is no longer the case. The rules-based world order has put a globally binding legal architecture in place that 195 nation-states of the United Nations are signatories to. Wars are at least no longer glorified for their own sake, nor seen as proof of one's camaraderie and heroism. World leaders now typically (though not always) opt for diplomacy *before* resorting to the use of violence to end disputes. There is certainly no shortage of international treaties and conventions. Wars of direct territorial annexation have now become the exception, rather than the rule.

It is this current world order based on a UN Charter that in theory prohibits warfare, the rise of mass media, the spread of democratic principles and mass literacy which make it impossible for rulers to simply force themselves onto unwilling groups of people, or to assimilate them into a common culture through coercion. Achieving national and cultural homogeneity through ethnic cleansing is not something that can get around international condemnation. The case of the Myanmar government and its Rohingya population is a prime example. Language, then, remains the most attractive tool for both nation-building and state-building in the post-industrial modern world. The three case studies presented in the thesis looked at three different attitudes towards the use of language by three different nationalist movements, which resulted in three different outcomes.

As argued in chapter three *Case Study 1: How Hebrew re-created the Jewish State*, when rigorous promotion of a single national language is combined with a powerful narrative about a shared past, the end result is likely to be the successful mobilisation and maintenance of a common national identity, despite internal ethnic diversity. The Zionist movement provided the narrative of Jewish struggle for independence as an ancient phenomenon, but its pioneers Leon Pinsker and Theodor Herzl had no plans to create homogenous linguistic communities. They had assumed that the narrative of Jewish suffering, diaspora and the yearning to return to Jerusalem and the hills of Zion would be sufficient to bind together the Jewish settlers in historic Palestine as one. What the early Zionist pioneers had paid little to no attention to was the presence of Sephardic (North African,

Greek and Turkish) Jews nor to Mizrahi (Middle Eastern, Persian and Subcontinental) Jews. It was ultimately the revival of Hebrew by Eliezer Ben Yehuda that managed to bring together Jews of Ashkenazi, Sephardic, Mizrahi, Ethiopian, and other ethnic varieties together as *Israelis*. In arguing as much, chapter three excludes the West Bank and the Gaza Strip as part of the Israeli nation because the Palestinian Arabs who live in these disputed territories are neither citizens of Israel, nor vote in Israeli elections. Only the Arab Israelis who reside within Israel proper and make up a fifth of the country's population do. So, the chapter focuses on the nation-building experience *within* Israel proper as both a Jewish and democratic state with civic rights extended to its Arab and Druze minorities.

As argued in chapter four *Case Study 2: How Urdu turned East Pakistan into Bangladesh*, when rigorous promotion of a single national language is combined with a powerful nationalist mythology that only some groups of the (aspiring) state can immediately relate to, but not others (because of the pressures of ethnic distinctness, a separate interpretation of the past and different language with its own separate script), then the national experiment can fail. The ethnic speakers of Pashto, Punjabi, Sindhi, Urdu, and other regional varieties managed to find common meaning in the notion that the Muslims of the Subcontinent were a single nation, because their languages either did not have written scripts, or had the modified right-to-left Arabic script, or made the shift from a non-Arabic to the Arabic script. They had interacted with each other through history. So, founder Muhammad Ali Jinnah's experiment to have Urdu only as the state language worked reasonably well for the West Pakistanis when combined with a shared national mythology. In this national mythology, the Arabic script was seen as the ultimate marker of the Muslim identity. The Bengalis had too distinct a sense of their own identity to simply be absorbed into the Pakistani national narrative. It was the fact that their individual and group identity was rooted in their own distinct Bengali language, written in a variety of the left-to-right Brahmi script seen by Muslims as a marker of the Hindu identity, that grounded their demands for language recognition. This was at first resisted by the Pakistani government and later granted in 1956. Though by that time it was too late. The end result was the eventual secession of Bangladesh which occurred in 1971.

As argued in chapter five *Case Study 3: How Russian ended the Soviet Experiment*, the early Soviet leaders knew from the beginning that they had inherited an ethnically and religiously diverse population from the Tsarist Russian Empire they replaced in 1917. There was an absence of a common national identity within the colossal landmass that became the Soviet Union. But since the Soviet Union was based on Marxist ideology, its pioneers were both egalitarian and optimistic in their thinking. Lenin had hoped that the ethnic, linguistic, and religious divisions would eventually be overcome, not through forced assimilation, but through the embrace of communist ideals of liberation from class struggles. By comparison to the non-negotiable attitudes of Eliezer Ben Yehuda in the case of Hebrew in Israel and Muhammad Ali Jinnah in the case of Urdu in Pakistan, Lenin went the *opposite* direction and thought that by allowing each of USSR's 15 socialist republics to celebrate their local languages, ethnicities, and regional cultures, they would come to respect the Soviet experiment without seeing it as a foreign occupier dominated by ethnic Russians.

Stalin was not different from other nationalists, in that, he *did* realise the need for a common language and a shared past to hold the Soviet nation together, the difference was, he wanted it to happen naturally. By the time Stalin took over and began Russification through the cyrillisation of ethnic languages within the USSR, people's senses of their ethnic distinctness had already been reinforced. While these sub-national differences were not the primary contributing factor for the collapse of the supra-national Soviet state, they did create a fragile national patchwork. By the time Gorbachev came into power in 1985 and began implementing economic and social reforms at the climax of the Cold War with the United States, the Soviet Union collapsed and fractured into 15 distinct nation-states.

The conclusion from the initial two chapters on nationalism and language, combined with the three comparative case studies of

Hebrew, Urdu and Russian is clear: From ancient city-states to medieval empires, rulers in the old world order sought to integrate the masses into common *political forms*. Dynasts tended to rule by divine right and demanded loyalty by use of force. Organising their subjects into a common cultural form was not always needed. Most ancient city-states and medieval empires were multiethnic and multireligious. People's cultural identities were *generally* defined by religion. Empires began to collapse as the nation-state emerged under the dynamic economic, social and political conditions of modernity. Neither exclusive appeals to religious identities nor demanded loyalties to undemocratic dynasties were viable tools for state building. It was a shared language that was needed.

It was when the multiethnic, multireligious empires had begun collapsing that shared language combined with a shared historical narrative became the most viable tools for parallel nation-building at the cultural level, and state-building at the political level. Both before and after statehood, nationalist movements have tended to utilise language to keep the nation (cultural form) bound together with the state (political form). In many cases it works. In other cases it partly works. In yet other cases it fails altogether. As seen in case study one, the Zionist nationalists had a powerful narrative about the past, while lexicographer Eliezer Ben Yehuda had the revived Hebrew language. The two worked hand in hand to integrate the ethnically diverse Ashkenazim, Sephardim, Mizrahim, Ethiopian, and other Jews into a common *cultural-political* form as Israelis. As seen in case study two, Muslim nationalists in the Subcontinent had a reactionary historical narrative that glorified the Urdu language written in a modified version of the right-to-left Arabic script. The Bengali language was written in the left-to-right Brahmi script, which Muslim nationalists associated as a marker of the Hindu identity. In the end they seceded to create Bangladesh. The formula worked for the rest of Pakistan's ethnicities, but not for the Bengalis because Muslim nationalists deployed a language and historical narrative that half its population did not relate to. As seen in case study three, Bolshevik nationalists lacked a historical narrative from the beginning, though they certainly had an idea of a triumphant future. The basis for creating the Soviet Union was ideological, as opposed to cultural. It was based on the idea of emancipation from class-based identities and as such, from class struggle. The Soviet Union *neither* had a historical narrative about a shared past, *nor* did its early pioneers make it a priority to enforce a common language on the population. After first allowing multiple nations and languages to grow within Soviet society, they began to gradually assimilate their non-Russian subjects into a common Russified Soviet identity. This reversal of language policies backfired. The formula failed because Soviet nationalism did not manage to effectively "imagine" a shared history nor, even more fundamentally, to implant a shared vernacular language.

No doubt, similar comparative analyses could be conducted across many other cases of nation-building and state-formation processes around the world. Members of a nation cannot opt-in or opt-out of an ethnicity because group membership here is usually determined by ancestry. It is either there by birth, or it is not. Members of a nation cannot simply convert to or apostate from a religion as that is a matter of life and death. Neither can people be expected to voluntarily give up their beliefs, nor can governments get away with forcing people to convert to a particular belief system as was the case during the heydey of Christian and Islamic rule from the early to late Middle Ages. Yet, in an age where the general intent of government is to rule by popular consent, there is a pressing need to mobilise the masses into a shared consciousness that is both cultural and political at the same time. Neither ethnicity nor religion can serve this purpose on their own. This is why the combination of a shared history as grounded in and articulated through a shared language has been such a powerful tool for nationalist movements since the rise of the nation-state in helping create and preserve national identities. It is hoped that the argument presented within this book will inspire other researchers to continue their exploration of other aspects of the combined study of nationalism and language, as well as to fill any gaps in our shared areas of research.

NOTES

1. Gellner, E. (1983). *Nations and Nationalism*. Cornell University Press, p.1
2. Ibid.
3. Greene, R. L. (2011). *You are what you speak: Grammar grouches, language laws and the politics of identity*. Black, p.133
4. Berlin, I., Hardy, H., Hausheer, R., & Marr, A. (2013). *The Proper Study of Mankind: An Anthology of Essays*. Vintage Books, p.590
5. Birgerson, S. M. (2002). *After the breakup of a multi-ethnic empire: Russia, successor states and Eurasian security*. Praeger, p.51
6. Ibid.
7. Minogue, K. R. (1967). *Nationalism*. Methuen, p.57
8. Ibid.
9. Renan, E. & Giglioli, M. F. (2018). *What is a Nation?: And other Political Writings*. Columbia University Press, p.19
10. Balakrishnan, G. & Anderson, B. R. (2012). *Mapping the Nation*. Verso, p.255
11. Hobsbawm, E. J. & Ranger, T. O. (1985). *The Invention of Tradition*. Cambridge University Press, p.1
12. Gellner, E. (1983). *op. cit.*, p.6
13. Smith, A. D. (1993). *National Identity*. University of Nevada Press, p.43
14. Kedourie, E. (1962). *Nationalism*. Praeger, p.75
15. Anderson, B. & Perkins, C. (1991). *op. cit.*, pp.5-6
16. Ibid., p.6
17. Lewis, B. (2001). *The Multiple Identities of the Middle East*. Schocken Books, p.81
18. See for instance the works of Nasif Al-Yaziji, Butrus Al-Bustani, Faris Shidyaq, Yaqub Sarruf, Faris Nimr, Jurji Zaydan, Sati' Al-Husri and Michel Aflaq.
19. Gellner, E. (1983). *op. cit.*, p.3
20. The concept of primordialism was first argued by Edward Shils and Clifford Geertz during the 1950s.
21. Gellner, E. (1983). *op. cit.*, p.3
22. Barfield, T. J. (2008). *The Dictionary of Anthropology*. Blackwell, p.445
23. Klabbers, J. (2016). *International Law Documents*. Cambridge University Press, p.2
24. Tilly, C. (1985). *Bringing the State back in*. Cambridge University Press, p.47
25. Ibid.
26. Klabbers, J. (2016). *op. cit.*, p.3
27. Senellart, M., Ewald, F., & Fontana, A. (2009). *Security, Territory, Population Lectures*

at the College De France, 1977–78. Palgrave Macmillan UK, p.109

28 Narak, K. (1954). *Identity and Continuity of States in Public International Law*, p.178

29 Wimmer, A. & Feinstein, Y. (2010, 10). The Rise of the Nation-State across the World, 1816 to 2001. *American Sociological Review,75*(5), p.765

30 Greene, R. L. (2011). *op. cit.*, pp.132-133

31 Fiala, A. G. (2004). *Practical Pacifism.* Algora Publishing, p.63

32 https://www.bbc.com/news/uk-scotland-29270441 (Retrieved on 2017, March 04)

33 https://www.statista.com/chart/11323/catalan-referendum_-90-back-independence/ (Retrieved on 2017, October 02)

34 It is often assumed that Pakistan was created by a form of religious Islamic nationalism. Yet this only tells half the story. If it was a form of Islamic nationalism, its membership would be open to all Muslims, including for instance, Arabs, Turks, Malays, Somalis, Indonesians and other ethnic or national groups. Islam does promote the concept of the 'ummah' and views all Muslims, regardless of ethnicity or race as being a single nation. Yet the form of religious nationalism subscribed to by Muslim nationalists in British India was limited to the ethnic groups within the Subcontinent. In this sense, it was a form of *regional* religious nationalism.

35 Gans, C. (2003). *The Limits of Nationalism.* Cambridge University Press, p.10

36 Most anglosphere nations offer migrants with desired professional skills to settle in their midst.

37 Rahman, T. (1997, 09). Language and Ethnicity in Pakistan. *Asian Survey,* 37(9), p.834

38 Israeli historian Shlomo Sand has attempted to discredit the validity of the Jewish national identity. His arguments do not strike me as sound.

39 Huntington, S. P. (1996). *The Clash of Civilisations and the Remaking of World Order.* Simon & Schuster Paperbacks, p.43

40 http://www.pewresearch.org/fact-tank/2013/08/13/spanish-is-the-most-spoken-non-english-language-in-u-s-homes-even-among-non-hispanics/ (Retrieved on 2015, March 06)

41 Dukes, P. (2001). *A History of Russia: Medieval, Modern, Contemporary, c. 882-1996.* Palgrave, p.44

42 https://www.washingtonpost.com/news/global-opinions/wp/2018/07/10/why-calling-france-the-last-african-team-in-the-world-cup-is-problematic/ (Retrieved on 2018, July 10)

43 Berlin, I., Hardy, H., Hausheer, R., & Marr, A. (2013). *op. cit.*, p.590

44 Gellner, E. (1983). *op. cit.*, p.6

45 https://www.continentaltelegraph.com/brexit/we-can-hope-brexit-as-the-beginning-of-the-end-of-the-european-ideal/ (Retrieved on 2019, January 26)

NOTES

46 Gellner, E. (1983). *op. cit.*, p.6
47 Ibid., p.2
48 This assertion is based on the way Israel defines itself. It is true that a fifth of its population are Arab Israelis with parliamentary representation, but Israel has continuously defined itself as a *Jewish* State. This makes its Jewish character the primary form of its national identity just as, in Great Britain's case, the *English* identity functions as first amongst equals with respect to the Scottish, Welsh and Irish identities. The Palestinian populations in the disputed territories of the West Bank and the Gaza Strip have not been factored into this assertion. The Palestinians see themselves as a separate nation and the Israelis see them as a separate nation.
49 Gellner, E. (1983). *op. cit.*, p.2
50 Wimmer, A., & Feinstein, Y. (2010, 10). *op. cit.*, p.764
51 Pomfret, R. W. (1995). *The Economies of Central Asia*. Princeton University Press, p.21
52 Wimmer, A., & Feinstein, Y. (2010, 10). *op. cit.*, p.765
53 See chapter four: Case Study 2 for a detailed discussion on the partition of the Subcontinent.
54 Wimmer, A., & Feinstein, Y. (2010, 10). *op. cit.*, p.785
55 Ibid.
56 Ibid.
57 Tapper, R. (2011). *Tribe and State in Iran and Afghanistan*. Routledge, p.194
58 Wimmer, A., & Feinstein, Y. (2010, 10). *op. cit.*, p.786
59 https://www.bbc.com/news/uk-scotland-29270441 (Retrieved on 2017, March 04)
60 https://www.statista.com/chart/11323/catalan-referendum_-90-back-independence/ (Retrieved on 2017, October 02)
61 Gellner, E. (1983). *op. cit.*, pp.4-5
62 Ibid.
63 http://www.pewglobal.org/2017/02/01/language-the-cornerstone-of-national-identity/ (Retrieved on 2017, February 01)
64 Birgerson, S. M. (2002). *op. cit.*, p.51
65 Ayres, A. (2009). *Speaking like a State: Language and Nationalism in Pakistan*. Cambridge University Press, p.3
66 http://www.2think.org/kom.shtml (Retrieved on 2015, January 04)
67 https://www.nextnature.net/2009/10/the-world-without-technology/ (Retrieved on 2018, December 28)
68 Mckeon, R. (1946, 10). Aristotle's Conception of Language and the Arts of Language. *Classical Philology, 41*(4), p.193

69   Safran, W. & Laponce J.A. (2005). *Language, Ethnic Identity and the State*. Routledge., p.1

70   Fishman, J. A. (1999). *Handbook of Language and Ethnic Identity*. Oxford University Press., p.80

71   http://penelope.uchicago.edu/josephus/ant-1.html (Retrieved on 2013, February 02)

72   https://www.bible.com/bible/111/GEN.11.NIV (Retrieved on 2017, April 21)

73   Kortlandt, F., Wiedenhof, J. M., Lubotsky, A. M., Schaeken, J., Derksen, R., & Siebinga, S. M. (2008). *Evidence and counter-evidence: Essays in honour of Frederik Kortland*. Rodopi, p.101

74   Ibid.

75   Trousdale, G. (2010). *An Introduction to English Sociolinguistics*. Edinburgh University Press, p.4

76   Ibid., p.5

77   Montgomery, M. (1995). *An Introduction to Language and Society*. Routledge, p.xxv

78   Fromkin, V. (2010). *An Introduction to Language*. Nelson Education, p.23

79   Ibid.

80   See the controversies that became manifest across two centuries in Europe with John Wyclif's efforts to translate the Bible in the late 14th century, through William Tyndale's efforts in 1520s to the eventual success of the King James version in 1611.

81   Sedley, D. N. (2003). *Plato's Cratylus*. Cambridge University Press, p.4

82   Saussure, F. D., Bouquet, S., & Sanders, C. (2008). *Writings in General Linguistics*. Oxford University Press, p.119

83   Hamilton, W. & Bowen, F. (1861). *The Metaphysics of Sir William Hamilton*. Allyn and Bacon, p.42

84   Grégoire, J. & Jewkes, M. (2015). *Recognition and Redistribution in Multinational Federations*. Leuven University Press, p.98

85   Ibid., p.98

86   Urdu and Hindi are essentially the same language that began to emerge in the past five centuries as the result of increased contact between Muslim invaders and merchants from Arabia, Persia and Central Asia on the one hand and the local Hindu princely states on the other. Urdu is written in a modified Nastaleeq blend of the right-to-left Arabic script while Hindi is written in the Devanagari blend of the left-to-right Brahmi script. This is dealt with in chapter four: Case Study 2. At one point the language was called Hindustani. The Urdu-Hindi divide widened over time due to the rise of distinct Muslim and Hindu nationalist movements in colonial India.

87   Fromkin, V. (2010). *op. cit.*, p.23

88   Fishman, J. A. (1999). *op cit.*, p.110

NOTES

89 Denton, R. E. (2010). *Studies of Identity in the 2008 Presidential Campaign*. Lexington Books, p.155

90 Orwell, G. (2017). *1984*. Houghton Mifflin Harcourt, p.23

91 Darwin, C. (1871). *The Descent of Man*. Murray, p.53

92 Grice, P. (1991). *Studies in the way of words*. Harvard University Press, pp.29-31

93 Sterkenburg, P. V. (2008). *Unity and Diversity of Languages*. Benjamins, p.24-25

94 Corballis, M. C. (2014). *The Recursive Mind: The Origins of Human Language, Thought and Civilisation*. Princeton University Press, p.23

95 Chomsky, N., & McGilvray, J. (2012). *The Science of Language Interviews with James McGilvray*. Cambridge University Press, p.71

96 Ibid., p.13

97 McWhorter, J. (2011). *The Power Of Babel: A Natural History of Language*. Cornerstone Digital, p.8

98 Chomsky, N. & McGilvray, J. (2012). *op. cit.*, p.17

99 Pinker, S. (1995). *The Language Instinct*. Penguin Group, p.333

100 Tomasello, M. (2010). *Origins of Human Communication*. MIT Press, p.2

101 Everett, D. L. (2013). *Language: The Cultural Tool*. Profile Books, pp.67-70

102 Ibid., p.46

103 Chomsky, N. & McGilvray, J. (2012). *op. cit.*, p.17

104 http://time.com/118522/pope-corrects-israeli-leader-actually-jesus-did-not-speak-hebrew/ (Retrieved on 2014, May 27)

105 Emerton, J. A. (1961). Did Jesus Speak Hebrew? *The Journal of Theological Studies*, XII(2), pp.189-202

106 The historical accuracy of the Babylonian exile story has been challenged. See Shlomo Sand, *The Invention of the Jewish People*, (Verson, 2009). Although the presence of Jewish communities in present-day Iraq and Iran would suggest there was some movement of Jewish people out of Jerusalem and towards the east.

107 Note that internal diversity within Jews goes beyond the four categories described here. Indian Jews were generally lumped together with other Mizrahim from Yemen or Iran, but Central Asian Jews from Uzbekistan or the Chinese Jews from Kaifeng (See Moshe Bernstein in the Bibliography) are in a category of their own. Many of these, today, live in Israel as 'Israeli' citizens speaking revived Hebrew as their first language.

108 https://www.reuters.com/article/us-pope-latin/pope-ditches-latin-as-official-language-of-vatican-synod-idUSKCN0HV1O2201 41006 (Retrieved on 2016, July 17)

109 Minogue, K. R. (1967). *op. cit.*, p.57

110 Ibid.

111 https://www.jpost.com/Jewish-World/Jewish-News/This-week-in-history-Revival-of-the-Hebrew-language (Retrieved on 2017, October 12)

112 Balakrishnan, G. & Anderson, B. R. (2012). *op. cit.*, p.255

113 https://www.haaretz.com/jewish/.premium-i-found-atheism-through-judaism-1.5382662 (Retrieved on 2018, April 24)

114 https://www.sefaria.org/Shulchan_Arukh,_Even_HaEzer.44.9?lang=bi (Retrieved on 2019, May 10)

115 It must be noted that Ethiopian Jews, also known as the Beta Israel, are recognised as Jews under Israel's Right of Return despite some divergent religious and cultural practices from normative Judaism. By contrast, the Chinese Jews whose religious and cultural practices far more closely resemble that of Jews globally have the status of gentiles due to their practice of patrilocal marriage.

116 The same emic approach is taken in the next case study on the Bengali language and the secession of Bangladesh from Pakistan in 1971. This is because both the Hebrew and Bengali cases are forms of cultural nationalism. Yet the third and last case study on the Soviet Union was more of an ideological experiment, as opposed to a cultural one, so it goes beyond the emic/etic distinction. (That said, empathy has been shown to the Soviet pioneers in studying their motivations.)

117 Originally Avram (high father) and later renamed Avraham (father of many). See Genesis 17:5 for details.

118 https://www.bible.com/bible/compare/GEN.12.1-10 (Retrieved on 2013, October 19)

119 Grant, M. (1997). *The History of Ancient Israel*. Phoenix, p.41

120 https://www.bible.com/bible/111/DEU.20.NIV (Retrieved on 2012, September 16)

121 Johnson, P. (2013). *History of the Jews*. Phoenix, p.62

122 http://www.unesco.org/new/en/social-and-human-sciences/themes/international-migration/glossary/nation-state/ (Retrieved on 2018, February 16)

123 Grant, M. (1997). *op. cit.*, p.111

124 https://www.haaretz.com/archaeology/why-are-jews-called-jews-1.5410757 (Retrieved on 2018, April 10)

125 https://www.bible.com/bible/111/JDG.12.NIV (Retrieved on 2015, January 04)

126 Grant, M. (1997). *op. cit.*, p.123

127 Groups of ancient Israelites worshipping other gods has been a recurrent theme throughout Jewish history. There are many examples. Moses goes up to Mt Sinai to receive the Ten Commandments and returns back to find the Israelites resorting to idolatry by worshipping the Golden Calf (See Exodus 32:4). Some Jews had worshipped the ancient deity Baal for instance and reminded through scripture that they could not have both Yahweh and Baal as their gods, that Yahweh was a "jealous" God who wanted to be worshipped alone. (See Deuteronomy

NOTES

6:4). These acts of theological defiance have often been evoked by Rabbis to explain Jewish suffering and persecution through the centuries. Judaism is strictly monotheistic and does not entertain any form of idolatry.

128   Levine, B. A. (2005). Assyrian Ideology and Israelite Monotheism. *Iraq, 67*(01), pp.411-427

129   Benor, S., & Hary, B. H. (2018). *Languages in Jewish Communities: Past and Present*. Walter De Gruyter, p.644

130   Spolsky, B. (2014). *The Languages of the Jews*. Cambridge University Press, p.28

131   Bullock, C. H. (2007). *Introduction to the Old Testament Prophetic Books*. Moody Press, p.340

132   Saenz-Badillos, A. (1993). *A History of the Hebrew Language*. Cambridge University Press, p.202

133   Bullock, C. H. (2007). *op. cit.*, p.345

134   Ibid.

135   Spolsky, B. (2014). *op. cit.*, p.38

136   Ibid., p.52

137   Ibid.

138   Further to Jesus Christ's inability to emancipate the Jews from Roman occupation, many other reasons have been outlined by both past and present Jewish scholars to explain why he is not considered the Messiah in Judaism. His alleged divinity is one of them. While there is no clear statement within the New Testament canon that demonstrates his divinity, there were some early Christian sects that began worshipping Jesus as divine, but it was not until the Council of Nicea in 325 CE that this belief was adopted as mainstream. The Mormons and Jehovah's Witnesses still continue to reject the divinity of Jesus believing him to be a prophet and a Messiah only, much like Muslims.

139   Spolsky, B. (2014). *op. cit.*, p.64

140   Benor, S. & Hary, B. H. (2018). *op. cit.*, p.644

141   Ostler, N. (2006). *Empires of the Word: A Language History of the World*. Harper Perennial, p.80

142   Bernstein, M. Y. (2017). *Globalisation, Translation and Transmission: Sino-Judaic Cultural Identity in Kaifeng, China*. Peter Lang AG, Internationaler Verlag der Wissenschaften.

143   Gil, M. (1984). Dhimmi Donations and Foundations for Jerusalem (638-1099). *Journal of the Economic and Social History of the Orient, 27*(2), p.156

144   Siecienski, A. E. (2016). *Constantine: Religious Faith and Imperial Policy*. Ashgate, p.3

145   Freeman, C. (2011). *AD 381: Heretics, Pagans and the Christian State*. Vintage Digital, p.92

146   Mundill, R. R. (2002). *England's Jewish Solution: Experiment and Expulsion, 1262-1290*. Cambridge University Press, p.26

147 Melton, J. G. (2014). *Faiths across time: 5,000 years of Religious History.* ABC-CLIO, p.1018

148 Ibid.

149 Spolsky, B. (2014). *op. cit.*, p.99

150 Brown, M. L. (1999). *Our Hands are Stained with Blood.* Destiny Image, p.93

151 Elazar, D. J. & Cohen, S. A. (1985). *The Jewish Polity: Jewish Political Organisation from Biblical times to the Present.* Indiana University Press, p.188

152 Breger, M. J. Reiter, Y., & Hammer, L. M. (2013). *Holy places in the Israeli-Palestinian conflict: Confrontation and coexistence.* Routledge, p.68

153 Lieu, J. M., & Rogerson, J. W. (2010). *The Oxford Handbook of Biblical Studies.* Oxford University Press, p.762

154 Ibid.

155 http://www.jewishagency.org/jewish-community/content/24408 (Retrieved on 2015, June 28)

156 https://www.bible.com/bible/compare/GEN.12.1-10 (Retrieved on 2013, October 19)

157 http://www.zionism-israel.com/js/Jewish_State_29.html (Retrieved on 2015, July 01)

158 http://www.jewishagency.org/herzl/content/25311 (Retrieved on 2015, February 11)

159 Mayer, K. (1968). The Jura Problem: Ethnic Conflict in Switzerland. *Social Research,* 35(4), pp.707-741

160 https://www.jewishvirtuallibrary.org/quot-auto-emancipation-quot-leon-pinsker (Retrieved on 2016, July 19)

161 Ibid.

162 Parfitt, T. (1972) The Use of Hebrew in Palestine 1800–1822. *Journal of Semitic Studies,* 17 (2), pp.237-252

163 http://www.benyehuda.us/miketz.htm (Retrieved on 2018, November 16)

164 Tapper, A. J. (2016). *Judaisms: A twenty-first-century introduction to Jews and Jewish identities.* University of California Press, p.202

165 Zuckermann, G. (2009, 06). Hybridity versus Revivability: Multiple Causation, Forms and Patterns. *Journal of Language Contact, 2*(2), p.48

166 Fox, A., & Blau, J. (1983, 03). *The Renaissance of Modern Hebrew and Modern Standard Arabic: Parallels and Differences in the Revival of Two Semitic Languages.* Language, p.32

167 Aytürk, I. (2010, 01). Revisiting the language factor in Zionism: The Hebrew Language Council from 1904 to 1914. *Bulletin of the School of Oriental and African Studies,73*(01), p.45

168 Shivtiel, A. (1985). Languages In Contact: The Contribution Of The Arabic Language To The Revival Of Hebrew. *Journal of Semitic Studies,* XXX(1), pp.95-113

NOTES

169 Fox, A., & Blau, J. (1983, 03). *op. cit.*, p.3

170 Contrast this with chapter four: Case Study 2 which discusses the deliberate and planned imposition of the Urdu language by Muslim nationalists in the Subcontinent to forge a shared 'Pakistani' national identity. See founding figure Muhammad Ali Jinnah's emphatic statement about Urdu being the state language. This was a top-down movement where the elites decided the linguistic fate of the nation.

171 Aytürk, I. (2010, 01). *op. cit.*, p.51

172 Ibid., p.63

173 Zuckermann, G. (2006, 03). A New Vision For Israeli Hebrew. *Journal of Modern Jewish Studies*, 5(1), pp.57-71

174 Millar, R. M. (2005). *Language, Nation and Power: An Introduction*. Palgrave Macmillan., p.140

175 Netanyahu, B. (2012). *The Founding Fathers of Zionism*. Balfour Books.

176 [The Official 700 Club]. (2015, Jul 28). *The Hope: Eliezer Ben-Yehuda* [Video File]. Retrieved from https://www.youtube.com/watch?v=NQvB-djqMag

177 Ibid.

178 Ibid.

179 Ibid.

180 Aytürk, I. (2010, 01). *op. cit.*, p.45

181 Kohn, H. (1961). *The Idea of Nationalism: A Study in its Origins and Background*. Macmillan, p.6

182 This reinforces my earlier point in chapter one that, as schools of thought, primordialism and modernism are not mutually exclusive as often assumed.

183 https://www.jpost.com/Jewish-World/Jewish-News/This-week-in-history-Revival-of-the-Hebrew-language (Retrieved on 2017, October 12)

184 https://www.newyorker.com/magazine/2015/06/29/the-great-divide-books-dalrymple (Retrieved on 2017, June 19)

185 Islam, N. (1981, 02). *Islam and National Identity: The Case of Pakistan and Bangladesh*, p.62

186 Rahman, T. (1997, 09). *op. cit.*, pp.833-839

187 Ahmed, S. (2004). *Bangladesh: Past and Present*. A. P. H. Publishing, p.129

188 Toor, S. (2011). *The State of Islam: Culture and Cold War politics in Pakistan*. Pluto Press, p.25

189 Jalal, A. (1999). *The Sole Spokesman: Jinnah, the Muslim League and the demand for Pakistan*. Cambridge University Press, p.266

190 Yegar, M. (1972). *The Muslims of Burma: A Study of a Minority Group*. Otto Harrassowitz, p.96

191 Ibid.

192	Ayres, A. (2009). *op cit.*, p16
193	Toor, S. (2011). *op. cit.*, p.18
194	Ibid., p.34
195	https://www.britannica.com/place/Bangladesh/The-arts#ref997951 (Retrieved on 2019, January 04)
196	Willford, A. C. (1991). *Religious resurgence in British India: Vivekananda and the Hindu Renaissance*, p.8
197	Islam, N. (1981, 02). *op. cit.*, p.57
198	Ibid.
199	Allison, D. (1998). *Text in Education and Society*. Singapore University Press, p.240
200	This it may be argued is unavoidable in order to mark out one's unique group identity.
201	Islam, N. (1981, 02). *op. cit.*, p.57
202	Ibid.
203	Ibid.
204	Toor, S. (2011). *op. cit.*, p.26
205	Ibid.
206	Ibid.
207	Ibid., p.27
208	Rahman, T. (1997, 09). *op. cit.*, pp.833-839
209	Islam, N. (1981, 02). *op. cit.*, p.71
210	http://www.southasiaanalysis.org/paper675 (Retrieved on 2018, September 08)
211	Toor, S. (2011). *op. cit.*, p.29
212	Ibid., p.30
213	Islam, N. (1981, 02). *op. cit.*, p.63
214	Khan, Z. (1982). March movement of Bangladesh: Bengali struggle for Political Power. *The Indian Journal of Political Science*, 33(3), pp.291-322
215	Toor, S. (2011). *op. cit.*, p.19
216	Ibid., p.23
217	Ibid.
218	Ibid.
219	Ibid., p.18
220	https://storyofpakistan.com/west-pakistan-established-as-one-unit (Retrieved on 2016, April 15)
221	https://nation.com.pk/13-Jan-2018/past-in-perspective?show=previewc=18388168508466929728 (Retrieved on 2018, January 13)
222	Umar, B. (1998). The Anti-Heroes of the Language Movement. *Economic and*

NOTES

       Political Weekly, 33(1), pp.636-637

223   Toor, S. (2011). *op. cit.,* p.34

224   Islam, N. (1981, 02). *op. cit.,* p.62

225   Schuman, H. (1972, 09). A Note on the Rapid Rise of Mass Bengali Nationalism in East Pakistan. *American Journal of Sociology, 78*(2), pp.290-298

226   Khan, Z. (1982). *op. cit.,* p.291-322

227   Islam, N. (1981, 02). *op. cit.,* p.60

228   https://www.thedailystar.net/news/six-points-and-june-7-1966 (Retrieved on 2013, June 06)

229   Ibid.

230   Talbot, I. (1998). *Pakistan: A Modern History.* St. Martin's Press, p.190

231   Glynn, S. (2015). *Class, ethnicity and religion in the bengali east end; a political history.* Manchester University Press, p.57

232   Ibid.

233   Ibid., p.58

234   Ibid.

235   Ibid.

236   https://www.bbc.com/news/world-asia-16207201 (Retrieved on 2015, January 04)

237   https://www.aljazeera.com/news/asia/2010/03/2010325151839747356.html (Retrieved on 2018, November 07)

238   Riaz, A. & Rahman, M. S. (2016). *Routledge Handbook of Contemporary Bangladesh.* Routledge/Taylor & Francis, p.43

239   Almond, G. A. & Coleman, J. S. (1970). *The Politics of Developing Areas.* Princeton University Press, p.161

240   Islam, N. (1981, 02). *op. cit.,* p.58

241   Ibid., p.59

242   http://news.bbc.co.uk/2/hi/south_asia/8425744.stm (Retrieved on 2017, August 10)

243   One side in this civil war, the "White Russians" enjoyed diplomatic and military support from external powers such as the United States, Japan, France, the United Kingdom, China, Poland, Italy, Greece and Serbia.

244   Smith, H. W. (2015). *The Oxford Handbook of Modern German history.* Oxford University Press, p.594

245   Wood, J. G. (1997). *Vietnam and the Indochina conflict / John Wood.* Macmillan, p.95

246   Malik, H. (1990). *Domestic determinants of Soviet foreign policy towards South Asia and Middle East.* Macmillan, p.29

247   Fukuyama, F. (1989). *The "End of History?".* United States Institute of Peace.

248   Grant, R. (2012). *World War II: Europe*. Britannica Digital Learning, p.50

249   https://nationalinterest.org/blog/the-buzz/how-north-korean-weapons-could-start-war-the-middle-east-23251 (Retrieved on 2017, November 18)

250   Musil, J. (1995). *The End of Czechoslovakia*. CEU Press, p.1

251   Bennett, C. (1998). *Yugoslavia's Bloody Collapse: Causes, Course and Consequences*. Hurst & Company, p.12

252   Kwon, H. (2004). *Divided Korea: Longing for reunification*. Center for Korean Studies. North Park University Theological Seminary, p.184

253   Schlesinger, A. M. (2004). *The Imperial Presidency*. Houghton Mifflin, p.128

254   Ibid., p.164

255   Williams, W. A. (1972). *The Tragedy of American Diplomacy*. Dell Publications, p.70

256   Gaddis, J. L. (2007). *The Cold War*. Penguin, p.12

257   Malia, M. E. (1994). *Soviet Tragedy: A History of Socialism in Russia*. Free Press, p.492

258   Ibid., p.42

259   Ibid., p.492

260   Remnick, D. (1993). *Lenin's Tomb: The Last Days of the Soviet Empire*. Viking, p.5

261   Huntington, S. P. (1996). *op. cit.*, p.212

262   http://www.pewforum.org/2006/08/18/five-years-after-911-the-clash-of-civilizations-revisited/ (Retrieved on 2013, September 09)

263   Amalrik, A. (1981). *Will the Soviet Union survive until 1984?*. Harper Colophon Books, p.17

264   Todd, E. (1979). *The Final Fall: An Essay on the Decomposition of the Soviet Sphere*. Karz, p.229

265   Miller, C. (2016). *The Struggle to save the Soviet Economy Mikhail Gorbachev and the Collapse of the USSR*. University of North Carolina Press, p.26

266   Suny, R. G. (1994). *The Revenge of the Past Nationalism, Revolution and the Collapse of the Soviet Union*. Stanford University Press, p.111

267   Milanovic, B. (1994, 03). Perspective. *Challenge*, 37(2), p.63

268   Ibid.

269   Ibid., p.62

270   Ibid.

271   Taubman, W. (2018). *Gorbachev: His Life and Times*. W.W. Norton & Company.

272   Breslauer, G. W. (2002). *Gorbachev and Yeltsin as Leaders*. Cambridge University Press.

273   Brown, A. (2010). *The Rise and Fall of Communism*. Vintage.

274   Milanovic, B. (1994, 03). *op. cit.*, p.63

275   Kotkin, S. (2009). *Armageddon Averted: The Soviet Collapse, 1970-2000*. Oxford

NOTES

University Press, p.3

276 Ibid., p.173

277 Ibid., p.106

278 Zubok, V. M. (2009). *A Failed Empire: The Soviet Union in the Cold War from Stalin to Gorbachev*. University of North Carolina Press, p.xvii

279 Plokhy, S. (2014). *The Last Empire the Final Days of the Soviet Union*. Basic Books, p.12

280 https://sourcebooks.fordham.edu/source/nestor.asp (Retrieved on 2015, May 04)

281 Dukes, P. (2001). *A History of Russia: Medieval, Modern, Contemporary, c. 882-1996*. Palgrave, p.7

282 https://community.dur.ac.uk/a.k.harrington/origirus.html (Retrieved on 2019, January 05)

283 Dukes, P. (2001). *op. cit.*, p.20

284 http://econc10.bu.edu/economic_systems/NatIdentity/FSU/Russia/prerevolution/vladimir.htm (Retrieved on 2018, September 25)

285 Dukes, P. (2001). *op. cit.*, p.11

286 Freeze, G. L. (2009). *Russia: A History*. Oxford University Press, p.13

287 Dukes, P. (2001). *op. cit.*, p.26

288 Ibid., p.44

289 Freeze, G. L. (2009). *op. cit.*, p.73

290 Comrie, B., Hewitt, B. G., & Payne, J. R. (1981). *The Languages of the Soviet Union*, CUP Archive, p.22

291 Freeze, G. L. (2009). *op. cit.*, p.85

292 Comrie, B., Hewitt, B. G., & Payne, J. R. (1981). *op. cit.*, p.21

293 Freeze, G. L. (2009). *op. cit.*, p.101

294 Comrie, B., Hewitt, B. G., & Payne, J. R. (1981). *op. cit.*, p.21

295 Freeze, G. L. (2009). *op. cit.*, p.110

296 Dukes, P. (2001). *op. cit.*, p.133

297 Ibid., p.134

298 Freeze, G. L. (2009). *op. cit.*, p.199

299 https://history.state.gov/milestones/1866-1898/alaska-purchase (Retrieved on 2017, December 06)

300 Dukes, P. (2001). *op. cit.*, p.153

301 Freeze, G. L. (2009). *op. cit.*, p.267

302 Comrie, B., Hewitt, B. G., & Payne, J. R. (1981). *op. cit.*, p.21

303 Myhill, J. (2006). *Language, Religion and National Identity*. John Benjamins Publishing, p.87

304	https://history.state.gov/milestones/1830-1860/opening-to-japan (Retrieved on 2017, December 09)
305	Dukes, P. (2001). *op. cit.*, p.352
306	Comrie, B., Hewitt, B. G., & Payne, J. R. (1981). *op. cit.*, p.21
307	Azimova, N., & Johnston, B. (2012, 09). Invisibility and Ownership of Language: Problems of Representation in Russian Language Textbooks. *The Modern Language Journal*, 96(3), p.341
308	Comrie, B., Hewitt, B. G., & Payne, J. R. (1981). *op. cit.*, p.1
309	Martin, T. (1998). *The Russification of the RSFSR. Cahiers Du Monde Russe: Russie, Empire Russe*, Union Soviétique, États Indépendants, 39(1), pp.99-100
310	Comrie, B., Hewitt, B. G., & Payne, J. R. (1981). *op. cit.*, p.22
311	Martin, T. (1998). *op. cit.*, p.100
312	Ibid.
313	Ibid.
314	Comrie, B., Hewitt, B. G., & Payne, J. R. (1981). *op. cit.*, p.22
315	Ornstein, J. (1959, 03). Soviet Language Policy. *South Atlantic Bulletin*, 24(4), p.12
316	Comrie, B., Hewitt, B. G., & Payne, J. R. (1981). *op. cit.*, p.23
317	Ibid., p.22
318	Fishman, J. A., & Sebeok, T. A. (1977). *Readings in the Sociology of Language*. Mouton, p.717
319	Ornstein, J. (1959, 03). *op. cit.*, p.12
320	Zuckermann, G. (2009, 06). Hybridity versus Revivability: Multiple Causation, Forms and Patterns. *Journal of Language Contact*, 2(2), p.48
321	Toor, S. (2011). *op. cit.*, p.18
322	Ornstein, J. (1959, 03). *op. cit.*, p.12
323	Martin, T. (1998). *op. cit.*, p.100
324	Ibid.
325	Ibid.
326	Ibid., p.103
327	Ibid., p.108
328	Ornstein, J. (1959, 03). *op. cit.*, p.12
329	Marples, D. R. (2011, 06). *op. cit.*, p.464
330	Ibid., p.103
331	Martin, T. (1998). *op. cit.*, p.103
332	Comrie, B., Hewitt, B. G., & Payne, J. R. (1981). *op. cit.*, p.24
333	Ibid., p.27
334	Ibid., p.31

NOTES

335 Martin, T. (1998). *op. cit.*, p.104
336 Ibid., p.103
337 Marples, D. R. (2011, 06). *op. cit.*, p.465
338 Martin, T. (1998). *op. cit.*, p.104
339 Ibid.
340 While Urdu did not work for the ethnic Bengalis for reasons extensively discussed in chapter four, it did manage to create a culturally homogenous landscape for the various ethnic groups within Pakistan proper itself.
341 https://www.onwar.com/aced/chrono/c1900s/yr10/fbasmachi1916.htm (Retrieved on 2018, December 27)
342 Martin, T. (1998). *op. cit.*, p.106
343 Ibid.
344 Ibid., p.107
345 Ibid.
346 Ibid.
347 Ibid., p.108
348 Ibid.
349 Ibid.
350 Ibid., p.110
351 Ibid.
352 Ibid.
353 Ibid.
354 Comrie, B., Hewitt, B. G., & Payne, J. R. (1981). *op. cit.*, p.22
355 Ibid.
356 Ibid.
357 Martin, T. (1998). *op. cit.*, p.110
358 Ibid.
359 http://ccat.sas.upenn.edu/~haroldfs/540/handouts/ussr/soviet2.html (Retrieved on 2018, December 11)
360 Martin, T. (1998). *op. cit.*, p.112
361 http://factsanddetails.com/central-asia/Uzbekistan/sub8_3d/entry-4710.html (Retrieved on 2018, November 05)
362 Azimova, N. & Johnston, B. (2012, 09). *op. cit.*, p.341
363 Marples, D. R. (2011, 06). *op. cit.*, p.465
364 Azimova, N. & Johnston, B. (2012, 09). *op. cit.*, p.341
365 Ibid.
366 Holbrook, J. R. (2018). *Moscow Memoir: An American Military Attaché in the USSR*

1979-1981. Authorhouse.

367 Marples, D. R. (2011, 06). *op. cit.*, p.464
368 Ibid.
369 Ibid., p.468
370 Ibid.
371 Ibid.
372 Milanovic, B. (1994, 03). *op. cit.*, p.63
373 Ibid.
374 Ibid.
375 Grenoble, L. A. (2011). *Language Policy in the Soviet Union.* Springer., p.vii
376 Differences between the various dialects of Chinese are often as varied as the differences between the Romance languages of Europe. While Spanish, Italian and French descend from a common Latin origin, their native speakers do not automatically understand each other by default. Just as in the Romance case knowing one does not mean you know the other, the same is true of Chinese languages. What standard Mandarin does is to provide the people of China a lingua franca to communicate with each other in, and at the same time, act as the social glue that binds the Chinese identity together. This is not to suggest that present-day Chinese society is free from ethnic tensions. The struggles over Tibet and the Muslim Uighurs show that China has its own share of internal strife, but compared to the Soviet case where the state collapsed, China is still on the world map and growing stronger by the day both economically and militarily.
377 https://www.bbc.com/news/uk-scotland-29270441 (Retrieved on 2017, March 04)
378 https://www.statista.com/chart/11323/catalan-referendum_-90-back-independence/ (Retrieved on 2017, October 02)
379 Martin, T. (1998). *op. cit.*, p.100

BIBLIOGRAPHY

Anderson, B., & Perkins, C. (1991). *Imagined Communities: Reflections on the Origin & Spread of Nationalism.* Verso.

The Antiquities of the Jews - Book I. (2013, February 02). Retrieved from http://penelope.uchicago.edu/josephus/ant-1.html

Azimova, N., & Johnston, B. (2012, 09). Invisibility and Ownership of Language: Problems of Representation in Russian Language Textbooks. *The Modern Language Journal,* 96(3).

Ahmed, S. (2004). *Bangladesh: Past and Present.* A.P.H. Publishing.

Ahsan, S. B. (2013, June 06). Six Points and June 7, 1966. Retrieved from https://www.thedailystar.net/news/six-points-and-june-7-1966

(2018, July 17). Retrieved from https://history.state.gov/milestones/1866-1898/alaska-purchase

Allison, D. (1998). *Text in education and society.* Singapore University Press.

Almond, G. A., & Coleman, J. S. (1970). *The Politics of Developing Areas.* Princeton University Press.

Attiah, K. (2018, July 10). Why calling France 'the last African team' in the World Cup is problematic. Retrieved from https://www.washingtonpost.com/news/global-opinions/wp/2018/07/10/why-calling-france-the-last-african-team-in-the-world-cup-is-problematic/

Ayres, A. (2009). *Speaking like a State: Language and Nationalism in Pakistan.* Cambridge University Press.

Aytürk, I. (2010, 01). Revisiting the language factor in Zionism: The Hebrew Language Council from 1904 to 1914. *Bulletin of the School of Oriental and African Studies,* 73(01), 45. doi:10.1017/s0041977x09990346

Balakrishnan, G., & Anderson, B. R. (2012). *Mapping the Nation.* Verso.

Bangladesh sets up war crimes court. (2018, November 07). Retrieved from https://www.aljazeera.com/news/asia/2010/03/2010325151839747356.html

Barfield, T. J. (2008). *The Dictionary of Anthropology.* Blackwell.

Bennett, C. (1998). *Yugoslavia's Bloody Collapse: Causes, Course and Consequences.* Hurst & Company.

Benor, S., & Hary, B. H. (2018). *Languages in Jewish Communities: Past and Present.* Walter De Gruyter.

Berlin, I., Hardy, H., Hausheer, R., & Marr, A. (2013). *The Proper Study of Mankind: An Anthology of Essays.* Vintage Books.

Bernstein, M. Y. (2017). *Globalisation, Translation and Transmission: Sino-Judaic Cultural Identity in Kaifeng, China.* Peter Lang AG, Internationaler Verlag der Wissenschaften.

(2018, November 16). Retrieved from http://www.benyehuda.us/miketz.htm

Bhaumik, S. (2017, August 10). Bengali 'should be UN language'. Retrieved from http://news.bbc.co.uk/2/hi/south_asia/8425744.stm

Birgerson, S. M. (2002). *After the Breakup of a Multiethnic Empire: Russia, Successor States and Eurasian Security.* Praeger.

Breger, M. J., Reiter, Y., & Hammer, L. M. (2013). *Holy places in the Israeli-Palestinian conflict: Confrontation and co-existence.* Routledge.

Breslauer, G. W. (2002). *Gorbachev and Yeltsin as Leaders.* Cambridge University Press.

We Can Hope – Brexit As The Beginning Of The End Of The European Ideal. (2019, January 26). Retrieved from https://www.continentaltelegraph.com/brexit/we-can-hope-brexit-as-the-beginning-of-the-end-of-the-european-ideal/

Brown, A. (2010). *The Rise and Fall of Communism.* Vintage.

Brown, M. L. (1999). *Our Hands are Stained with Blood.* Destiny Image.

Bullock, C. H. (2007). *Introduction to the Old Testament Prophetic Books.* Moody Press.

Cannon, B. (2018, April 24). You don't need to believe in God to believe in Judaism. Retrieved from https://www.haaretz.com/jewish/.premium-i-found-atheism-through-judaism-1.5382662

Chomsky, N. (1969). *Aspects of the Theory of Syntax.* Massachusetts Institute of Technology.

Chomsky, N., & McGilvray, J. (2012). *The Science of Language Interviews with James McGilvray.* Cambridge University Press.

Comrie, B., Hewitt, B. G., & Payne, J. R. (1981). *The Languages of the Soviet Union.* CUP Archive.

Corballis, M. C. (2014). *The Recursive Mind: The Origins of Human Language, Thought and Civilisation.* Princeton University Press.

Dalrymple, W. (2017, June 19). *The Mutual Genocide of Indian Partition.* Retrieved from https://www.newyorker.com/magazine/2015/06/29/the-great-divide-

BIBLIOGRAPHY

books-dalrymple

Darwin, C. (1871). *The Descent of Man*. Murray.

Denton, R. E. (2010). *Studies of Identity in the 2008 Presidential Campaign*. Lexington Books.

Deuteronomy 20, New International Version (NIV) | The Bible App. (2012, September 16). Retrieved from https://www.bible.com/bible/111/DEU.20.NIV

Dias, E. (2014, May 27). Pope Francis Corrects Benjamin Netanyahu on Jesus Speaking Hebrew. Retrieved from http://time.com/118522/pope-corrects-israeli-leader-actually-jesus-did-not-speak-hebrew/

Dukes, P. (2001). *A History of Russia: Medieval, Modern, Contemporary, c. 882-1996*. Palgrave.

Dummett, M. (2015, January 04). Bangladesh War: The article that changed history. Retrieved from https://www.bbc.com/news/world-asia-16207201

Elazar, D. J., & Cohen, S. A. (1985). *The Jewish Polity: Jewish political organisation from Biblical times to the present*. Indiana University Press.

Emerton, J. A. (1961). Did Jesus Speak Hebrew? *The Journal of Theological Studies*, XII(2), 189-202. doi:10.1093/jts/xii.2.189

Everett, D. L. (2013). *Language: The Cultural Tool*. Profile Books.

(2018, December 27). Retrieved from https://www.onwar.com/aced/chrono/c1900s/yr10/fhasmachi1916.htm

Fiala, A. G. (2004). *Practical Pacifism*. Algora Publishing.

Fishman, J. A., & Sebeok, T. A. (1977). *Readings in the Sociology of Language*. Mouton.

Fishman, J. A. (1999). *Handbook of Language and Ethnic Identity*. Oxford University Press.

Fox, A., & Blau, J. (1983, 03). The Renaissance of Modern Hebrew and Modern Standard Arabic: Parallels and Differences in the Revival of Two Semitic Languages. *Language*, 59(1), 233. doi:10.2307/414088

Freeman, C. (2011). *AD 381: Heretics, Pagans and the Christian State*. Vintage Digital.

Freeze, G. L. (2009). *Russia: A History*. Oxford University Press.

Fromkin, V. (2010). *An Introduction to Language*. Nelson Education.

Fukuyama, F. (1989). *The "End of History"?* United States Institute of Peace.

Gaddis, J. L. (2007). *The Cold War*. Penguin.

Gans, C. (2003). *The Limits of Nationalism*. Cambridge University Press.

Gellner, E. (1983). *Nations and Nationalism*. Cornell University Press.

Grant, R. (2012). *World War II: Europe*. Britannica Digital Learning.

Grenoble, L. A. (2011). *Language Policy in the Soviet Union*. Springer.

Grice, P. (1991). *Studies in the Way of Words*. Harvard University Press.

Grégoire, J., & Jewkes, M. (2015). *Recognition and Redistribution in Multinational Federations*. Leuven University Press.

Genesis 12:1-10-13 The Message (MSG). (2013, October 19). Retrieved from https://www.bible.com/bible/compare/GEN.12.1-10

Genesis 11, New International Version (NIV) | The Bible App. (2017, April 21). Retrieved from https://www.bible.com/bible/111/GEN.11.NIV

Gil, M. (1984). Dhimmi Donations and Foundations for Jerusalem (638-1099). *Journal of the Economic and Social History of the Orient*, 27(2), 156. doi:10.2307/3632101

Gilad, E., Hasson, N., Rozovsky, L., Khoury, Y. K., Bar, Z., Hecht R., Reuters Associated. (2018, April 10). Why are Jews called Jews? Retrieved from https://www.haaretz.com/archaeology/why-are-jews-called-jews-1.5410757

Glynn, S. (2015). *Class, Ethnicity and Religion in the Bengali East End; a Political History*. Manchester University Press.

Gonzalez-Barrera, A. (2015, March 06). Spanish is the most spoken non-English language in U.S. homes, even among non-Hispanics. Retrieved from http://www.pewresearch.org/fact-tank/2013/08/13/spanish-is-the-most-spoken-non-english-language-in-u-s-homes-even-among-non-hispanics/

Grant, M. (1997). *The History of Ancient Israel*. Phoenix.

Greene, R. L. (2011). *You are what you speak: Grammar grouches, language laws and the politics of identity*. Black.

Hamilton, W., & Bowen, F. (1861). *The metaphysics of Sir William Hamilton*. Allyn and Bacon.

Hays, J. (2018, November 05). Crimean Tatars and Meskhetian Turks in Uzbekistan. Retrieved from http://factsanddetails.com/central-asia/Uzbekistan/sub8_3d/entry-4710.html

Hobsbawm, E. J., & Ranger, T. O. (1985). *The Invention of Tradition*. Cambridge University Press.

Holbrook, J. R. (2018). *Moscow Memoir: An American military attaché in the USSR 1979-1981*. Authorhouse. [The Official 700 Club]. (2015, Jul 28).

The Hope: Eliezer Ben-Yehuda [Video File]. Retrieved from https://www.youtube.com/watch?v=NQvB-djqMag

Huntington, S. P. (1996). *The Clash of Civilisations and the Remaking of World Order.* Simon & Schuster Paperbacks.

Husain, S. S., & Tinker, H. R. (2019, January 04). Bangladesh. Retrieved from https://www.britannica.com/place/Bangladesh/The-arts#ref997951

Islam, N. (1981, 02). Islam and National Identity: The Case of Pakistan and Bangladesh. *International Journal of Middle East Studies,* 13(01), 55-72. doi:10.1017/s0020743800055070

Jalal, A. (1999). *The Sole Spokesman: Jinnah, the Muslim League and the demand for Pakistan.* Cambridge University Press.

Jewish Languages. (2015, June 28). Retrieved from http://www.jewishagency.org/jewish-community/content/24408

The Jewish State Theodor Herzl's Program for Zionism. (2015, July 01). Retrieved from http://www.zionism-israel.com/js/Jewish_State_29.html

Johnson, P. (2013). *History of the Jews.* Phoenix.

Judges 12, New International Version (NIV) | The Bible App. (2015, January 04). Retrieved from https://www.bible.com/bible/111/JDG.12.NIV

Kedourie, E. (1962). *Nationalism.* Praeger.

Khan, Z. (1982). March movement of Bangladesh: Bengali struggle for Political Power. *The Indian Journal of Political Science,* 33(3): 291-322.

Klabbers, J. (2016). *International Law Documents.* Cambridge University Press.

(2015, January 04). Retrieved from http://www.2think.org/kom.shtml

Kohn, H. (1961). *The Idea of Nationalism: A Study in its Origins and Background.* Macmillan.

Kortlandt, F., Wiedenhof, J. M., Lubotsky, A. M., Schaeken, J., Derksen, R., & Siebinga, S. M. (2008). *Evidence and counter-evidence: Essays in honour of Frederik Kortland.* Rodopi.

Kotkin, S. (2009). *Armageddon Averted: The Soviet Collapse, 1970-2000.* Oxford University Press.

Kwon, H. (2004). *Divided Korea: Longing for reunification. Center for Korean Studies.* North Park University Theological Seminary.

Levine, B. A. (2005). Assyrian Ideology and Israelite Monotheism. *Iraq,* 67(01), 411-427. doi:10.1017/s0021088900001455

Lewis, B. (2001). *The Multiple Identities of the Middle East.* Schocken Books.

Lieu, J. M., & Rogerson, J. W. (2010). *The Oxford Handbook of Biblical Studies.* Oxford University Press.

Liu, J., & Liu, J. (2013, September 09). Five Years After 9/11, The Clash of Civilisations Revisited. Retrieved from http://www.pewforum.org/2006/08/18/five-years-after-911-the-clash-of-civilizations-revisited/

Malia, M. E. (1994). *Soviet Tragedy: A History of Socialism in Russia*. Free Press.

Martin, T. (1998). The Russification of the RSFSR. *Cahiers Du Monde Russe: Russie, Empire Russe, Union Soviétique, États Indépendants,* 39(1).

Malik, H. (1990). *Domestic determinants of Soviet foreign policy towards South Asia and Middle East.* Macmillan.

Mayer, K. (1968). The Jura Problem: Ethnic Conflict in Switzerland. *Social Research,* 35(4): 707-741.

Marples, D. R. (2011, 06). Review Article. *Canadian Slavonic Papers,* 53(2-4

McCarthy, N. & Richter, F. (2017, October 02). Infographic: Catalan Referendum: 90% Back Independence. Retrieved from https://www.statista.com/chart/11323/catalan-referendum_-90-back-independence/

Mckeon, R. (1946, 10). Aristotle's Conception of Language and the Arts of Language.*Classical Philology, 41*(4), 193-206. doi:10.1086/362975

McWhorter, J. (2011). *The Power Of Babel: A Natural History of Language.* Cornerstone Digital.

Montgomery, M. (1995). *An Introduction to Language and Society.* Routledge.

Melton, J. G. (2014). *Faiths Across Time: 5,000 Years of Religious History.* ABC-CLIO.

Milanovic, B. (1994, 03). Perspective. *Challenge,* 37(2), 61-64. doi:10.1080/05775132.1994.11471737

Minogue, K. R. (1967). *Nationalism.* Methuen.

Miller, C. (2016). *The struggle to save the Soviet economy Mikhail Gorbachev and the collapse of the USSR.* University of North Carolina Press.

Millar, R. M. (2005). *Language, Nation and Power: An Introduction.* Palgrave Macmillan.

Mitchell, T. (2017, February 01). Language: The Cornerstone of National Identity. Retrieved from http://www.pewglobal.org/2017/02/01/language-the-cornerstone-of-national-identity/

Mundill, R. R. (2002). *England's Jewish solution: Experiment and expulsion, 1262-1290.* Cambridge University Press.

Musil, J. (1995). The End of Czechoslovakia. CEU Press.

Myhill, J. (2006). *Language, Religion and National Identity.* John Benjamins Publishing.

Narak, K. (1954). *Identity and Continuity of States in Public International Law.*

The Nation. (2018, January 13). Past in Perspective. Retrieved from https://nation.com.pk/13-Jan-2018/past-in-perspective?show=previewc=18388168508466929728

(2018, February 16). Retrieved from http://www.unesco.org/new/en/social-and-human-sciences/themes/international-migration/glossary/nation-state/

(2015, May 04). Retrieved from https://sourcebooks.fordham.edu/source/nestor.asp

Netanyahu, B. (2012). *The Founding Fathers of Zionism*. Balfour Books

(2017, December 09). Retrieved from https://history.state.gov/milestones/1830-1860/opening-to-japan

(2019, January 05). Retrieved from https://community.dur.ac.uk/a.k.harrington/origirus.html

Ornstein, J. (1959, 03). Soviet Language Policy. *South Atlantic Bulletin, 24*(4).

Ostler, N. (2006). *Empires of the Word: A Language History of the World*. Harper Perennial.

Orwell, G. (2017). 1984. Houghton Mifflin Harcourt.

Parfitt, T. V. (1972). The Use Of Hebrew In Palestine 1800–1822. *Journal of Semitic Studies,* 17(2), 237-252. doi:10.1093/jss/17.2.237

Pinker, S. (1995). *The Language Instinct*. Penguin Group.

Plokhy, S. (2014). *The Last Empire the Final Days of the Soviet Union*. Basic Books.

Pomfret, R. W. (1995). *The Economies of Central Asia*. Princeton University Press.

Pope ditches Latin as official language of Vatican Synod. (2016, July 17). Retrieved from https://www.reuters.com/article/us-pope-latin/pope-ditches-latin-as-official-language-of-vatican-synod-idUSKCN0HV1O220141006

Rabbis & Religion. (2015, February 11). Retrieved from http://www.jewishagency.org/herzl/content/25311

Rahman, T. (1997, 09). Language and Ethnicity in Pakistan. *Asian Survey, 37*(9), 833-839. doi:10.1525/as.1997.37.9.01p02786

Remnick, D. (1993). *Lenin's Tomb: The Last Days of the Soviet Empire*. Viking.

Renan, E. & Giglioli, M. F. (2018). *What is a Nation?: And other Political Writings*. Columbia University Press.

Riaz, A. & Rahman, M. S. (2016). *Routledge Handbook of Contemporary Bangladesh*. Routledge/Taylor & Francis Group.

Roblin, S. (2017, November 18). How North Korean Weapons Could Start a War (in the Middle East). Retrieved from https://nationalinterest.org/blog/the-buzz/how-north-korean-weapons-could-start-war-the-middle-east-23251

Safran, W. & Laponce J.A. (2005). *Language, Ethnic Identity and the State*. Routledge.

Saussure, F. D., Bouquet, S., & Sanders, C. (2008). *Writings in General Linguistics*. Oxford University Press.

Saenz-Badillos, A. (1993). *A History of the Hebrew Language*. Cambridge University Press.

Schlesinger, A. M. (2004). *The Imperial Presidency*. Houghton Mifflin.

Schuman, H. (1972, 09). A Note on the Rapid Rise of Mass Bengali Nationalism in East Pakistan. *American Journal of Sociology*, 78(2), 290-298. doi:10.1086/225325

Scottish Referendum: Scotland votes 'No' to independence. (2017, March 04). Retrieved from https://www.bbc.com/news/uk-scotland-29270441

Sedley, D. N. (2003). *Plato's Cratylus*. Cambridge University Press.

Shivtiel, A. (1985). Languages In Contact: The Contribution Of The Arabic Language To The Revival Of Hebrew. *Journal of Semitic Studies*, XXX(1), 95-113. doi:10.1093/jss/xxx.1.95

Shulchan Aruch, Even HaEzer 44:9. (2019, May 10). Retrieved from https://www.sefaria.org/Shulchan_Arukh,_Even_HaEzer.44.9?lang=bi

Siecienski, A. E. (2016). *Constantine: Religious faith and Imperial policy*. Ashgate.

Smith, A. D. (1993). *National Identity*. University of Nevada Press.

Spolsky, B. (2014). *The Languages of the Jews*. Cambridge University Press.

Story of Pakistan. (2016, April 15). West Pakistan Established as One Unit. Retrieved from https://storyofpakistan.com/west-pakistan-established-as-one-unit

Senellart, M., Ewald, F., & Fontana, A. (2009). *Security, Territory, Population Lectures at the College De France, 1977–78*. Palgrave Macmillan UK.

Smith, H. W. (2015). *The Oxford Handbook of Modern German History*. Oxford University Press.

(2018, December 11). Retrieved from

http://ccat.sas.upenn.edu/~haroldfs/540/handouts/ussr/soviet2.html

Suny, R. G. (1994). *The Revenge of the Past Nationalism, Revolution and the Collapse of the Soviet Union*. Stanford University Press.

Sterkenburg, P. V. (2008). *Unity and Diversity of Languages*. Benjamins.

Talbot, I. (1998). *Pakistan: A Modern History*. St. Martin's Press.

BIBLIOGRAPHY

Tapper, R. (2011). *Tribe and State in Iran and Afghanistan*. Routledge.

Tapper, A. J. (2016). *Judaisms: A twenty-first-century introduction to Jews and Jewish identities*. University of California Press.

Taubman, W. (2018). *Gorbachev: His life and times*. W.W. Norton & Company.

Texts Concerning Zionism: "Auto-Emancipation". (2016, July 19). Retrieved from https://www.jewishvirtuallibrary.org/quot-auto-emancipation-quot-leon-pinsker

This week in history: Revival of the Hebrew language. (2017, October 12). Retrieved from https://www.jpost.com/Jewish-World/Jewish-News/This-week-in-history-Revival-of-the-Hebrew-language

Tilly, C. (1985). *Bringing the State back in*. Cambridge University Press.

Todd, E. (1979). *The Final Fall: An Essay on the Decomposition of the Soviet Sphere*. Karz.

Trousdale, G. (2010). *An Introduction to English Sociolinguistics*. Edinburgh University Press.

Tomasello, M. (2010). *Origins of Human Communication*. MIT Press.

Toor, S. (2011). *The State of Islam: Culture and Cold War politics in Pakistan*. Pluto Press.

Umar, B. (1998). The Anti-Heroes of the Language Movement. *Economic and Political Weekly*, 33(1): 636-637.

Urdu controversy is dividing the nation further. (2018, September 08). Retrieved from http://www.southasiaanalysis.org/paper675

(2018, September 25). Retrieved from http://econc10.bu.edu/economic_systems/NatIdentity/FSU/Russia/prerevolution/vladimir.htm

Willford, A. C. (1991). *Religious resurgence in British India: Vivekananda and the Hindu Renaissance*.

Williams, W. A. (1972). *The Tragedy of American Diplomacy*. Dell Publications.

Wimmer, A., & Feinstein, Y. (2010, 10). The Rise of the Nation-State across the World, 1816 to 2001. *American Sociological Review*, 75(5).

The World Without Technology. (2018, December 28). Retrieved from https://www.nextnature.net/2009/10/the-world-without-technology/

Wood, J. G. (1997). *Vietnam and the Indochina Conflict*. Macmillan.

Yegar, M. (1972). *The Muslims of Burma: A Study of a Minority Group*. Otto Harrassowitz.

Zubok, V. M. (2009). *A Failed Empire: The Soviet Union in the Cold War from Stalin to Gorbachev*. University of North Carolina Press.

Zuckermann, G. (2009, 06). Hybridity versus Revivability: Multiple Causation,

Forms and Patterns. *Journal of Language Contact*, 2(2).

Zuckermann, G. (2006, 03). A New Vision For Israeli Hebrew. *Journal of Modern Jewish Studies,* 5(1), 57-71. doi:10.1080/14725880500511175

NOTES

NOTES

NOTES

www.ingramcontent.com/pod-product-compliance
Lightning Source LLC
Chambersburg PA
CBHW052058300426
44117CB00013B/2192